CORNELL SCIENTIFIC INQUIRY SERIES

TEACHER EDITION

Watershed Dynamics

NATIONAL SCIENCE TEACHERS ASSOCIATION

CORNELL SCIENTIFIC INQUIRY SERIES

TEACHER EDITION

Watershed Dynamics

BY THE ENVIRONMENTAL INQUIRY LEADERSHIP TEAM
WILLIAM S. CARLSEN
NANCY M. TRAUTMANN
CHRISTINE M. CUNNINGHAM
MARIANNE E. KRASNY
ADAM WELMAN

WITH TEACHERS
HARRIET BECK (WELLSVILLE HIGH SCHOOL)
HARRY CANNING (NEWARK VALLEY HIGH SCHOOL)
MARK JOHNSON (ITHACA HIGH SCHOOL)

AND CORNELL SCIENTISTS
EUGENIA BARNABA
REUBEN GOFORTH
SUSAN HOSKINS

NATIONAL SCIENCE TEACHERS ASSOCIATION
ARLINGTON, VIRGINIA

NSTA Press
National Science Teachers Association

Claire Reinburg, Director
Andrew Cocke, Associate Editor
Judy Cusick, Associate Editor
Betty Smith, Associate Editor

ART AND DESIGN Linda Olliver, Director
PRINTING AND PRODUCTION Catherine Lorrain-Hale, Director
    Nguyet Tran, Assistant Production Manager
    Jack Parker, Desktop Publishing Specialist
*sci*LINKS Tyson Brown, Manager
    David Anderson, Web and Development Coordinator

NATIONAL SCIENCE TEACHERS ASSOCIATION
Gerald F. Wheeler, Executive Director
David Beacom, Publisher

Library of Congress has cataloged the Student Edition as follows:
Watershed dynamics / by the Environmental Inquiry Leadership Team, William S. Carlsen ... [et al.].— Student ed.
    p. cm. — (Cornell scientific inquiry series)
  ISBN 0-87355-213-X
  1. Watersheds—Study and teaching (Secondary)—Activity programs. 2. Watershed ecology—Study and teaching
(Secondary)—Activity programs. 3. Water quality—Study and teaching (Secondary)—Activity programs. I. Carlsen, William S.
II. Series.
  GB1002.25.W28 2004
  551.48—dc22

2004002042

This material is based on work supported by the National Science Foundation under Grant No. 96-18142. Any opinions, findings, conclusions, or recommendations expressed in this material are those of the authors and do not necessarily reflect the views of the National Science Foundation.

Contents
TEACHER EDITION

vi

ACKNOWLEDGMENTS

We would like to recognize the contributions to this volume that have been made by Environmental Inquiry (EI) staff and collaborators, as well as participants in an earlier project, the Institute on Science and the Environment for Teachers (ISET). Several of the activities in this volume were initially developed, modified, and tested in the ISET program.

Among the staff of the EI and ISET programs were many Cornell graduate students and graduate preservice teachers who assisted with the development of these resources, including Cherish Brigham, Pamela Emerson, Dan Chiao, Christopher Grange, Jennifer Hahn, Kate Hester, Tracey Kast, Moon Kim, and Thad Schug. In addition to other duties as staff graduate assistants, Michael Arquin, Valery Hussain, Dwight Schuster, and Dave Thomas drafted early versions of some of the protocols and activities.

Curriculum writing and pilot testing of watershed materials took place in schools in New York City, Rochester, and other communities through a Cornell University graduate course, the *Curriculum Design Laboratory*. Students who contributed to this publication through that course include Matthew Anthes-Washburn, Gregory Bartus, Stephen Costanza, Jamilla Cutliff, Tabitha Dionne, Mark Dollard, Thomas Glickman, Jeremy Haas, Jacaranda Henkel, Amy Heusinkveld, Tracey Kast, Joshua Kraus, Nicole Ladue, Heather Peterson, Contanza Phillips, Jesse Rodrigues, David Saunders, Jeremiah Smith, Erin Tompkins, and Andrzej Wolski.

Over 200 teachers piloted materials and provided us with feedback, which we appreciated greatly. We want to recognize the particular contributions of Jack Balcome, William Beal, Anthony (Bud) Bertino, Pat Carroll, Terry Dunlap, Naima Freitas, Kim Gilbertson, Mark Johnson, Cass Loomis, Mark Nelson, John Signorelli, Doug van Etten, and Mary van Wert. Harry Canning developed the prototype for our design challenge, and Harriet Beck drafted the initial WHEBIP/land use activity. Mark Johnson developed and pilot-tested resources to support the study of local watersheds using airphotos.

Artwork for this volume was created by Jane McDonald of Sunset Design.

Funding for this work was provided by grants from the Teacher Enhancement Program and the Instructional Materials Development program of the National Science Foundation. We thank NSF program officers Trish Morse, David Campbell, and George deBoer for support though the funding, writing, and production process. Additional support came from the New York State Education Department.

A number of Cornell scientists and extension agents provided technical support, ideas, materials, and instruction during the development and piloting of these materials. Special thanks to Stephen Brown, Karen Edelstein, Barbare Peckarsky, and Reuben Goforth. Eugenia (Jeannie) Barnaba and Susan Hoskins provided leadership related to remote sensing and land use analysis.

This book benefited from detailed and constructive reviews by Jeannie Barnaba, John Durant, Anne Gallagher, Susan Hoskins, Marci Meixler, and Linda Wagenet.

Watershed Dynamics was produced by NSTA Press, and included the participation of director Claire Reinburg, project editor Andrew Cocke, art director Linda Olliver, production director Catherine Lorrain-Hale, assistant production manager Nguyet Tran, with sciLINKS prepared by manager Tyson Brown and Web development coordinator David Anderson.

Finally, we thank our families for their support for and participation in watershed investigations. Paddling a canoe is always more fun with someone else.

NATIONAL SCIENCE TEACHERS ASSOCIATION

INTRODUCTION

ENVIRONMENTAL INQUIRY

Watershed Dynamics is part of the Environmental Inquiry (EI) curriculum series developed at Cornell University to enable high school students to conduct authentic environmental science research. The goals of EI are for students to

1. Develop research skills

2. Use their newly acquired skills to conduct research projects of their own design focusing on topics relevant to their local communities

3. Participate in communities of peer student scientists

4. Enhance their understanding of scientific content and process

Rather than learning science as a static body of facts, EI students experience the research process through which scientific understandings are formed and continually revised. Instead of memorizing a "scientific method," they discover for themselves the multifaceted nature of scientific research. By studying problems relevant to their communities, they discover interconnections between science and society.

MEETING THE STANDARDS

The contemporary movement for science education reform calls for the teaching of science to more closely reflect the way in which science is practiced. According to the National Science Education Standards, the central strategy for teaching science should be to engage students in authentic inquiry or research:

> Students at all grade levels and in every domain of science should have the opportunity to use scientific inquiry and develop the ability to think and act in ways associated with the processes of inquiry, including asking questions, planning and conducting investigations, using appropriate tools and techniques to gather data, thinking critically and logically about the relationships between evidence and explanations, constructing and analyzing alternative explanations, and communicating scientific arguments.[1]

The Science as Inquiry standards[2] call for all students to develop the following abilities:

▶ Identify questions and concepts that guide scientific investigations

▶ Design and conduct scientific investigations

▶ Use technology and mathematics to improve investigations and communications

---

[1] National Research Council (NRC). 1996. *National Science Education Standards.* Washington, DC: National Academy Press, p. 105.

[2] NRC pp. 175–176.

▶ Formulate and revise scientific explanations and models using logic and evidence

▶ Recognize and analyze alternative explanations and models

▶ Communicate and defend a scientific argument

Using a stepwise approach, EI research helps students gain all of these abilities as they design and carry out investigations, exchange ideas about their results and interpretations with peer student scientists, and make recommendations for future experiments. Students engaged in EI ecological research also will learn concepts and skills covered in other Standards, including Science in Personal and Social Perspectives, History and Nature of Science, Life Science, Science and Technology, and other areas (Table 1).

AUDIENCE

The Cornell Scientific Inquiry Series was written for 9th and 10th grade students, including those who have not historically enrolled in traditional college-preparatory science courses but are now expected to pursue academically demanding programs of study. In a growing number of schools, integrated science or environmental science is being taught or considered as an introductory high school science course for some students. *Watershed Dynamics* is designed to be useful in that type of course. EI research is also a good motivator for students who have not yet studied the foundational scientific disciplines. With its emphasis on local resources, community problems, and genuinely unsolved scientific puzzles, EI takes a very different approach than the common "go slow" strategy of many basic-level commercial science textbooks. The challenge of carrying out authentic research and reporting the results to others—beyond the classroom—enhances self-esteem in students who are not accustomed to thinking of themselves as scientists.

Watershed Dynamics activities and units have also been used successfully in more conventional biology, chemistry, Earth science, environmental science, and general science courses, and as resources for individual student research, by students ranging from 8th graders through those in Advanced Placement Environmental Science courses.

TABLE 1
National Science Education Content Standards Addressed in *Watershed Dynamics*

National Science Education Standards (National Research Council, 1996)	Protocol 1: Watershed Field Survey	Protocol 2: Object Recognition Using Maps and Airphotos	Protocol 3: Delineating a Watershed	Protocol 4: Analyzing Stream Integrity Using Remote Sensing Data	Protocol 5: Collecting Aquatic Invertebrates	Protocol 6: Simplified Stream Biota Test	Protocol 7: Index of Biotic Integrity Using Aquatic Invertebrates	Protocol 8: Measuring Stream Discharge	Protocol 9: Aquatic Chemistry	Protocol 10: Computer Modeling with STELLA	Interactive Research	Stormwater Treatment Design Challenge
Unifying Concepts and Processes in Science												
Systems, order, and organization	●	●	●	●	●	●	●	●	●	●	●	●
Evidence, models, and explanation	●	●	●	●		●	●	●	●	●	●	●
Constancy, change, and measurement	●	●	●	●		●	●	●		●	●	●
Science as Inquiry												
Abilities necessary to do scientific inquiry	●	●	●	●	●	●	●	●	●	●	●	●
Understandings about scientific inquiry	●	●		●	●	●	●	●	●	●	●	●
Physical Science										●	●	
Life Science												
Interdependence of organisms				●	●	●	●					
Behavior of organisms				●	●	●		●				
Earth and Space Science	●	●	●					●				
Science and Technology												
Abilities of technological design										●	●	●
Understandings about science and technology	●			●						●	●	●
Science in Personal and Social Perspectives												
Population growth	●										●	
Natural resources	●	●					●		●		●	
Environmental quality	●	●	●	●	●	●	●	●	●		●	●
Natural and human-induced hazards	●	●		●	●	●	●	●	●	●	●	●
Science and technology in local, national, and global challenges	●	●		●	●	●	●	●	●	●	●	●
History and Nature of Science												
Science as a human endeavor	●	●	●	●				●		●	●	●
Nature of scientific knowledge	●	●	●	●	●	●	●	●		●	●	●
Historical perspectives		●		●							●	

WHY WATERSHED DYNAMICS?

Students engaged in this EI curriculum learn basic concepts of watershed dynamics, a fairly complex science. With all of the challenges that schools face, why include watershed dynamics in a secondary science program?

RELEVANCE

One important reason for studying watershed dynamics at the high school level is its relevance to everyday life. Clean water is essential to life. Water is a renewable resource, but water quality depends heavily upon human actions and natural processes in the environment. Watershed studies can help students understand where their drinking water originates, what a watershed is, and how aquatic systems function. *Watershed Dynamics* also investigates the relationship between human actions in the environment and the effects of those actions on the biology, chemistry, and hydrology of water resources. How does building a parking lot affect nearby streams? Should rural communities provide drinking water to larger urban communities, and if so, who should pay for watershed protection? Why is it important to preserve wetlands? In learning about land use and water quality, students will become better prepared to make reasoned decisions about issues such as these.

Watershed dynamics offers the opportunity to connect classroom science to relevant issues in all types of communities—rural, suburban, and urban. People living in rural areas usually drill wells to get the water they need. What do engineers and builders need to know about watersheds in order to drill wells successfully? The residents of large cities may get their water from reservoirs a hundred miles away. How do agricultural practices affect the water in lakes and rivers used by people for drinking and recreation?

CONNECTIONS

Another reason for including watershed dynamics in high school science is that it provides a natural link between scientific disciplines, including biology, chemistry, geology, environmental science, and human health. School sciences are often presented as discrete fields of study. By highlighting the natural links and common themes, watershed dynamics can make all of these fields more interesting. Study of watershed dynamics also highlights the connections among science, social science, and public policy. For example, when students interpret the results of their studies of land use and water quality, they can better understand how the interplay between scientific data and human judgment shapes public policy decisions such as zoning, flood control, and the regulation of agricultural practices.

Watershed Dynamics can be used in conjunction with other curricula in the Environmental Inquiry series. For example, students can combine their knowledge and skills of macroinvertebrate sampling and water chemistry with the bioassay protocols featured in *Assessing Toxic Risk* (2001; the first publication in the Cornell Scientific Inquiry Series) to investigate suspected toxic sediments from streams, rivers, and lakes.

RESEARCH AND ENGINEERING DESIGN OPPORTUNITIES

One of the great challenges for science teachers is providing students with opportunities for authentic open-ended investigations that are safe and feasible to perform at the high school level. EI protocols are ideally suited to student research. Not only are many of the protocols simple and inexpensive to carry out, they also are authentic scientific techniques that can be used to investigate issues relevant to the local community.

Using remote sensing and monitoring procedures, students can carry out the same types of tests used by scientists in universities, government, and industry. Although scientists have access to budgets and equipment far beyond the reach of secondary schools, they use similar procedures to reveal an integrated picture of aquatic environments. For example, scientists use riparian inventories and watershed delineation techniques to determine how land use affects stream quality. With very few modifications, students can carry out the same procedures to answer questions of their own design.

Scientific experiments often lead to more questions than they answer. After each experiment, students are likely to come up with several more questions that can be addressed through further experimentation. Given the time and freedom to carry through with some of these ideas, students will be able to experience the creativity inherent in research and to experience firsthand the joy of practicing science.

In addition to research opportunities, *Watershed Dynamics* also contains an Engineering Design Challenge. In this activity, students work with classmates to build a stormwater retention device that meets certain specified criteria and operates within stated constraints. The Challenge provides students with the opportunity to integrate information presented in the introductory text with skills and knowledge they have gained from the protocols. By presenting their final solution to classmates, and then reviewing the design of fellow students, students will gain an appreciation of how these issues are approached in everyday situations in their local communities.

CRITICAL THINKING

Students often believe that scientific work is a process that produces unambiguous results. This misconception may lead to confusion or suspicion when students observe scientists publicly disagreeing about issues like long-term implications of global warming, food safety, or the causes of cancer. How can opposing views in an argument be "scientific?" Students who engage in Environmental Inquiry will learn that good scientific work involves both careful attention to standard methods and creativity in responding to real-world problems. They will discover that different research teams approach problems in different ways, even when they begin with the same "standard" methods. Students' own work will be influenced by how they frame their problems, what resources they have on hand, and whether other students in their schools have studied the problem before. For example, students investigating an urban river may not be able to safely wade into the water, so they will need to use collection methods different from those used to study a seasonal rural stream.

In interpreting the results of their investigations, students will find that they need to think carefully about how conclusions are justified. In grappling with such questions, students are forced to identify their assumptions and to think critically about different explanations. Initially they may jump to conclusions, then realize through classroom discussions and peer review that other interpretations are possible or that further experiments are needed before a final conclusion can be reached. They may also discover that new data force them to revise or discard explanations that adequately accounted for earlier data. These struggles are similar to the ones that engage professional scientists as they interpret and present the results of research.

There are many excellent resources for studying aquatic systems and for understanding watersheds, and we encourage you to draw upon other resources as you craft your own local solution to the challenge of understanding watershed dynamics. In creating the activities and investigations for this book, we have tried to complement the best currently available resources with some fresh material, integrative activities, and approaches to research that will help your students understand science the way it is practiced.

Table 2 lists intended learning outcomes for students engaged in EI watershed research and engineering designs.

TABLE 2
Intended Learning Outcomes

Skills: Students will gain the ability to

▶ Conduct scientific research, starting with well-defined protocols and progressing to open-ended research projects

▶ Define a research question related to watershed science, then plan and carry out a study to address this question using protocols, field investigations, or other types of studies

▶ Work collaboratively to design experiments and devices, interpret results, and critically analyze ideas and conclusions

▶ Engage in engineering design: plan, construct, and test a device; assess its cost; and then present and critique the results with fellow students

▶ Analyze data and draw conclusions about watershed processes

▶ Write a concise and accurate summary of methods, results, and conclusions

▶ Engage in peer review to exchange constructive criticism of fellow students' data analyses, interpretations, and conclusions

▶ Use commentary from fellow students to revise or justify research reports and presentations

Concepts: Students will gain the understanding that

▶ Watershed dynamics concerns the study and management of the complex interactions among water, land, atmosphere, and the organisms living within the drainage area of a river, stream, or other water body.

▶ The management of watersheds is a complex process that involves communication between people with many different ideas, values, needs, and resources

▶ Watershed science is multidisciplinary, related to societal concerns, and has important impacts on how water is used by humans, plants, animals, and other organisms living in watersheds

▶ Concerned students, citizens, and organizations can play important roles in watershed science and watershed management

▶ Field studies, remote sensing, computer modeling, and laboratory experiments all contribute to our understandings of ecological systems and how they respond to change

▶ Remote sensing and computer modeling provide useful tools for assessing land uses and evaluating the impact of various management practices

▶ Land uses and management practices affect stormwater runoff characteristics such as pH, dissolved oxygen, and nutrient concentrations, and consequently have important effects on streamwater quality and aquatic habitats

▶ Scientists and engineers work both individually and collaboratively, reviewing each other's work to provide feedback on experimental design and interpretation of results

▶ Scientific understandings are tentative and subject to change with new discoveries. Peer review among scientists helps sort genuine discoveries from incomplete or faulty work

▶ Aquatic organisms have species-specific habitat requirements concerning chemical, physical, and biological properties

▶ The living and nonliving components of ecosystems change over time and respond to disturbances

▶ The diversity and abundance of stream invertebrates can often be used to assess water quality

LEVELS OF INQUIRY

Environmental Inquiry (EI) is organized into two levels of inquiry modeled after research activities conducted by professional scientists. Students first learn standard research methods, or *protocols,* and carry out other related activities. Then they explore possibilities for using these protocols to address relevant research or technological design questions. After planning and carrying out *interactive research* experiments and design projects, students present and discuss their results with their peers and possibly with interested community groups.

EI research involves progressively increasing levels of student responsibility for the design of investigations. There also is a progression in interaction among students as they learn to critically analyze their results, argue among alternative interpretations, and communicate their findings to fellow student scientists (see Figure 1).

FIGURE 1
Levels of Inquiry in EI

NOTE: Many different sequences are possible, depending on student ability levels and interests as well as considerations of time and curriculum.

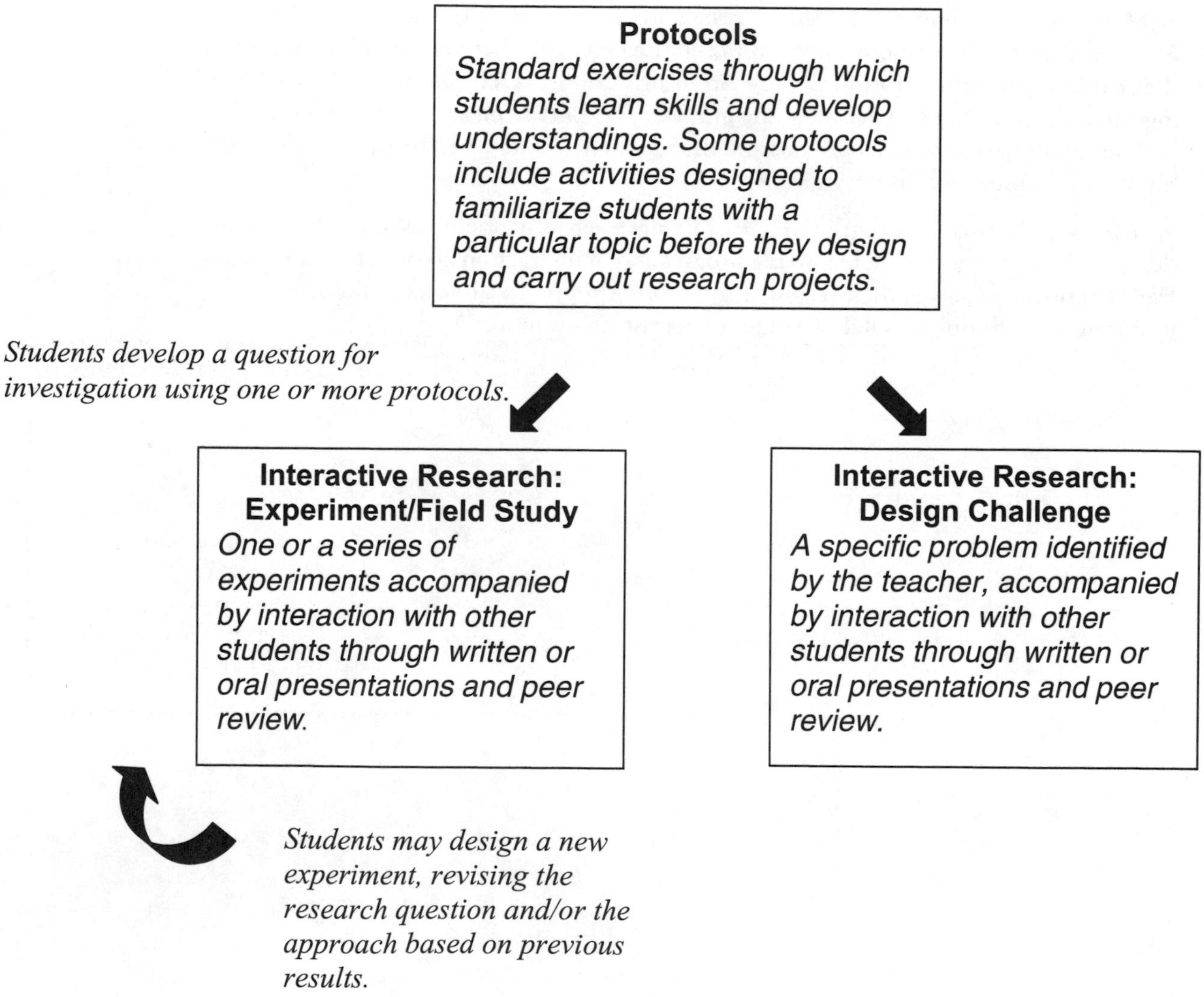

Protocols
Standard exercises through which students learn skills and develop understandings. Some protocols include activities designed to familiarize students with a particular topic before they design and carry out research projects.

Students develop a question for investigation using one or more protocols.

**Interactive Research:
Experiment/Field Study**
One or a series of experiments accompanied by interaction with other students through written or oral presentations and peer review.

**Interactive Research:
Design Challenge**
A specific problem identified by the teacher, accompanied by interaction with other students through written or oral presentations and peer review.

Students may design a new experiment, revising the research question and/or the approach based on previous results.

GUIDING PROTOCOL-LEVEL INQUIRY

Protocol Labs introduce students to standard laboratory and field methods and help students to develop the basic skills and understandings that they will need to explore watershed dynamics. Protocols differ from traditional school laboratory exercises in that *the teacher should not already know the precise outcome* of a Protocol Lab investigation. EI protocols tend to be procedurally "cookbook," just as much routine work in science is methodologically invariant. However, EI protocols are applied to novel questions, areas, streams, or watersheds. In this respect, their use is scientifically authentic. The **Protocol Planning Form** (p. 130) will help your students decide which protocols are appropriate for different questions.

Collaborative work is integral to EI research, including at the protocol level (Table 3). This collaboration includes the process of peer review, through which students exchange feedback about their work. Although peer review is used primarily at the interactive research level, students who have completed a protocol can critique each other's results and conclusions and exchange written feedback using the **Research Report Peer Review Form** (p. 159). This step introduces students to the benefits of exchanging constructive criticism, both to sharpen their own thinking and to provide advice to their peers.

TABLE 3
Collaboration and Peer Review at the Protocol Level

Activity	Collaborative and Individual Work	Peer Review Process
Planning to use a protocol	Students work individually or collaboratively to fill out the **Protocol Planning Form** (p. 130).	N.A.
Carrying out a protocol	Students work in groups to conduct a protocol.	N.A.
Analyzing and presenting the results	Students work individually or collaboratively to report and analyze their data, then write individual lab reports.	Groups pair up to discuss and compare results using the **Research Report Peer Review Form** (p. 159).

Related Activities

In Protocols 4 and 10, we have included activities that familiarize students further with a particular topic before they begin designing and carrying out research projects. These activities involve interpretation of datasets, computer simulations, and hands-on modeling activities. Although these activities begin with very specific step-by-step instructions, they prepare students for subsequent investigations in directions of their own choosing. After testing an initial set of specified scenarios, students can then investigate scenarios that they create in order to analyze or extend the underlying model or to explore new directions of inquiry.

CONDUCTING INTERACTIVE RESEARCH

After mastering relevant protocols, students work in groups to plan and conduct field studies or experiments. Attention is given to choosing a research question, designing suitable experiments or fieldwork, and then interpreting and communicating the results. Students *interact* initially by seeking advice from each other as they plan their experiments, then later by presenting their findings in oral or written form, engaging in peer review, and discussing possible interpretations of their research results. Forms in the Student Edition will assist them in planning and carrying out the collaborative and review processes in "Interactive Research: Field Studies and Experiments" (Table 4).

One of the goals of Interactive Research is to dispel the common misconception among students that scientific work is pursued in isolation. Students generally do not realize the extent to which scientists work together to discuss ideas, share findings, give each other feedback, and collaborate on joint projects. Scientists also communicate with larger, non-science communities. Scientific findings inform public decision-making and, in turn, community priorities help shape scientific research agendas.

Field Studies and Experiments

At the interactive research level, students work in groups to plan and conduct field studies or experiments, then communicate their findings and build on each other's experiences as they carry out the following processes:

▶ Narrowing down an interesting research question

▶ Planning appropriate experiments or fieldwork

▶ Sharing observations and advice with other students who are conducting similar studies

▶ Discussing various possible interpretations of research results

▶ Presenting findings in oral or written form

▶ Participating in peer review of research presentations

▶ Recommending ideas and approaches for future experiments

TABLE 4
Collaboration and Peer Review in Field Studies and Experiments

Activity	Collaborative Work	Peer Review Process
Planning an experiment	Students work together to brainstorm research ideas, then fill out **Choosing a Research Topic** (p. 144) and **Interactive Research Planning Sheet #1** or **#2** (pp. 147 and 149).	Student groups are paired up to discuss and refine research plans using the **Experimental Design Peer Review Form** (p. 158).
Carrying out the experiment	Students work in groups to conduct experiments.	N.A.
Analyzing and presenting the results	Students collaborate to analyze their data, then write research reports using the **Research Report Form** (p. 154) or create posters using the **Poster Guidelines** (p. 157).	Students present their research results, then exchange feedback using the **Research Report Peer Review Form** (p. 159) or **Poster Peer Review Form** (p. 160). Final reports incorporate changes generated through peer review.

Stormwater Treatment Design Challenge

The goal of a Design Challenge—a second type of Interactive Research—is to design and construct a device or process for solving a practical problem, and to execute that design under financial and other constraints. Design Challenges emphasize engineering rather than experimentation. Working within provided specifications, students create, build, and test a design they have chosen as optimal in balancing performance with costs and other non-technical design constraints. In addition to demonstrating their device, student teams evaluate their device's performance, construction costs, and other strengths and weaknesses. This process is included in Interactive Research because students demonstrate their devices publicly and participate in the process of peer review (see Table 5).

One aspect of science that is difficult to replicate in a classroom is that scientific investigation is an iterative and social process, with each scientist learning from the work of both preceding and contemporary researchers. Before embarking on new research, scientists typically begin by reviewing what others have published. As they progress, they discuss their findings informally with colleagues and formally through the peer review process. The Interactive Research level of EI provides analogous opportunities for high school students to share findings and discussions with their peers.

TABLE 5
Collaboration and Peer Review in a Design Challenge

Activity	Collaborative Work	Peer Review Process
Designing alternatives and choosing the best alternative	In response to a teacher-specified design problem, students work in groups to brainstorm ideas and then choose the best alternative using the **Design Selection Matrix** (p. 171) and present it to the teacher using the **Design Proposal Form** (p. 172).	N.A.
Building and using a device	Students work in groups to build, test, refine, and then run a wastewater treatment unit.	N.A.
Analyzing and presenting the results	Students collaborate to evaluate the effectiveness of their device and to plan a presentation of their work.	Students demonstrate their device and their assessment of its performance, then exchange feedback using the **Presentation Assessment Form** (p. 174).

TABLE 6
Watershed Dynamics Examples at the Protocol and Interactive
Research Levels of Environmental Inquiry

Inquiry Level	Description	*Watershed Dynamics* Examples
Protocol labs and related activities	Students learn standard laboratory and field methods and apply them to novel problems. Students interpret, predict, and test new ideas through additional activities such as computer simulation and modeling.	Through fieldwork and data analysis, students use one protocol to calculate flow in one segment of a local stream. The students use another protocol to assess changes in land use practices in the stream's watershed through analysis of contemporary and historical airphotos. Using modeling software, students study the effects of changes in land use practices on stream flow after a storm event.
Interactive Research	**Field Studies and Experiments:** Students rethink questions and methods, then plan and conduct an experiment or field study. They present their findings, discuss possible interpretations of their results, and get feedback from their peers, either face-to-face or electronically.	A class divides into several groups to conduct an interdisciplinary study of a local stream. Each group formulates its own research question and collects data during an all-day field trip. Back at school, the teams pool their findings, then prepare and present oral reports on their investigations.
	Design Challenge: In response to a teacher-specified design problem, students work in groups to plan and construct a device, assess its performance, determine the construction cost, and explain and demonstrate the device to others. They also participate in peer review of other groups' design solutions.	Students build, test, and evaluate devices for treating simulated stormwater, using a standard construction kit of readily acquired materials. They demonstrate their devices in a public assembly and evaluate the performance of other teams' devices.

GUIDING STUDENT INQUIRY

ABOUT THE *TEACHER EDITION*

In the *Teacher Edition* we have included information that will help you guide your students through the background text, protocols, activities, interactive research possibilities, and design challenges that make up the four sections of the Student Edition:

Section 1—Understanding Watershed Dynamics

Four chapters introducing students to watersheds, land use, streams, and related research, monitoring, and management.

Section 2—Protocols: Introduction to Research

Ten protocols providing specific instruction on research techniques related to the study of watersheds. This section also includes three activities that involve data manipulation or computer modeling software and specifically relate to an individual protocol.

Section 3—Interactive Research: Field Studies and Experiments

Suggestions and forms that guide students through the development of relevant, interesting, and interactive research projects that use the protocols in Section 2.

Section 4—Interactive Research: Stormwater Treatment Design Challenge

An engineering design challenge in which students design and develop a device for treating simulated stormwater runoff. The design challenge requires students to draw on knowledge gained from the introductory text and protocols.

Sections 2, 3, and 4 include forms designed to guide students through the processes of planning a research or design project, analyzing and presenting their results, and engaging in peer review.

UNDERSTANDING WATERSHED DYNAMICS

The first chapter of the Student Edition introduces students to watersheds and how humans interact with them. The subsequent chapters examine land use practices and effects, stream ecology, and how aquatic systems can be monitored, modeled, or studied by scientists, local governments, and other interested parties.

At the end of each chapter we have provided several discussion questions. Model responses to some of the questions are provided below.

MODEL RESPONSES TO DISCUSSION QUESTIONS

Chapter 1: Introduction to Watershed Dynamics

▶ Historically, wetlands have often been considered "wasted" land that can be drained, filled, and used as "new" land for development and construction. What are some possible ecological consequences of this type of development strategy?

Potential ecological consequences include reduction in groundwater recharge (which may in turn affect base flow), reduction in the uptake of dissolved chemicals, increases in the stream velocity (which may scour downstream), increased flooding, and the loss of important habitat for aquatic birds and other organisms.

Chapter 2: What's in a Watershed?

▶ What are some of the advantages of remote sensing compared with field sampling?

On the plus side, remote sensing can be a very cost-effective way to gather information on land uses over a large area. It can be used to study areas that might be inaccessible otherwise (because of rugged terrain, remoteness, private ownership, or other factors). Remote sensing may reveal features that are not readily apparent on the ground (such as old stream channels). Historical airphotos can also reveal structures or natural features that are no longer evident, such as old landfills.

Chapter 3: Biological Communities in Streams

▶ Why would it matter if input of untreated sewage or manure killed all of the pollution-sensitive invertebrates in a stream?

These organisms are important elements of aquatic food webs; if they are lost, so is the work that they do by eating other things and the resource that they provide by being eaten (e.g, by trout). This can affect not only aquatic organisms, but species that rely on aquatic organisms, such as insect-eating birds or fish-eating people.

▶ Why does it make sense to use aquatic invertebrate populations to assess streamwater quality?

Ecologically, many of these species spend most of their lives in the water; and many are very sensitive to unhealthy conditions, such as low levels of dissolved oxygen. Because they typically live for relatively long times (weeks, months, or years), their presence not only corroborates field testing of water quality at the time they are collected; they also provide evidence of historical water quality, at least in the recent past. Also, as noted in the previous question, these organisms are often important at the lower levels of food webs, and their presence or absence helps determine the presence or absence of other organisms. On a pragmatic level, aquatic invertebrates are easy to collect and, with practice, to identify to higher-level taxonomic groups.

▶ What are some possible limitations of assessing streamwater quality using invertebrate sampling?

Species vary in their sensitivity to pollutants. Some stoneflies that are found only in highly oxygenated water are quite tolerant of low pH. Consequently, they are useful as indicators of organic pollution, but their presence does not necessarily indicate a healthy stream. Other limitations of using invertebrates in water quality assessment include the relatively high cost of monitoring, the need for monitors to be trained in identification, and the fact that, unlike chemical or flowrate monitoring, biological monitoring cannot easily be automated.

Chapter 4: Physical Characteristics of Streams

▶ Why do some streams flow year-round, and others dry up during the summer months?

A stream will flow year-round if rainfall is frequent or groundwater reaches the surface year-round somewhere upstream. Much of this is determined by climate and terrain, but human activities in a watershed can also affect base flow. For example, if wetlands or stream meanders are removed, or the landscape is made less permeable (e.g., by paving), the water table will drop because groundwater is not being recharged at its former rate. It should be noted that many seasonal streams and wetlands are naturally so, and may indeed serve an important ecological function by being seasonal. Wetter doesn't always mean better.

▶ What steps could be taken to reduce the impact of development on flood levels after large storms?

The overall imperviousness of the landscape can be reduced by planting trees or other plants (this can even be done on the tops of buildings, so-called green roofs). Technologies can be installed to retain stormwater temporarily and permit it to seep into the ground. It also makes sense to look upstream: Working with upstream neighbors to develop and enforce sensible land use practices reduces post-storm water levels downstream.

Chapter 5: Stream Chemistry

▶ What makes some lakes more susceptible than others to the effects of acid precipitation?

The effects of acid precipitation are reduced if the water is buffered, or alkaline. Buffering is caused by the presence of carbonate, bicarbonate, or hydroxide ions, typically because there is limestone or similar minerals in the soil and/or bedrock beneath the lake or elsewhere in the watershed.

▶ What impacts would you expect to see in a lake if it received runoff containing high concentrations of fertilizer nutrients?

Typically, this condition would stimulate the growth of macrophytes, especially in shallow areas, as well as free-floating algae. The shoreline may become so choked with vegetation that it is no longer navigable or swimmable. The water would probably become more turbid (less clear) and it would be more difficult to see the bottom. In extreme cases, fish kills might occur on hot summer nights, from subsurface anoxia that arises from high rates of organic decomposition.

Chapter 6: Modeling and Management

▶ What can we do with models that we cannot accomplish through experiments in the lab or field?

Models can be used to evaluate the effects of factors that cannot be easily manipulated in an experiment, such as the number of people living in a watershed or the amount of rain that falls in a particular storm. Models can be used to add or remove factors systematically, in order to understand their importance. Models also allow people to evaluate the potential effects of expensive interventions (e.g., upgrading a wastewater treatment plant) before investing in them. Models also permit the investigation of events that are rare but important, such as 100-year floods.

▶ After we build a model, how do you think we could test it to evaluate the accuracy of its predictions?

Typically, models are evaluated by comparing their predictions to natural events or by testing their predictions experimentally. Models are also evaluated by testing them in different settings.

PROTOCOLS
INTRODUCTION TO RESEARCH

The protocols and activities in this book provide students with tools to map and explore watersheds; to collect stream organisms and use their collection to assess water quality; to measure the discharge of streams; to examine the chemistry of streamwater; and to use computer software to model watershed processes. After becoming familiar with one or all of these protocols, students can use them to design and carry out research projects in local watersheds.

Many of the protocols in this book require students to work near or wade into streams, rivers, and other bodies of water. Because even shallow, slowly flowing streams may have deep areas or slippery bottoms, it is important to review safety precautions with your students before beginning each protocol.

PROTOCOL 1—WATERSHED FIELD SURVEY

Students will explore and conduct a field survey of a local watershed or sub-watershed small enough to tour by foot and/or bus. An area of no more than 4 square miles is best if part of your survey will be by vehicle, less if you will be doing it entirely by foot. If you are not sure how to delineate the watershed your students will visit, first explore your site on foot, and then use Protocol 3 to delineate it with a topographical map. In selecting a study watershed, we recommend consulting with local resources (e.g., county extension agent, watershed management council) that may already be involved in watershed research monitoring or education. They may also be able to assist you with watershed delineation.

Before beginning the protocol, you will need to prepare a map (e.g., USGS topographic map) of your study area and label it with up to 18 lettered (A–R) observation points. If you plan to do Protocol 2 in the future, examine the airphotos you will use and choose observations points that will help students orient themselves to the landscape (e.g., water towers, railroads, rivers). Some points should be landscape features that will be visible during the field trip, and others should be areas that may impact water quality (e.g., parking lots, drains). You may also want to provide scale information on your maps, and if you have enlarged or reduced them, you (or your students) will need to recalculate the scale.

In addition to the qualitative analysis in Protocol 1, we have also developed protocols for quantitative analyses of land use. To access these protocols visit the *Watershed Dynamics* section of our Web site (*http://ei.cornell.edu/watersheds*).

PROTOCOL 2—OBJECT RECOGNITION USING MAPS AND AIRPHOTOS

Students will use topographic maps and airphotos to learn skills for recognizing objects that affect watersheds. Each student group will need at least one contour map and one airphoto. If possible, complete Protocol 1 first and use those maps with Protocol 2. Note that both Table 2.2 (Protocol 1—Watershed Field Survey) and Table 2.3 (Protocol 2— Object Recognition Using Maps and Airphotos) permit you to reference up to 18 features, which you'll need to label "A" through "R" on the map beforehand.

Free airphotos are viewable online for most of the United States. However, for Protocol 2 we recommend using higher resolution paper prints, which you can purchase from a number of sources (see Sources of Airphotos, Maps, and Supplies, p. 76). Airphotos printed from original negatives have much higher resolution than the digitized photographs on the Internet, and your students will be able to make out much smaller landscape features. If handled carefully and stored out of sunlight between uses, these photos will last for decades.

If you order print airphotos, we suggest photo-enlarging your study area to make photos that are large enough for 2–3 students to examine at the same time (18" square is a good size). We also recommend ordering photos of the same area taken at different dates. It may be possible to obtain photos for watersheds as old as the 1930s and as recent as the present day. Finally, you may want to provide scale information for the airphotos as well as the maps, such as, "In the 1938 photograph, l cm = 60 m." Alternatively, calculating the scale can be an exercise left to the students. This will be easy to do if an athletic playing field (or other structure of known dimensions) appears in the photo.

PROTOCOL 3—DELINEATING A WATERSHED

This protocol leads students through the process of delineating the boundaries of a watershed. Depending on your local topography, this task may be relatively simple or it may be difficult for even an expert. One way to make it more straightforward is to begin by focusing on a small sub-watershed that provides water to an *order 1* stream segment (i.e., the section of a stream from the point where surface flow begins to the point where it is joined by another stream). Stream *order* is defined and illustrated in the Student Edition. Label the downstream end of the stream segment "A," and the upstream end, "B."

We include a map that you can use (Figure 2) and a solution (Figure 3), but if you have local maps, we strongly suggest that you mark your own points on a landscape that will be familiar to your students. It is not necessary for all students to use the same points A and B (or even the same maps), but because they will be checking their answers against other groups' solutions, you should try to ensure that there are some duplicates of each A-B setup.

After they delineate their watershed, students will measure its area. A photocopy-ready 1/100 square kilometer grid suitable for use with 7.5-minute USGS topographic maps is reproduced in Figure 4. Alternatively, students can design a measurement method of their own, and are asked to describe it in the activity's last question.

If you decide to use the map we provide (Figure 2) you have several options as you move on to Protocol 4:

▶ Have your students complete Protocol 3 a second time, this time using a local map. Then proceed to Protocol 4.

▶ Provide a solution for your local watershed (such as your own delineation or a delineation done by previous students) to use in Protocol 4.

▶ Work through Protocol 4 together as a class, displaying a delineated watershed map with an overhead projector and drawing more heavily on students' experiences during their field surveys than on their analysis of airphoto imagery.

FIGURE 2
Sample Map, from Sherman Quadrangle, USGS

FIGURE 3
Solution of the Sample Map (Sherman Quadrangle, USGS)

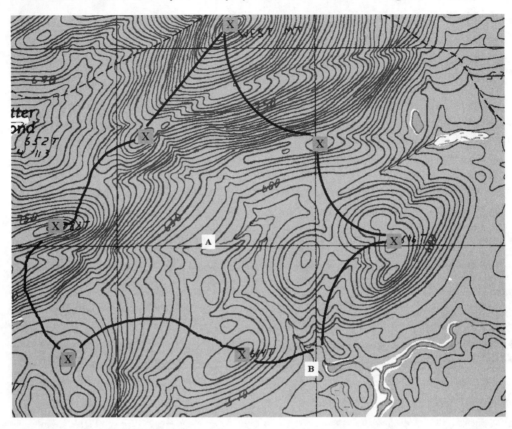

FIGURE 4
Area Grid

1 square = 1/100 sq. km on a 7.5-minute USGS topographic map

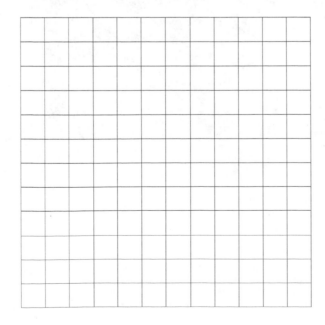

PROTOCOL 4—ANALYZING STREAM INTEGRITY USING REMOTE SENSING DATA

Protocol 4 involves the assessment of stream integrity through the use of remote sensing data and the "Watershed Habitat Evaluation and Biotic Integrity Protocol" (WHEBIP). Your students will need access to maps and airphotos of their study area. If they are not familiar with the area in the maps and photos, you may want to provide them with land use maps (see "Sources of Airphotos, Maps, and Supplies," p. 76).

If your students completed Protocol 2 (Object Recognition Using Maps and Airphotos), we recommend that you use the same airphotos and again focus on a local watershed. You may wish to have all of your students analyze the same stream segment, or you may choose to have different student groups calculate WHEBIP scores for different stream segments. If you select the latter approach, we recommend that you have at least two student groups characterize each segment, then compare and discuss their results.

If your students completed Protocol 3 (Delineating a Watershed), we recommend that they use the delineated watershed transparencies and score the enclosed stream segment. An alternative is to apply WHEBIP to a stream segment in an alternative region (e.g., the entire area covered by an airphoto), or an area bounded by easily defined features (e.g., highways, geographic coordinates). This option may be especially useful if your watersheds are very small or extend over multiple airphotos or maps. Should you make this modification, simply explain to your students that whenever the protocol's instructions refer to "watershed" or "drainage basin" they should refer to the alternative region you've selected.

You may wish to modify the written instructions for Protocol 4 so they refer to specific maps, airphotos, or other materials you use in your local studies. An editable version of the protocol can be downloaded from the EI Web site (*http://ei.cornell.edu/watersheds*).

Finally, note that while WHEBIP has been carefully evaluated in a couple of watersheds, it is not a decades-old protocol that has been used and validated in many different types of watersheds by many different researchers. Its newness is one of the reasons we decided to adapt it for use in this curriculum. As you work with your students, we hope you will point out WHEBIP's provisional status and challenge your students to critique the method in the context of their local studies. For example, is there something about your local watershed that renders aspects of the protocol irrelevant? You may also wish to explain that in a colleague's study, for example, part of the research involved carefully assessing stream integrity using conventional (ground-based) methods and statistically correlating them with the WHEBIP scores calculated from remote sensing. In convincing colleagues of the merits of a new method, scientists must often demonstrate that the new method produces data comparable to accepted methods.

Activity 4.1—Stream Integrity and Aquatic Communities

In this activity, your students will make comparisons between WHEBIP (Protocol 4) and other types of stream assessment data. Because these data demonstrate the variability found in most ecological research, completing this activity will help your students interpret data from research they may conduct after working with *Watershed Dynamics* protocols.

The protocol instructions allow for two possibilities. If you do not have easy access to computers, or if your students are either unfamiliar or not ready to work with graphing software, you may wish to complete this activity using the graphs we have provided (Figures 5–10). If you would like your students to develop their own graphs, we have provided the necessary raw data in paper form (p. 35), as well as on the EI Web site (information on downloading data and graphs is provided below).

Before beginning this activity, your students should be familiar with Protocol 4, Analyzing Streamside Habitats Using Remote Sensing Data. We also suggest that you have your students read the "Background" section and answer the first seven questions on the Worksheet as homework the day before beginning this activity.

Graphs Created by Students in Activity 4.1

(1) Comparison of WHEBIP and RCE Habitat Scores (Figure 5)

The relationship between RCE (Riparian, Channel, and Environmental inventory) and WHEBIP scores is very strong, suggesting that WHEBIP is a useful tool for assessing stream integrity. Nevertheless, as your students examine this graph, you may want to challenge them to brainstorm other potentially important stream and riparian characteristics that might be missed during remote sensing (e.g., depth, velocity, presence of riffles, or stream sections under trees)—and therefore invisible from above.

(2) Invertebrate Biotic Integrity (InvertBI) and Habitat (Figure 6)

The measure of invertebrate biotic integrity used here is a modified version of the Family Biotic Index (Hilsenhoff 1988). You may wish to discuss with your students the limitations of an index like this one that is sensitive primarily to *organic pollution*, such as the release of untreated sewage. The InvertBI measure of biotic integrity would be unsuitable for identifying streams polluted by acidic precipitation, a form of *inorganic pollution*.

(3) Percent Pollution Intolerant = Invertebrates (InvertPI) and Habitat (Figures 7 and 8)

Students inspecting Figure 7 may suggest that it looks like there are actually two different sets of data in the graph, one with a generally upward progression, and one with virtually no pollution-intolerant organisms. In fact, if you graph only the samples from headwater (order 1 or 2) stream segments, as we have done in Figure 8, the relationship between stream integrity and InvertPI is much stronger, because most of the sites with few or no pollution-intolerant individuals were larger, main channel streams. In the Table 7 data (and the file available on the EI Web site), headwater sites have the prefix "HW" and main channel sites have the prefix "MC."

(4) Fish Species Richness and Habitat (Figure 9)

One possible reason for the weak (not statistically significant) downward trend in this graph is that although headwater streams may have excellent integrity ratings, they may be too shallow to support larger fish species.

(5) Fish Biotic Integrity (FishBI) and Habitat (Figure 9)

The fish biotic integrity metric is based on Karr's (1981) Indices of Biotic Integrity, modified to reflect specific conditions found in the French Creek watershed. There is a statistically significant upward trend in these data.

Step 8 in the activity directs students to add linear trend lines to two graphs: (1) WHEBIP by RCE and (2) WHEBIP by Fish Species Richness. Because there is a strong relationship between WHEBIP and RCE, developing a linear trend line for this graph is reasonably straightforward. However, the relationship between WHEBIP and Fish Species Richness is less strong, and therefore trend lines may be difficult to draw—and your students' results may be highly variable. Depending on the abilities of your students, you may want to lead a discussion of variability and relationships in data series. In case you or your students are interested, the R^2 of the first graph is 0.866 (highly correlated and statistically significant), and the R^2 of the second graph is only 0.165 (low correlation, not statistically significant).

ONLINE FILES ARE AVAILABLE ON EI'S WEB SITE

You can download Excel and text files containing the raw data and graphs used in Activity 4.1 from the *Watershed Dynamics* section of the EI Web site (*http://ei.cornell.edu/watersheds*). To each of the Excel graphs reproduced in this book, we have added a regression (trend) line and a correlation coefficient; more advanced students may be interested in further statistical analyses of these data. Feel free to adapt these files to best suit your needs.

FIGURE 5
Graph of WHEBIP and RCE (Activity 4.1)

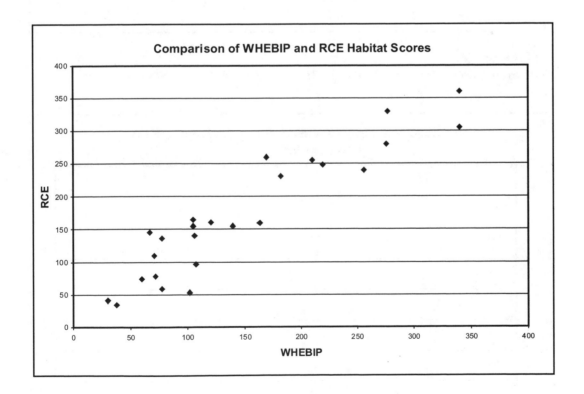

FIGURE 6
Graph of WHEBIP and InvertBI (Activity 4.1)

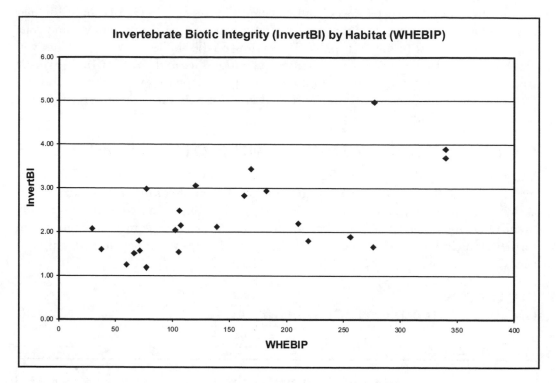

FIGURE 7
Graph of WHEBIP and InvertPI (Activity 4.1)

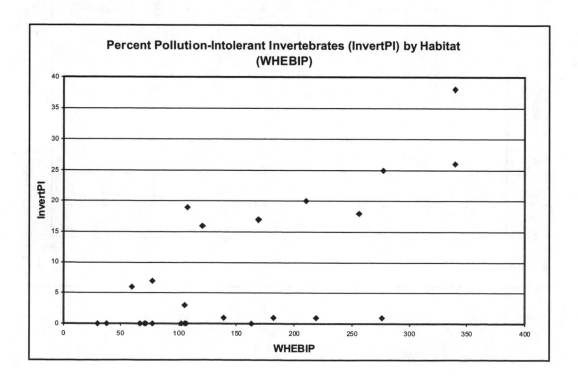

FIGURE 8
Graph of WHEBIP and InvertPI, Headwater Sites

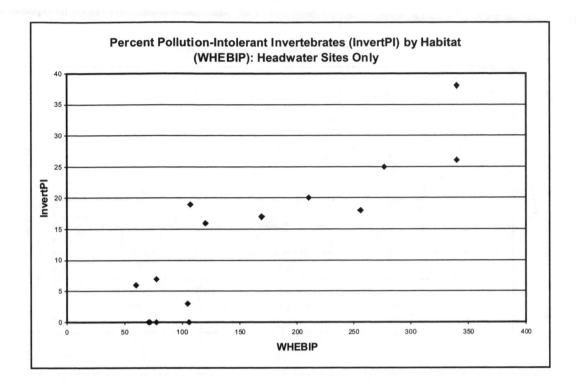

FIGURE 9
Graph of WHEBIP and Fish Species Richness (Activity 4.1)

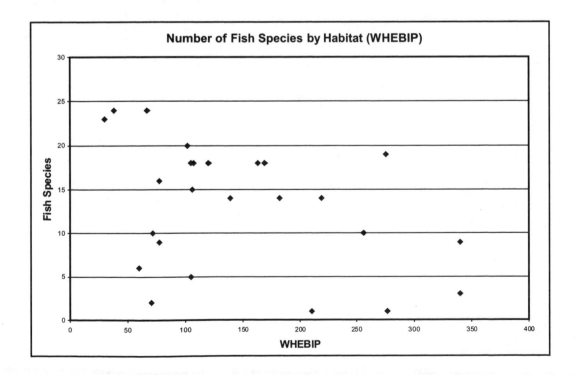

FIGURE 10
Graph of WHEBIP and FishBI (Activity 4.1)

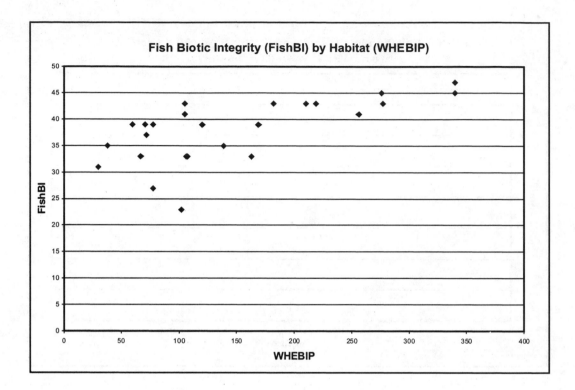

TABLE 7
Dataset for Activity 4.1

Sample site	WHEBIP	RCE	InvertBI	InvertPI (%)	Fish Species (#)	FishBI
HW1	340	360	3.70	26	9	47
HW2	169	260	3.44	17	18	39
HW3	107	97	2.15	19	18	33
HW4	120	161	3.06	16	18	39
HW5	277	330	4.97	25	1	43
HW6	210	255	2.20	20	1	43
HW7	78	136	2.98	7	9	39
HW8	60	74	1.26	6	6	39
HW9	340	305	3.90	38	3	45
HW10	72	78	1.57	0	10	37
HW11	106	140	2.48	0	15	33
HW12	78	59	1.19	0	16	27
HW13	105	155	1.55	3	5	41
HW14	71	110	1.81	0	2	39
HW15	256	240	1.90	18	10	41
MC1	102	53	2.05	0	20	23
MC2	139	155	2.13	1	14	35
MC3	105	165	1.55	0	18	43
MC4	38	34	1.61	0	24	35
MC5	163	160	2.83	0	18	33
MC6	67	145	1.52	0	24	33
MC7	276	280	1.67	1	19	45
MC8	219	248	1.80	1	14	43
MC9	182	231	2.94	1	14	43
MC10	30	41	2.07	0	23	31

PROTOCOLS 5–7—MACROINVERTEBRATES AND WATER QUALITY

Protocol 5 provides a general method for collecting aquatic invertebrates, and Protocols 6 and 7 use these collected organisms to analyze streamwater quality. Protocol 6 is very simple and yields only a rough estimate of water quality, while Protocol 7 is more involved and provides a more refined analysis (see Figure 11). None of these protocols requires knowledge of invertebrate taxonomy beyond that represented in the Stream Invertebrate ID Sheet (p. 81, Student Edition). Note: If strong currents or water depth preclude going into the water, the protocols may be used with invertebrates collected using artificial substrates (see below).

After examining and counting stream invertebrates, many students will be interested in returning them—alive—to the stream from which they were collected. To reduce mortality, use lots of fresh water in holding containers and process samples in the coolest available areas (e.g., in the shade). Consider using nested plastic boxes, and continuously replace the water in the lower box with fresh, cool water from the stream. Finally, if you add ice to the lower box and use an aquarium bubbler in the upper box, you may even be able to keep samples alive in a heated classroom for several hours before returning them to the stream. This final step will be especially useful if you collect invertebrates during the winter, but wish to examine them in the warmth of your classroom.

If you would like to store invertebrates for future classes, you will need to preserve them in alcohol. An easy storage method is to place invertebrates in small vials of rubbing alcohol (or 70% ethanol). After they have been in the alcohol for about 24 hours, replace the solution with fresh alcohol. This is necessary because the water in your invertebrate samples dilutes the initial alcohol to levels unacceptable for long-term storage. After replacement, your samples can be stored indefinitely. Be sure to store them in a safe place, as alcohol is flammable.

Before you begin these protocols, you may wish to find out if other groups are doing similar measurements or if there are potential resources available at the local, watershed, or state level. Contact local watershed management officials or the EPA's "Adopt Your Watershed" program (*http://www.epa.gov/adopt*) for more information. Another reason to do background research before beginning your studies is that some states require that you obtain a collecting permit to sample stream invertebrates. A local environmental conservation officer can help you determine what you need.

FIGURE 11
Using Protocols 5, 6, and 7

Conduct this protocol first...   **...Then conduct one of these protocols**

Protocol 6. *Simplified Stream Biota Test.* Look for stoneflies, mayflies, and caddisflies. Then use the enclosed, simple chart to classify the stream water quality.

Protocol 5. *Collecting Benthic Macroinvertebrates.* Instructions for collecting samples and doing preliminary sorting and identification

Protocol 7. *Index of Biotic Integrity.* Collect 100 invertebrates. Determine: (1) How many taxa are there? (2) How abundant is the most common of these? (3) How many of the species are mayflies, stoneflies, and caddisflies? Then use the chart to calculate and interpret the IBI score.

ARTIFICIAL SUBSTRATES

Most students enjoy going into the water to collect invertebrates (Protocol 5), but sometimes that just isn't possible. An alternative approach is to place artificial substrates in the stream for 4–6 weeks, then retrieve them along with the invertebrates that have moved in. The animals are then rinsed off or manually removed for identification.

There are several different types of artificial substrates, the most common being multiplate samplers (hardboard disks bolted together to make a many-layered sandwich with spaces between the disks) and rock baskets (wire baskets filled with stones). Samplers are typically anchored with a cord to a spot on shore from which the sampler can later be retrieved. You'll want to remove the samplers from the water carefully, to minimize the number of animals that abandon their home when it is disturbed.

Artificial substrates have advantages and disadvantages compared to collecting with nets. On the plus side, they provide standardized microhabitats even where such habitats don't exist, such as on the bottom of a stream that has no loose stones. If you have multiple study sites along a stream, such as upstream and downstream of a suspected pollution source, artificial substrates may help you distinguish between habitat effects and toxic effects.

On the minus side, measures of invertebrate diversity taken from artificial substrates can't be directly compared with measures taken from conventional netting methods. If you plan to use artificial substrates, use them at all of your study sites. This doesn't preclude netting at some sites; in fact, having data from multiple sampling methods may provide a richer picture of stream conditions. Artificial substrates are available from commercial suppliers (see References, p. 77), but constructing substrates can be a great project for students. You may wish to start with conventional designs, and then create a Design Challenge of your own.

Rock baskets can be made in any size out of a variety of different materials. Chicken wire is cheap but will puncture your fingers when you work with it, so we suggest using a larger gauge mesh (such as "hardware cloth"). Galvanized, plastic, or vinyl-coated wire will last for many years. You can form a cylinder-shaped basket and two circular end pieces, or fold the wire into a box shape with rectangular end pieces. The components can be clipped together easily with plastic cable ties. Be sure to hinge one side so you can open the basket: Use cable ties on one side and clip the other side with a removable fastener. Fill the basket with rocks that are just large enough to stay put.

PROTOCOL 8—MEASURING STREAM DISCHARGE

In this protocol, students will measure both streamwater velocity and discharge using a variant of a velocity-area float method. Although the protocol calls for using an orange, you may find a cork useful in shallow streams.

If you or your students are involved in long-term stream monitoring research, you may find that, after using Protocol 8 to understand how discharge measurements are taken, *routinely* monitoring discharge takes more time than you have available. Accordingly, you may be able to use flow data collected by others to assist you in long-term studies. The following are resources you may be able to use:

(1) Inspect bridge footings on your study stream. If you see a scale painted down to the water surface, contact your local highway department and ask whether a stage-discharge graph has been made. With the graph, you will be able to measure discharge indirectly by simply reading the water level.

(2) Locate a nearby, automated gauging station. If there is no station on your specific stream, there may be one on a comparable stream nearby, or on a lower reach, which could serve as a proxy. Involve your students in evaluating the suitability of the proxy: Is precipitation highly variable in your local area? Are land use practices near the gauging station comparable to those around your study site? If conditions are similar, data from the proxy can be used in your studies.

(3) Finally, the USGS provides an excellent set of online tools to support the analysis of water data from sites all over the country. Their Web site (*http://water.usgs.gov*) provides access to real-time data from over 1.5 million sites, including telemetry-equipped monitoring stations. You can easily access historical stream discharge data, lake and other surface water data, and groundwater information.

PROTOCOL 9—AQUATIC CHEMISTRY

In this protocol, students develop a question or questions about the chemistry of their study stream, take samples from the stream, use commercially available test kits or probes to analyze the samples, and then analyze their result to learn what they mean.

Using chemical test kits without first developing research questions can often lead to unsatisfactory results. Accordingly, the most important part of the protocol is choosing a question *before* taking samples. Questions can be as simple as, "What is the pH of the stream behind our school right now?" or as complex as, "How do the dissolved oxygen levels of two streams in our community vary over time?" To help students generate questions, you may want to lead a classroom discussion about streams, streamwater variables, and test kits or probes. The Interactive Research section (pp. 133–175) of the Student Edition might in help this process.

Once students have generated questions and chosen their study sites, you will need to determine what chemical test kits or probes you will use. You may decide to limit your students to questions that can be answered by kits and probes already available to them, or you may consider purchasing new ones. There are many commercially avail able kits and probes (see p. 77 for contact information) to suit just about any school budget, from simple "drop in a tablet" tests to sophisticated methods that use laptop computers and probes.

After measuring samples with test kits and/or probes, students will be instructed to organize their data in a way that is most useful to answering their questions. If questions are simple or few samples were taken, the results may already be appropriately organized in the Data Forms (p. 104). If questions are more complicated, or more than one variable was measured, students may need to experiment to determine the best organizational scheme.

After the data are organized, the protocol instructs students to create graphs. If graphing these types of data is new to your students, you may find it helpful to lead a classroom discussion about appropriate types of graphs. The "Analyzing Data" section of the Teacher Edition (pp. 53–57), which provides information on planning ahead, graphing, data variability, and data interpretation, contains information that may be useful for this discussion.

Finally, students will use the Aquatic Chemistry Reference Sheet (pp. 102) to learn what their test kit results actually mean in terms of streamwater suitability for different types of aquatic organisms. Though this reference sheet provides useful information about several common streamwater variables, it is by no means a final resource. If your students have additional questions about their results, point them towards SciLinks or the local library. You may also want to have students refer to the Aquatic Chemistry Reference Sheet for help in planning their original questions.

PROTOCOL 10—COMPUTER MODELING WITH STELLA

This protocol is slightly different from the others in that it is not so much a tool to measure watershed variables as it is an activity that will introduce students to computer modeling. This process will prepare students to develop simple models of their own, which may be a useful component of watershed research or monitoring. The protocol also is a useful introduction to Activities 10.1 and 10.2, which incorporate more complicated watershed models developed by the Environmental Inquiry team.

This protocol has three parts. In the first part, students conduct an activity in which they examine how water flows out of a container, and how the amount of water in the container affects that flow rate. This physical modeling exercise provides a simple, hands-on experience with a concrete model of a dynamic system. In the second part, students explore the basics of STELLA software and build a computer model of the system used in Part 1. With the STELLA model, they explore the relationship between the rate that water flows out of a container and the amount of water present in the bucket, eventually making the system more complex by having an inflow (recharge). In the third part, students further expand the simple model and explore some of the more advanced components of STELLA.

INITIAL SUGGESTIONS FOR PART 1

▶ Allow the students to choose their own container and hole size and shape. This will encourage divergent treatments and provide a motivation for exploring additional factors at a later time.

▶ Allow students to determine what volumes to test. This will motivate them to think through an experimental design issue. Keep in mind that this could make comparisons between groups difficult, depending on your method of comparison.

▶ Students may create a setup where a poor measurement of the instantaneous rate is obtained because too much water drains out (e.g., 400 mL drains from a starting volume of 600 mL). Allow this to happen, and then ask the students to consider if there is a problem.

WRAP-UP SUGGESTIONS FOR PART 1

▶ When they are done, have your students compare the results from different groups. Ask them what patterns emerged.

▶ Discuss the difficulties that students encountered in determining what range of volumes to use, and how many trials to run.

▶ Discuss the challenges that students had in carrying out the experiment. How could they improve their approach?

▶ Discuss graphing techniques. How did students determine what scales to use? How did they use the graph to make their prediction? Did they draw a straight line through their data? Did their line go through the origin? Would they make different decisions if they made their graphs again?

▶ Point out leaks (e.g., water running down your hand), and ask students to suggest ways to test if they are significant and ways to minimize them if they are.

▶ Ask students whether hole shape or size affected the way flowrate increased with volume.

▶ Have students compare similar volumes and hole size in different shaped bottles (wide versus thin). Ask students if volume is the only factor.

▶ Discuss other possible factors affecting the flowrate. You might be surprised at what they come up with (starting volume, hole size, bottle shape, temperature, adhesion, atmospheric pressure, etc.).

▶ An example graph is provided in Figure 12.

INITIAL SUGGESTIONS FOR PARTS 2 AND 3

▶ Run through the model yourself beforehand, experimenting with STELLA's features and familiarizing yourself with the program. This will help you anticipate questions your students may have.

▶ Because computer modeling is abstract in its nature, reminding the students of the physical system they are modeling may help your students understand the model better.

WRAP-UP SUGGESTIONS FOR PARTS 2 AND 3

▶ During discussion, you can build upon the physical modeling exercise and compare and contrast it with the STELLA model. For example, you might point out that making the STELLA model more realistic also had the added effect of making the model more complex. How complex should the model be? What is a good trade-off between realism and complexity? Point out that watershed managers and other model users constantly wrestle with this issue.

FIGURE 12
Example Graph of Flow vs. Volume

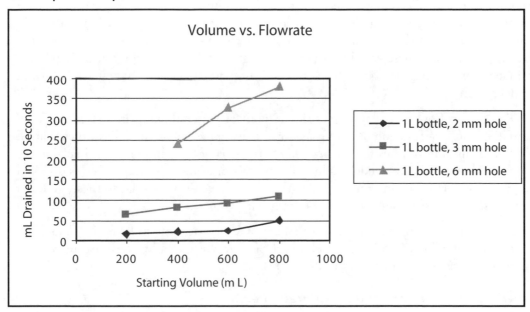

OTHER NOTES FOR PARTS 2 AND 3

▶ This activity is designed for use with a range of class periods and student abilities. If getting through the entire activity in one period is not possible, an ideal stopping point is between Parts 2 and 3. For ambitious students, you might let them continue on with Part 3 and see how far they can get. You might also have them explore the model in greater depth, asking them to record how changing variables (such as leak rate or flowrate) may affect the model.

DOWNLOADING STELLA SOFTWARE

STELLA software is produced by High Performance Systems, Inc. (HPS). HPS offers a free "demo" version that allows you and your students to conduct this protocol and use the EI models presented in Activities 10.1 and 10.2; however, you will likely need to purchase the software should you wish to proceed beyond these activities.

Because HPS occasionally updates its demo-downloading procedure, we provide only general instructions here. First, visit the HPS Web site (*http://www.hps-inc.com*). Then follow links to or search for the "Demo" or "Download Demo" version of STELLA. Should you have difficulty, you may wish to contact HPS for help via their Web site.

Once you have successfully downloaded the software, you should install it, open it up, and explore how it works. The HPS Web site may have a tutorial or "How It Works" animation that may be useful to first-time users. Before using STELLA with your students, you will likely find it useful to run through Protocol 10 and one or both of the Activities. Be sure to install STELLA on the computers your students will be using.

Activity 10.1—Modeling Land Use and Streamflow

In this activity, students use STELLA software to model streamflow in a watershed after a rain event. The watershed has four types of land use: urban, suburban, farm, and forest. When using the model, students can alter both the land use distribution and rainfall amount. They can also make predictions regarding how the stream will respond to these variables. Because land usage is the most important factor affecting whether water will enter streams as runoff or subsurface flow (i.e., how long it will take water to travel to the stream), by altering these variables students will gain an understanding of their relative influences on streamflow. Note that total land use percentage must equal 100% for the model to run.

The Streamflow model simulates the amount of water flowing in a stream after a rainfall event, as a function of land usage in the watershed. The model assumes that all rainfall eventually reaches the stream via overland runoff or underground subsurface flow. In other words, the model assumes that no water evaporates, transpires, is diverted to sewers, or is retained in groundwater. All models have limits similar to these, and you may wish to discuss these types of limitations with your students.

In Question 10 on the student Worksheet, we suggest that students use data from their own watershed. If you cannot obtain data from your area, we have included land use percentages for a community in New York State.

Downloading the Model and Related Files

To download a copy of the Activity 10.1 STELLA model, visit the EI Web site at *http://ei.cornell.edu/watersheds*. We have also provided online information regarding the technical components and troubleshooting tips for the model.

Critiquing the Model

You may want to conclude this section with a brief discussion about the benefits and potential misuses of modeling. The following are possible discussion questions:

▶ Why would a STELLA model be useful in this situation?

▶ Were the model results useful? Did the model give a plausible answer to the original predictions?

▶ What are some of the assumptions that were made in the design of the model?

▶ What additional factors might be added to a model like this to make it more accurate? What else would we need to know and include in our model? (For example, to add evaporation and transpiration, we would need to estimate the rates of these processes and include variables like seasonality).

▶ Why do scientists use models, in general? What kinds of things do we need to be aware of when using models?

Activity 10.2—Modeling the Management of a Watershed to Limit Eutrophication

In this activity students first learn how four watershed factors (population, land use, agricultural practices, and wastewater treatment efficiency) affect cultural eutrophication of a simulated lake. Eutrophication indicators in the model include Secchi depth (a measure of turbidity), dissolved oxygen, and algal density. Students then use the model to measure lake responses in three different scenarios. After completing each scenario they are asked to make general recommendations to a fictional town board. The scenarios were designed to allow students to explore them in any order, and to complete just one or all three.

▶ **Scenario 1**—students model how increasing human population growth affects the depth to which algae grow, turbidity of the water column, and lake-bottom dissolved oxygen levels.

▶ **Scenario 2**—students examine how agricultural practices and the amount of watershed land used in agricultural affect eutrophication.

▶ **Scenario 3**—using specific budget constraints, students model the most effective way to limit cultural eutrophication.

Downloading the Model and Related Files

To download a copy of the Activity 10.2 STELLA model, visit the *Watershed Dynamics* page of the EI Web site at *http://ei.cornell.edu/pubs/wd.asp*. We have also provided online information regarding the technical components and troubleshooting tips for the model.

Model Responses to Activity Worksheet Questions

All of the activities contain worksheets with questions for students. While many of these questions ask for answers that are likely to diverge widely (e.g., predictions), others have answers that will remain relatively constant for all students. We have provided model answers to many of those questions below.

Activity 4.1—Stream Integrity and Aquatic Communities

1. Review WHEBIP scoring and consider hypothetical Streams 1 and 2. Stream 1 has a WHEBIP score of 248, and Stream 2 has a score of 175. Which is likely to be a healthier habitat for stream plants and animals? Why?

    Stream 1 is likely to be a healthier habitat for streams plants and animals. Though Streams 1 and 2 both have "Very Good" Stream Integrity Ratings, Stream 1 approaches "Excellent," and Stream 2 is close to being rated "Good." As we learned in the background section of Activity 4.1, stream integrity is an indictor of water quality and the types of organisms that live in streams. Stream 1's higher integrity rating suggests that it is more likely to have better water quality and healthier habitat.

2. List three things you might find in a stream segment's drainage basin that would tend to increase the area's WHEBIP score.

    The possible answers to this question are numerous. To evaluate answers, refer to Table 4.5 (Student Edition, Protocol 4). Those variables with a higher subscore (appearing near the top of each category) will increase a watershed's WHEBIP score.

5. Without using any actual numbers, describe the differences between the communities in these two streams. Which community has greater diversity?

The community in Stream 3 has greater diversity. (Please note that our intention here is to elicit students' commonsense understanding of "diversity"; that is why the question is asked without first defining the term. If you grade this exercise, we encourage you to keep that in mind and to be generous in assigning credit to students' commonsense responses.)

Mathematically, diversity reflects the number of species in an area ("species richness") as well as the relative abundance of individuals of the different species. Stream 3 has four different "species" (three of which have several individuals in the sample), and Stream 4 has only two, with one species predominating. Note that our sample from Stream 4 yielded more organisms (absolute abundance), but Stream 3 had both more species and greater relative abundance across species.

6. In your own words, describe what you think *diversity* and *abundance* mean.

Diversity *reflects the number of species in an area, while* abundance *refers to the number of individuals present in an area. The popular media (and even some science texts) often equate richness (number of species) and diversity (technically, a function that includes both the number of species and their relative abundance).*

7. Would it make a difference ecologically if the triangles represented stonefly nymphs, which require high levels of dissolved oxygen, instead of aquatic worms, which require very little dissolved oxygen? In your own words, describe differences between the terms *biotic integrity* and *diversity*.

Diversity *reflects the number of species in an area.* Biotic integrity *is a measure of diversity that gives more weight to organisms that characteristically live in healthy systems. In other words, if Habitat A and Habitat B have the same number of species, but those living in Habitat A are typically found in well-oxygenated streams, then Habitat A has a higher biotic integrity.*

8. After studying your graph of WHEBIP by RCE, does it appear that both methods rate the same stream similarly? For example, if the WHEBIP method rates one stream as excellent, does the RCE method rate it the same way, or very differently? Explain.

The graph suggests that the methods rank stream segments similarly: As WHEBIP scores increase, RCE scores generally also increase. For example, a stream with a WHEBIP score of 139 has an RCE score of 155, and another stream with a WHEBIP score of 340 has an RCE score of 360. The relationship appears to be very strong.

On a more technical level, the statistical correlation between WHEBIP and RCE is significant at $p < .005$. The second RCE graph in the teacher's version of the Excel workbook plots the linear regression line and the value of R-squared. R^2 in this case is 0.8655, which means that 87% of the variance in RCE can be predicted from the WHEBIP score. By comparison, the critical value of the correlation coefficient for a sample size of 25 (one-tailed, $p < .05$) is 0.323; that means that coefficients larger than 0.323 are statistically significant.

9. Describe what happens to InvertBI as WHEBIP scores *increase*. Explain why you think this is happening.

There is a modest positive correlation: As habitat integrity increases, invertebrate biotic integrity increases. If you'd like to demonstrate this to statistically savvy students, do the following: in Microsoft Excel 2002, open the "InvertBI" chart and from the Chart pulldown menu, select "Add Trend Line," type "Linear," options "Display R-squared value on chart." The regression line has a positive slope and an R-squared of .37, indicating that 37% of the variance in InvertBI is accounted for by WHEBIP. This is statistically significant. On a less technical level, you might draw your students' attention to the extreme values for each scale: The lowest values of each scale are found for sites that have low scores for the other scale, and the highest values of each scale are associated with high values for the other scale.

10. Describe what happens to InvertPI as WHEBIP scores *increase*. Explain why you think this is happening.

Your students may decide that there are two trend lines in this graph (Chart "InvertPI"), one with a strong upward slope and one that hugs the bottom of the graph, with the percentage of pollution-intolerant invertebrates varying little with habitat. This interpretation appears to be supported by the data. Chart "InvertPI_2" displays the data from only headwater (upstream) segments. This second graph shows a strong correlation between InvertPI and WHEBIP, with the percentage of pollution-intolerant invertebrates increasing with habitat integrity. The points that have been omitted are from stream segments that carry greater volumes of water, collected over a larger land area. Apparently, local habitat integrity is a poor predictor of InvertPI for these larger segments.

11. Describe what happens to the number of fish species in streams as the WHEBIP score *increases*. Explain why you think this is happening.

As WHEBIP scores increase, the number of fish species in a stream appears to decrease, though this relationship does not appear to be a strong one. Perhaps this is because headwater streams tend to have higher quality habitat (and consequently higher WHEBIP scores), but are too shallow to support larger fish.

12. Describe what happens to FishBI in streams as WHEBIP score *increases*.

As WHEBIP scores increase, FishBI scores increase. This makes sense because streams with better water quality are more likely to sustain pollution-intolerant fish species.

Activity 10.1—Modeling Land Use and Streamflow

3. What initial conditions have been set for land use practices? In other words, what percent of the landscape in the model is farmland, forest, suburbs, and urban?

In the initial STELLA model conditions, 100% of the land use is "forest."

7. How did the streamflow change when the land use was changed from 100% forest to 100% urban? What's different about the graphs?

When the land use was changed to 100% urban, the streamflow response was much quicker and peak flow was higher. Rainfall reached the stream faster when land use was 100% urban. This occurs because more of the landscape is impervious, and a greater fraction of the rainfall becomes surface runoff instead of subsurface flow.

11. Look at page 2 of the graph and compare the findings from the three simulations. How did streamflow change as land use changed over time? Explain.

It appears that in 1910 and 1992 streamflow generally responded a bit more quickly to rainstorms than it did in 1600. However, the graphs are fairly similar. (Obviously, if you use local watershed data, students' answers will differ.)

14. Now consider a developer who wants to create a subdivision with many new houses in your town. Your town currently has land use percentages of 23% farm, 65% forest, 7% urban, and 5% suburban. How would you change these percentages to model the impact the developer might have on streamflow? How do you think the streamflow will respond to these changes?

I would lower the % Forest by 10% and increase the % Suburban by 10% to reflect the developer's impact. I would expect the hydrograph to peak a little bit earlier under these conditions. When I ran the model the hydrograph did peak earlier, but it was a small difference.

15. The city is buying some old buildings located next to a stream, bulldozing the buildings, and planting trees to create forest. How do you predict streamflow will respond to these changes? Why? Explain.

After these changes, I think streamflow peaks will shift a little bit later. In other words, precipitation will take a while longer to get to the stream after the forest begins to grow.

16. Why do you think streamflow patterns matter in terms of water quality and quantity? Why would it matter to town residents if all the rainwater washed out of the watershed in streamflow very quickly or more slowly?

Streamflow response matters to watershed residents for several reasons. For example, if run-off after a storm is quick and volumes are high, the potential for flooding is greater. Additionally, if more water rushes over impervious surfaces, into streams and out of the watershed, less is left to seep into the ground and replenish aquifers used for drinking water. Faster streamflow increases streambank erosion and may scour stream channels, rendering them inhospitable to some aquatic organisms. In municipalities that treat water collected by storm sewers, treatment capacity is more likely to be exceeded by fast-draining landscapes.

Activity 10.2—Modeling the Management of a Watershed to Limit Eutrophication

Scenario I

1. Tuscaville expects significant population growth in the next decade. You know that more people means more sewage, and that more sewage means more phosphorus discharged into Tuscaloosa Lake. What do you predict will happen to **Algal Density** in the lake as the population of Tuscaville increases? Why? Explain.

I predict that that if greater amounts of phosphorus enter Tuscaloosa Lake, algal density levels will rise. Most lake algae are phosphorus-limited, so an increase in phosphorus will increase their ability to grow in greater numbers.

4. As **Algal Density** increases, what changes do you think you might observe in Lake Tuscaloosa's appearance? Why?

As algal densities increase, I would expect Secchi depth to decrease. Greater algal density results in lower water clarity, which corresponds to a lower Secchi depth. This means that it is less likely that you will be able to see the bottom in many areas. The water will look green or murky.

6. As a lake becomes less clear, the Secchi depth decreases. Recall that a Secchi depth of less than 2 meters indicates a eutrophic lake, while a Secchi depth of more than 5 meters indicates an oligotrophic lake (between 2 m and 5 m Secchi depths, lakes are known as "mesotrophic"). Based on the Secchi Depth line, as the population in Tuscaville increases, does the lake become more or less eutrophic?

According to this model, as the population increases, the Secchi depth decreases and the lake becomes more eutrophic.

7. What could be done to the treatment plant to offset the increased level of phosphorus from more sewage? Explain.

If the treatment plant only performs primary and secondary treatment, it could be modernized to include tertiary treatment. In tertiary treatment, additional nutrients such as phosphorus are removed from the effluent.

8. Based on your answer above, try to reduce the rate at which **Secchi depth** declines. With a population of 70,000, how efficient must the wastewater treatment plant be to preserve a Secchi depth of at least 10 m 90 days after ice-out?

The treatment plant has to be about 75% efficient to keep Secchi depth greater than 10 meters 90 days after ice-out.

Scenario II

5. What generally happens to **DO on Bottom** as **Algal Density** increases?

As algal density increases, the dissolved oxygen on the lake bottom generally decreases.

6. What causes this general pattern in **DO on the Bottom** of the lake?

As algal density increases, the amount of dead algal biomass (which settles to the bottom) also increases. Bacterial populations that feed on dead algal biomass then increase and use up oxygen. Furthermore, because light can no longer penetrate to the bottom of the lake, photosynthesis cannot take place. Therefore, DO levels generally decrease as algal levels increase.

Scenario III

5. Given your limited budget, what did you find to be the best mix of remedies to keep Lake Tuscaloosa from becoming eutrophic? Were you able to find a "solution" to this problem? Will it be necessary for the Town Board to spend more money?

Answers to this question will vary considerably. You may want to ask students to get together in small groups to explain and defend their solutions.

INTERACTIVE RESEARCH:
FIELD STUDIES AND EXPERIMENTS

A common misconception among students is that scientists are social loners who work in isolation with little connection to each other or society. Through **interactive research**, students experience some of the ways in which professional scientists work together to discuss ideas, share findings, and collaborate on joint projects. In the process, they experience scientific inquiry and expand their understanding of the nature of science.

PEER REVIEW

Before students begin the process of choosing a research topic and conducting experiments, it is useful to consider how peer review fits into the process. Professional scientists rely on peer review to separate fact from falsehood and good science from bad in the continuous search for new understandings about how the world works. Peer review also plays a key role in determining which research endeavors receive funding, which conference papers get accepted, and which articles get published in the most prestigious journals. Finally, peer review helps scientists to focus their thinking and improve their writing as they respond to comments from professional colleagues.

In schools, peer review of student research reports can provide similar opportunities for students to think critically as they question their own and each other's experimental designs, assumptions, results, interpretations, and conclusions. Peer review is an integral component of interactive research (Figure 13). After students have planned an experiment, they will benefit from meeting in pairs or small groups to discuss their ideas and exchange written feedback. A more formal type of peer review comes after students have completed their experiments. At this point, peer review provides a forum for critical evaluation of research results and helps students to improve the quality of their reports or poster presentations.

FIGURE 13
Peer Review in Interactive Research

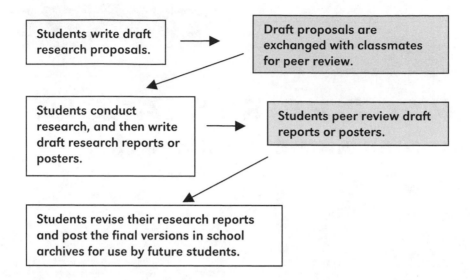

STEPS IN CONDUCTING INTERACTIVE RESEARCH

Once students are familiar with the introductory chapters and the concept of peer review and have gained experience with the protocols, they are ready to engage in interactive research projects. Below we explain how each of these steps fits into the interactive research process:

- Choosing a research topic
- Planning and conducting experiments using protocols
- Analyzing data
- Interpreting results
- Designing presentations

CHOOSING A RESEARCH TOPIC

Scientists build on each other's work

One of the elements of science that is difficult to replicate in high school classrooms is the idea that scientific investigation is a cumulative process, with each scientist learning from the work of earlier and contemporary researchers. Before embarking on a new research endeavor, scientists typically begin by talking with colleagues, attending conferences, and reading related publications to learn what has already been accomplished and what questions remain unanswered.

The interactive research level of EI aims to provide analogous opportunities for high school students to base their research questions on what has already been learned in previous experiments. When time constraints make it impossible to carry out a series of experiments, students can still experience the cumulative and interactive aspects of research without having to carry out every step of the process themselves. For example, if you save student research reports from one year to the next, students can design their experiments based on results and recommendations made by previous student researchers, then conclude by making their own recommendations to next year's students. Rather than each class starting their research from square one, students model professional scientific practice by starting with an analysis of what has already been accomplished in the field. In carrying out these steps, students not only improve their understandings of their own research, they also gain a broader understanding of the ways in which scientists work both individually and collaboratively. Knowing that future researchers will actually use their work helps reshape students' work from "just another assignment for the teacher" to authentic scientific research.

Research commonly begins with informal explorations

Contrary to popular belief, scientists do not routinely launch into research by stating and then testing a hypothesis. In many cases, they begin with a period of exploration, observation, and discovery that gradually leads to ideas about fruitful areas of investigation. If you can fit exploratory research into your class schedule, it will provide a chance for students to apply curiosity, imagination, and creativity to science rather than having to follow a predetermined set of rules. This period of trial and error also will help students to discover for themselves some of the basic principles of experimental design, such as the need for replicates and controls.

Based on considerations of curriculum, scheduling, and student ability levels, interactive research may consist of a single investigation or a series of iterations. Ideally, students carry out preliminary investigations, and then use the results of these explorations to reassess their focus and experimental design. They might decide to carry out additional exploratory level investigations or to use what they have learned to design a more rigorous experiment with a clearly defined hypothesis, dependent and independent variables, and replicates for each treatment. These explorations may lead to modifications of their research topic.

DEVELOPING TOPIC IDEAS

After your students have gained experiences using one or more of the protocols, they are ready to conduct interactive research projects. First, they need to develop research topics. One approach is to give your students a great deal of freedom to develop their own research questions. Or you may decide to specify a particular topic such as stream assessment and allow them to develop questions in that context. Other ideas include having a classroom discussion about the ideas for interactive research projects listed in Figure 14, or brainstorming about ideas students developed as they conducted protocols. However you proceed, encourage your students to consider previous research results as they consider their topics.

Forms

▶ **Choosing a Research Topic (p. 144)** guides students through the process of choosing a research question that is both feasible and interesting.

FIGURE 14
From Protocols to Interactive Research

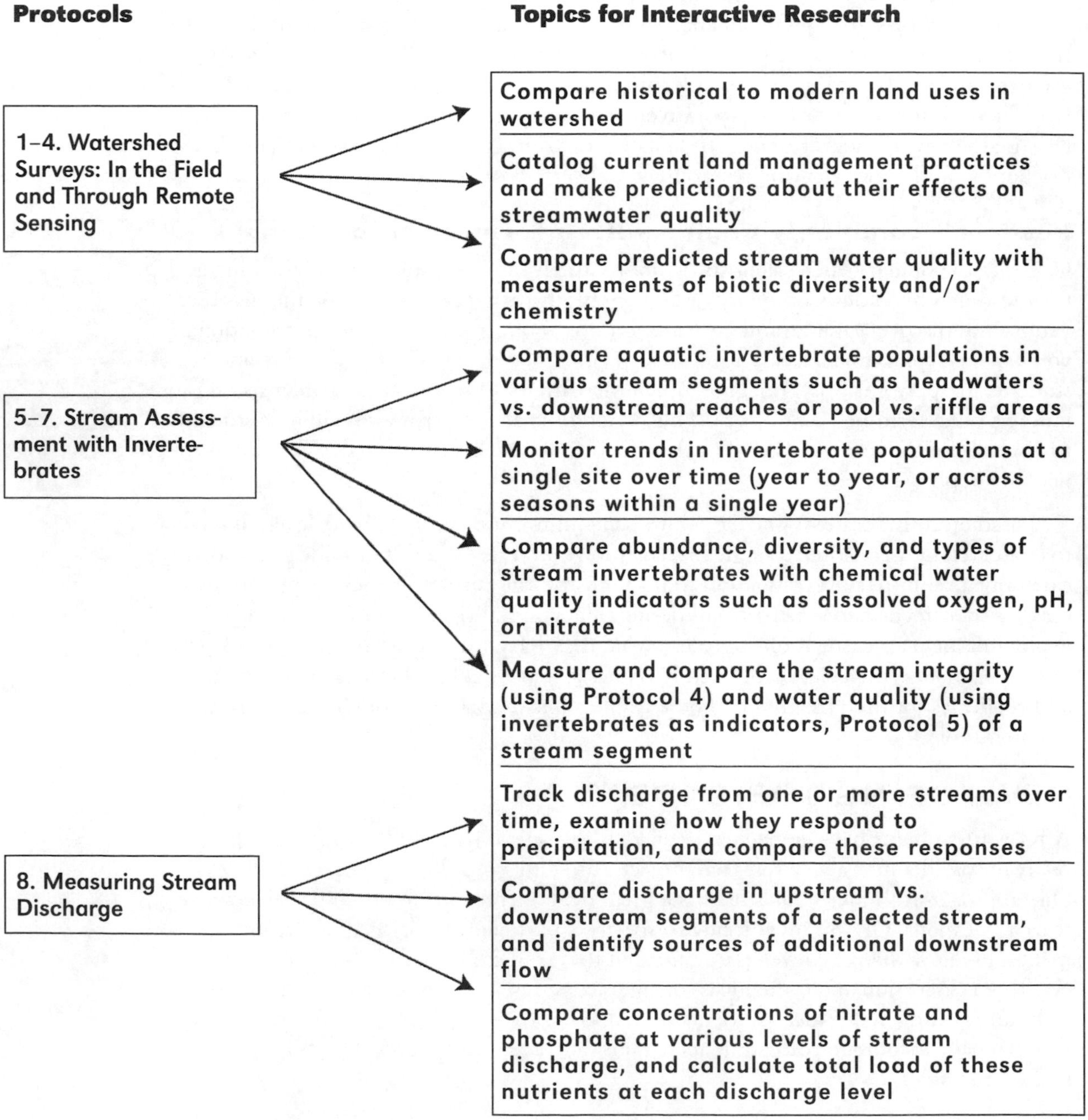

Protocols   **Topics for Interactive Research**

1–4. Watershed Surveys: In the Field and Through Remote Sensing

- Compare historical to modern land uses in watershed
- Catalog current land management practices and make predictions about their effects on streamwater quality
- Compare predicted stream water quality with measurements of biotic diversity and/or chemistry

5–7. Stream Assessment with Invertebrates

- Compare aquatic invertebrate populations in various stream segments such as headwaters vs. downstream reaches or pool vs. riffle areas
- Monitor trends in invertebrate populations at a single site over time (year to year, or across seasons within a single year)
- Compare abundance, diversity, and types of stream invertebrates with chemical water quality indicators such as dissolved oxygen, pH, or nitrate
- Measure and compare the stream integrity (using Protocol 4) and water quality (using invertebrates as indicators, Protocol 5) of a stream segment

8. Measuring Stream Discharge

- Track discharge from one or more streams over time, examine how they respond to precipitation, and compare these responses
- Compare discharge in upstream vs. downstream segments of a selected stream, and identify sources of additional downstream flow
- Compare concentrations of nitrate and phosphate at various levels of stream discharge, and calculate total load of these nutrients at each discharge level

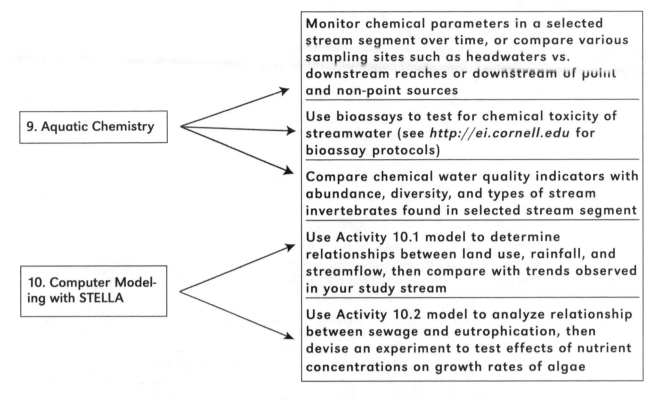

9. Aquatic Chemistry	Monitor chemical parameters in a selected stream segment over time, or compare various sampling sites such as headwaters vs. downstream reaches or downstream of point and non-point sources
	Use bioassays to test for chemical toxicity of streamwater (see *http://ei.cornell.edu* for bioassay protocols)
	Compare chemical water quality indicators with abundance, diversity, and types of stream invertebrates found in selected stream segment
10. Computer Modeling with STELLA	Use Activity 10.1 model to determine relationships between land use, rainfall, and streamflow, then compare with trends observed in your study stream
	Use Activity 10.2 model to analyze relationship between sewage and eutrophication, then devise an experiment to test effects of nutrient concentrations on growth rates of algae

PLANNING AND CONDUCTING EXPERIMENTS USING PROTOCOLS

Once students have narrowed their research question(s), they are ready to conduct their own research using appropriate protocols. If they are interested in making modifications to any of the protocols, they should first discuss this with you. Encourage them to consider issues like consistency and variability as they conduct protocols. We have developed two forms—one for exploratory level and another for rigorously designed experiments—to help students plan their experiments.

Forms

▶ Interactive Research Planning Form 1 (p. 147)

▶ Interactive Research Planning Form 2 (p. 149)

ANALYZING DATA

> If the result confirms the hypothesis, then you've made a measurement. If the result is contrary to the hypothesis, then you've made a discovery.
>
> —Enrico Fermi

Planning Ahead

When students are planning their own experiments, it is helpful for them to think about how to organize and present their results. They might start by labeling the columns and rows in a table or spreadsheet, indicating how they will summarize the data, for example by calculating the mean of all replicates within a single treatment. Students also could begin by drawing an empty graph showing what independent variable will be portrayed on the *x*-axis and what dependent variable on the *y*-axis. It may seem premature to think about data analysis before conducting an experiment, but going through this process may help students discover potential problems in their experimental designs before it is too late to make changes.

Choosing the Appropriate Type of Graph

After data have been collected, the best way to decide on data analysis methods is to start by considering the specific research question being addressed. For example, analysis of trends over time requires a different approach than determining whether one treatment is different from another (or from a control). Students may be surprised to learn that different types of graphs are useful for different purposes. To analyze trends over time, a line graph may be appropriate. The lines connecting data points represent predictions of values in between the ones that have been measured. For example, a line graph is a useful way to portray changes in streamflow over time (Figure 15).

FIGURE 15
Line Graphs Show Patterns Over Time

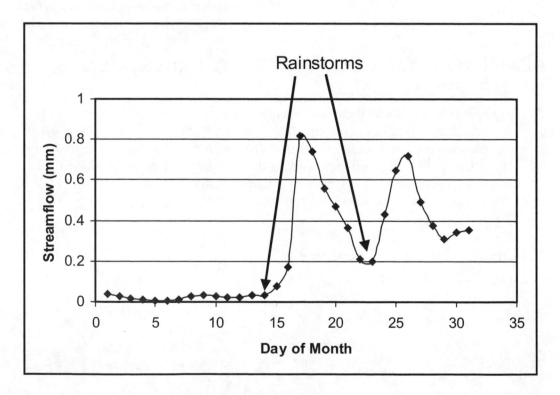

If there is no logical connection between data points, then a bar graph may be more appropriate. This is the case when you are comparing two or more sites (or, in an experiment, the differences between treatments). For example, consider stonefly abundance in sections of a stream immediately below and immediately above a potential point source (Figure 16).

FIGURE 16

Bar Graphs Show Differences between Treatments (Sites)

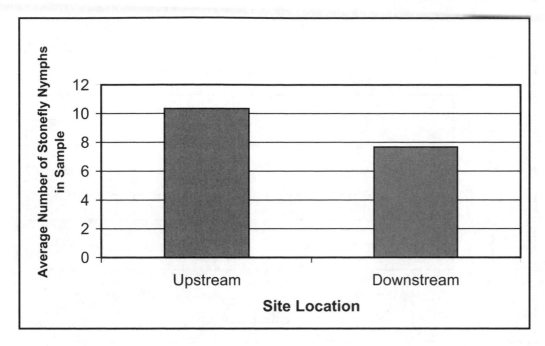

A LOOK AT VARIABILITY

A standard approach in analyzing research data is to compare the variability *within* each treatment with the variability *between* treatments. For example, if the data from Figure 16 were graphed as individual points rather than means, it would become apparent that there is some overlap in values between the two treatments (see Figure 17). This highlights the desirability of using replicates whenever feasible.

FIGURE 17
Graphs of Individual Data Points Show Variability Within Treatments (Sites)

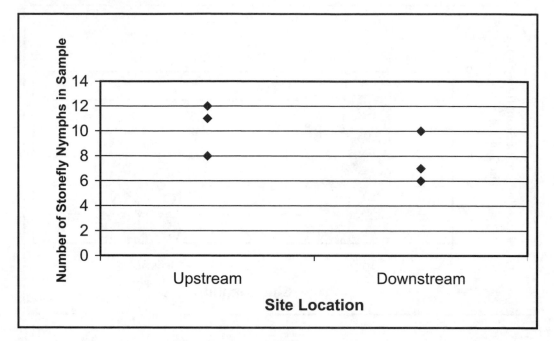

Students who are ready for higher level statistics can calculate standard deviations using scientific calculators or computer spreadsheet programs, then draw a bar representing ± 1 standard deviation around each mean (Figure 18). Standard deviation provides a measure of the degree of variability within the data collected for each treatment. The larger the standard deviation, the greater the spread between the individual data points making up the mean. Standard deviations can be used to compare the variability within each treatment to the apparent differences between treatments. Students who have studied statistics may prefer to perform t-tests or an analysis of variance to calculate the statistical significance of apparent differences between treatments or between a treatment and the control.

FIGURE 18
Bar Graphs with ± 1 Standard Deviation Also Show Variability

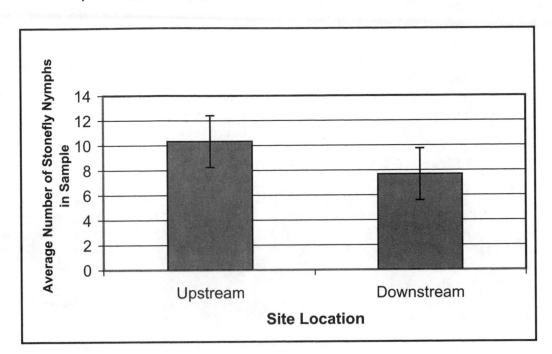

Some of the variability in data may be due to the fact that there is unavoidable biological variability in substrate, flow dynamics, and benthic insect distribution, even at a single location. However, in any experiment, there is always some variability that can be controlled by the experimenter (e.g., exactly following the protocol each time). Identifying these potential sources of variability will help students to figure out which types are unavoidable and which can be reduced through careful attention to method.

INTERPRETING RESULTS

> The most exciting phrase to hear in science, the one that heralds new discoveries, is not "Eureka!" (I found it!) but "That's funny. ..."
>
> —Isaac Asimov

After students have summarized their data, they will be ready to try to figure out what conclusions they can reach. A common misconception among students is that experiments should always reveal definitive answers to the research question. In reality, many experiments only partially answer the original question, and often the question changes as the research proceeds through several rounds of experiments. Perhaps the original question was not narrowly enough defined, or the methods were inadequate. Or perhaps everything went according to plan, but more trials are needed before conclusions can be reached.

It is important for students to recognize that they have not failed if their experiment didn't work out as expected. In fact, sometimes the most unexpected results lead to the most interesting discoveries. The results of an experiment, even when seemingly ambiguous or contradictory, often lead to new insights, new questions, and new investigations. Scientific research rarely ends with definitive answers—more commonly, the results of each experiment suggest ideas for further studies. If students have learned something from their experiment, then it was a success. The important thing is for them to evaluate their findings at each stage of the process and to apply what they have learned to decisions about next steps. Even if they will not be carrying out further experiments themselves, they can leave recommendations for future students.

DESIGNING PRESENTATIONS

Public discussion of the explanations proposed by students is a form of peer review of investigations, and peer review is an important aspect of science. Talking with peers about science experiences helps students develop meaning and understanding. Their conversations clarify the concepts and processes of science, helping students make sense of the content of science.

—*National Science Education Standards*, p. 174

The final step in research is to communicate the findings in a way that can be understood and used by others. When students present their research findings, they can benefit from presenting to an audience rather than just turning in a report for a grade. After exchanging peer reviews, students should be encouraged to consider using this feedback to revise their research reports. To assess their understanding of the peer review process, you might ask them to address questions such as the following in their final write-ups:

▶ What peer review comments did you receive?

▶ Did you agree with these comments? Why or why not?

▶ How did you use the comments in preparing your final report?

Inevitably, some of your students will receive peer reviews that are not helpful, possibly even tactless or otherwise inappropriate. A classroom discussion about this problem can be used to point out that such weaknesses can occur in professional scientific review as well, but the goal for all peer reviewers should be to provide constructive criticism in order to promote better science. Science as a "way of knowing" relies upon a norm of *organized skepticism*. Criticism is essential, but accomplishing this in a way that is helpful is something that must be learned.

Forms

▶ **Research Report Form** (p. 154)

▶ **Poster Guidelines** (p. 157)

▶ **Research Report Peer Review Form** (p. 159)

▶ **Poster Peer Review Form** (p. 160)

▶ Alternatively, you might choose to work with your students to devise your own peer review form based on criteria such as those listed in the example Assessment Criteria for Student Research (p. 66).

INQUIRY TEACHING TIPS

Choosing a Research Topic

Some students may have generated ideas as they conducted protocols. These students and others may benefit from the classroom discussions mentioned above in which they use their ideas or your suggestions to brainstorm research topics. For others, the process of choosing a question and designing related experiments may be new or frustrating—especially for students who are accustomed to (and often successful with) more traditional verification-type lab exercises.

Don't worry if your students seem frustrated initially with this assignment. In fact, you might even want to alert them ahead of time that you expect that! After a period of floundering and hoping that you will help them to find the "right" answer, your students will gain confidence and become accustomed to the idea of being responsible for open-ended inquiry.

Questions about Protocols

Even though we have included step-by-step instructions for the protocols, questions about exactly what to do will invariably arise while students are carrying them out. Some teachers are caught off guard by these questions and don't know how to respond. If this happens to you, don't panic. Making decisions about how to carry out research procedures is something scientists face all the time. Although they often consult with other scientists or the scientific literature, sometimes they have to devise their own solutions. As long as the solutions are well developed and the relevant details are reported in the methods section of the research report, modifying protocols is acceptable—indeed, it's often how scientific breakthroughs are made.

Thus, you can use students' questions to engage the students themselves in finding or developing suitable answers on their own. In this way you can help students model how professional scientists answer such questions. If students pose questions about methods while they are conducting research, we suggest two approaches to answering them. First, refer students back to the protocol. Do they understand the background information? Are they familiar with relevant sections of the introductory chapters? Are they following the steps correctly? Second, if the protocols don't provide answers, work with your students to develop or find answers. Perhaps the protocol in question needs a slight modification to work with their research question. Or maybe a protocol is too general and needs to be made more specific—or vice versa. The important thing is that students don't rush to make decisions.

If several students or student groups will be compiling their data, it is important that all students understand and follow decisions made about procedures. If one group proceeds with one understanding, and another uses the protocol in a different way, it might not be possible to compile or compare the results. Standardized, consistent procedures are also important when students are comparing different sites, treatments, or years.

If your students will be sharing their data with professional scientists or community or government groups, it is especially important that the protocols followed are clear and consistent. In fact, contacting the scientist or group may provide answers to student questions.

Finally, no matter how the students proceed, make sure they *fully record exactly what they do*. This way, if questions arise during the analysis, students can refer to the notes. Furthermore, when new students are continuing this research or doing similar research in subsequent years, they can refer to these notes—and long-term comparisons will thus be more valid.

INTERACTIVE RESEARCH:
STORMWATER TREATMENT DESIGN CHALLENGE

In this technological design project, students work together to design and devise a solution to a stormwater retention and treatment problem in a fictional city. Participating in a technological design project requires that students gather and process information, generate and analyze ideas, present results, and probably most difficult of all, get practice working effectively in teams. One of the benefits of this teamwork is that students learn firsthand the value of skills in conceptualization, design, and construction. Another is that successful completion of the design requires them to meet criteria while addressing conflicting constraints. The students who come up with the most creative design solutions often are not the same students who excel at book learning.

A partial design parts list with prices, which the students will use to select parts to construct their specific design, is included in the Student Edition. Suggested additional parts with prices are listed on the **Suggested Extra Parts List for the Stormwater Design Challenge,** page 63. Students may inquire about these as they develop their designs. Finally, note that in addition to specific design criteria that all students must follow, a set of restrictions has been added to the scenario that will help generate design alternatives.

SUMMARY OF THE PROCEDURE

Step 1. Define the Problem

This step is designed to lead students through the problem-solving cycle in an iterative fashion that allows students to identify the general problem specifications as well as the constraints. First, students are introduced to a scenario and an initial statement of the problem. Second, you then may want to encourage your students to conduct additional library or Internet research or provide them with more information on stormwater retention and treatment. It is important that careful reading and data recording by the students be stressed throughout this step and the rest of the challenge.

Step 2. Identify Design Solutions and Select the Best Alternative

This step gives students the opportunity to brainstorm design ideas and eventually choose the one they feel will best address the problem. It is important for you to stress that all possible ideas should be considered and recorded. Each team of students should generate at least two design options. In order to select the best alternative, students must determine the advantages and disadvantages of each alternative device or modifications to an existing design. To do this, the students will create a qualitative or quantitative scale to judge each of their alternatives against the same set of criteria. An example rubric in the Student Edition (p. 166) shows how they can then select the best alternative based on the results of the analysis. Emphasis should be placed on the need to make trade-offs in selecting alternative designs and the reasoning used to make the decisions.

Step 3. Build, Test, and Use the Best Design

As students assemble their systems they will need to test them at various stages of development, probably over lab sinks or other areas that can accommodate spills. Students will most likely find it necessary to make modifications in their designs to overcome problems such as leaks, treatment constraints, and drainage volumes. Emphasis should be placed on the methods developed for judging alternative choices that were established in Step 2.

Step 4. Evaluate the Constructed System

Students will use the Presentation Rubric Worksheet to evaluate their system and record their assessment in laboratory notebooks. You may wish to use this rubric to assist in grading student performance.

Step 5. Plan Your Presentation

It is important for students to consider that these types of projects are not complete until results have been presented to a broader audience. Accordingly, they should design and deliver a classroom presentation that is designed to convince their audience that their device meets all the established criteria. You may want to include a discussion of the attributes of a quality presentation, including advantages of multimedia tools such as PowerPoint. Students should use a copy of the **Presentation Assessment Form** (Student Edition, p. 174) as they prepare for their presentation.

Step 6. Present Your Work

Students present their results to a classroom audience, followed by a question-and-answer period. Afterward, a **Presentation Assessment Form** (Student Edition, p. 174) should be provided to each member of the audience, including the teacher. We suggest that each team then meet with the teacher to review the results of the self-assessment, peer assessment, and teacher assessment. This will supply students with essential feedback to adequately judge the quality of their work.

MAKING SYNTHETIC STORMWATER

We suggest that you provide students with a standard stormwater recipe that will be used in evaluating designs, but that you change your recipe from year to year. That will help keep the challenge "fresh" for students in subsequent years. Obviously, you'll want the concoction to be safe to handle and relatively easy to clean up if it is spilled outside of the treatment system. Stormwater commonly contains solids, dissolved organic material, road salt, fertilizers, and chemicals that leak from automobiles, such as motor oil and antifreeze. A classroom-friendly formulation might include, per liter:

▶ Soil or potting soil—provides solid particles and suspended sediments (10 g)

▶ Sand—provides solid particles (5 g)

▶ Cornstarch—provides dissolved and suspended organic matter (5 g)

▶ Houseplant fertilizer—provides nutrients (a few drops of liquid fertilizer)

▶ Table or road salt—chemical runoff from road deicing (5 g)

▶ Vegetable oil—safe alternative to motor oil (10 mL)

Suggested Extra Parts List for the Stormwater Design Challenge

Material	Cost per item ($)
Nylon	0.10/(15 cm x 15 cm)
Cotton	0.02/g
Sponge	0.05/cm^2
Poly-fish filter	0.03/g
Activated charcoal	0.05/g
Charcoal brick	0.03 ea.
Peat moss	0.01/g
Coffee filter	0.02 ea.
Kitty litter	0.04/100 g
Vermiculite	0.02/100 g
Cork sheet	0.06/cm^2
Paper towel	0.01/sheet
Gauze pads	0.30/(8 cm^2)
Cheese cloth	1.00/(30 cm x 30 cm)
Modeling clay	0.05/gm
Straw, soil, clay, sand, wood chips, cardboard, rocks, rubber cement	Free

ASSESSMENT

PERFORMANCE ASSESSMENT

Although sample test questions are included on pages 70–71, student performance in EI research is best assessed using worksheets and other written records assembled by students as they go through the processes of designing and conducting experiments, interpreting and presenting results, and engaging in peer review.

In assessing student research, bear in mind that clearly defined "right" or "wrong" answers rarely exist. Instead, the goal of assessment is to evaluate the process used by the students and the conceptual understandings they have achieved through their research experiences. Laboratory journals, worksheets, draft reports, and responses to peer reviews all will provide evidence of the progress that students have made in thinking critically, synthesizing information, and carrying out scientific research. The following pages outline possible assessment criteria for student research, as well as example assessment rubrics for posters and written reports. These can be downloaded in electronic form from the EI Web site (*http://ei.cornell.edu*) so that you can make adaptations to meet the needs of your particular students and their projects.

The peer review process provides both opportunities and challenges for assessment. Through peer review, some of the assessment responsibility can be shifted from the teacher to the students themselves—an important step in promoting self-regulated learning. Once students become familiar with peer review, they are likely to become motivated to work harder and to look more critically at their own work because they begin to anticipate the expectations of other students carrying out projects similar to their own.

Since it probably will be too cumbersome to keep track of all the comments exchanged by students, we suggest you concentrate on determining how students respond to the feedback they receive. This approach helps to overcome any worries among students about whether it is fair to be evaluated by someone other than their teacher. If they don't agree with reviewers' suggestions, that's fine, as long as they can justify their position. In their final research reports, you can direct students to summarize the comments they received from peer reviewers, whether they agreed with these critiques, and how they used them in revising their work.

EXAMPLE ASSESSMENT RUBRICS FOR EI STUDENT RESEARCH

Assessment Criteria for Student Research

Criteria such as these can be used to create a checklist for students and a grading rubric for completed research portfolios.

Identify a Researchable Question

❏ Develop a researchable question, including a clear statement of why this question is relevant to watershed dynamics.

❏ Review previous work in the field, including Internet as well as print sources.

❏ Formulate a hypothesis that addresses the research question, and predict experimental results.

Plan the Investigation

❏ Identify treatments and a control.

❏ Plan to vary only one independent variable at a time.

❏ Plan adequate replicates of each treatment.

❏ Describe appropriate tools and techniques to gather, interpret, and analyze the data within constraints of time and resources.

❏ Identify safety concerns and precautions that will be taken.

Conduct the Research

❏ Carry out one or a series of experiments, using proper equipment and safety precautions.

❏ Record data and observations at appropriate intervals.

❏ Document any decisions made about experimental design or data collection as the experiment progresses.

Analyze the Data

❏ Summarize data clearly using tables and graphs.

❏ Identify trends and outlying data that do not fit the trends.

❏ Identify potential sources of variability.

Interpret the Results and Formulate Conclusions

❏ Compare actual results to predicted results.

❏ Clearly state the meaning of the results in terms of the original research question.

❏ Identify possible improvements in the experimental design.

❏ Suggest new directions for future research.

Present the Project and Engage in Peer Review

❏ Effectively communicate the experimental design and results to a peer audience.

❏ Defend or revise conclusions based on consideration of alternative explanations of research results.

❏ Revise written report or poster presentation when appropriate based on reviewers' comments.

Assessment Rubrics for Poster Presentations

Name(s) of student(s) _____

Date _____

ASSESSMENT SCALE
1—Inadequate in meeting requirements of the task
2—Minimal in meeting requirements of the task
3—Adequate in meeting requirements of the task
4—Superior in meeting requirements of the task

Poster Presentation Criteria	Evaluation	Points
The poster includes these sections: Title, Research Question, Hypothesis, Procedure, Results, Conclusions, and Acknowledgments (if appropriate)	1 2 3 4	
The purpose is clearly stated in the research question and hypothesis.	1 2 3 4	
The procedure is described clearly enough to be reproduced.	1 2 3 4	
Results and conclusions are displayed in a sequence that is easy to follow.	1 2 3 4	
The display is neat, clearly labeled, and easy to read.	1 2 3 4	
The ideas fit together and make sense.	1 2 3 4	
	TOTAL	

Comments:

ASSESSMENT SCALE
"?" = Not enough information available to evaluate this question.
Assign 5 points for each "Yes" and 0 points for each "No" or "?".

Experimental Design Criteria	Evaluation	Points
The experiment was appropriately designed to test the stated hypothesis.	Yes No ?	
Only one independent variable was changed at a time.	Yes No ?	
There was a control, which was exposed to the same conditions as the treatments except for the independent variable.	Yes No ?	
Adequate replicates were provided for each treatment.	Yes No ?	
The conclusions appear well supported by the data.	Yes No ?	
	TOTAL	

Comments:

Assessment Rubric for Written Reports

Name(s) of student(s)_____

Date_____

```
ASSESSMENT SCALE
1—Inadequate in meeting requirements of the task
2—Minimal in meeting requirements of the task
3—Adequate in meeting requirements of the task
4—Superior in meeting requirements of the task
```

Criteria	Evaluation	Point
Introduction		
States a researchable question, and clearly explains why this question is relevant to watershed dynamics.	1 2 3 4	
Summarizes previous work in the field, if applicable.	1 2 3 4	
States a hypothesis that addresses the research question and expected results.	1 2 3 4	
Procedure		
Experiment is appropriately designed to address the research question.	1 2 3 4	
Describes procedures clearly enough to be replicated.	1 2 3 4	
Includes data and observations recorded at appropriate intervals.	1 2 3 4	
Uses proper equipment, techniques, and safety precautions.	1 2 3 4	
Includes independent and dependent variables and a control.	1 2 3 4	
Changes only one independent variable between treatments.	1 2 3 4	
Provides adequate replicates of each treatment.	1 2 3 4	
Results		
Summarizes data clearly using tables and graphs.	1 2 3 4	
Identifies trends and outlying data.	1 2 3 4	
Discusses potential sources of variability.	1 2 3 4	

Conclusions					
Compares actual results to predicted results.	1	2	3	4	
Clearly discusses meaning of the results in terms of the original research question.	1	2	3	4	
Makes conclusions that are well supported by the data.	1	2	3	4	
Identifies possible improvements in the experimental design.	1	2	3	4	
Suggests new directions for future research.	1	2	3	4	
Defends or revises conclusions based on consideration of alternative explanations of research results.	1	2	3	4	
Overall Report					
Displays understanding of experimental design.	1	2	3	4	
Displays understanding of applicable concepts in watershed dynamics.	1	2	3	4	
Includes clear discussion of use of peer review comments in revising the research report, or logical argument for why peer suggestions were not followed.	1	2	3	4	
Appropriately cites written and/or Internet references.	1	2	3	4	
Is neat, organized, and well written.	1	2	3	4	
Organizes ideas clearly.	1	2	3	4	
Uses proper spelling and grammar.	1	2	3	4	
				TOTAL	

SAMPLE TEST QUESTIONS

1. Which of the following best defines the term *watershed?*

    (a) Region of land surrounding a mountain

    (b) *Region of land draining into a stream, river, pond, lake, or other body of water*

    (c) All of the land downstream of a section of stream or river

    (d) Land that borders streams, rivers, ponds, and other bodies of water

2. As a landscape becomes more urbanized, which of the following changes would be most likely to increase the chance of flooding?

    (a) Greater water use by residents would increase the level of the water table

    (b) Increased property values make the consequences of flooding more expensive

    (c) Greater water use by residents would lower the water table

    (d) *Water would flow into streams much faster because the landscape is less permeable*

3. Which of the following would not be considered remote sensing?

    (a) *Traveling a long distance to a watershed to collect data*

    (b) Using a satellite to make infrared images of the Earth

    (c) Taking pictures of a forest from an airplane

    (d) Making a videotape of the Earth's surface from the space shuttle

4. The important ecological area along the edges of a stream is called the

    (a) Watershed

    (b) Stream channel

    (c) Ecotone

    (d) *Riparian zone*

5. An aquatic plant, an insect that eats it, and the fish that eats the insect could be referred to as

    (a) A producer, a carnivore, and a consumer

    (b) A consumer, a producer, and a producer

    (c) A producer, a decomposer, and a consumer

    (d) *A producer, a consumer, and a consumer*

6. The primary difference between insects that undergo complete metamorphosis and insects that undergo incomplete metamorphosis is that

    (a) Only incomplete metamorphosis occurs among aquatic species

    (b) Incomplete metamorphosis takes less time

    (c) The adults of insects that undergo complete metamorphosis never live in the water, but the larvae do

    (d) *Insects that undergo incomplete metamorphosis do not have a pupal stage*

7. A biology class collected invertebrates from the bottom of a stream. The best evidence that their stream's water quality was excellent would be

   (a) *The presence of insects that cannot tolerate polluted water*

   (b) A large number of snails, midge larvae, and alderfly larvae

   (c) The absence of animals that trout eat, such as mayflies

   (d) That the invertebrates could be easily kept alive in a tub of water

8. Compared to cold water, warm water can hold less

   (a) *Oxygen*

   (b) Nitrates

   (c) Phosphates

   (d) Chloride

9. The use of road salt is most likely to increase the amount of which of the following in nearby streams?

   (a) Oxygen

   (b) Nitrates

   (c) Phosphates

   (d) *Chloride*

10. Cultural eutrophication is most likely to occur in a lake that receives runoff water that contains high levels of which of the following?

    (a) Oxygen

    (b) Nitrates

    (c) *Phosphates*

    (d) Chloride

11. A scientist uses a computer program to simulate the effects of different land use practices on runoff in a watershed. This activity would most correctly be described as

    (a) Peer review

    (b) *Modeling*

    (c) Experimentation

    (d) Field studies

12. Describe some of the most important information that regional planners and policy makers would need in order to develop a watershed management plan.

13. A watershed that was previously farmland is returning to forest. As this process continues, what are the likely consequences for organisms living in the streams that cross this landscape?

REFERENCES

WATERSHED STUDIES

Baron, J. S., N. L. Poff, P. L. Angermeier, C.N. Dahm, P. H. Gleick, N.G. Hairston, Jr., R. B. Jackson, C. A. Johnston, B. D. Richter, and A. D. Steinman. 2003. Sustaining healthy freshwater ecosystems. *Issues in Ecology* (10). Available online at *www.esa.org/sbi/sbi_issues*.

Carpenter, S., N. F. Caraco, D. L. Correll, R. W. Howarth, A. N. Sharpley, and W. H. Smith. 1998. Nonpoint pollution of surface waters with phosphorus and nitrogen. *Issues in Ecology* (3). Available online at *www.esa.org/sbi/sbi_issues*.

Environmental Protection Agency. Online training in watershed management. Washington, DC: EPA. Available online at *www.epa.gov/watertrain*.

Environmental Protection Agency. 1997. Volunteer stream monitoring: A methods manual. Washington, DC: EPA. Available online at *www.epa.gov/volunteer/stream*.

Federal Interagency Stream Restoration Working Group. 1998. Stream corridor restoration: Principles, processes, and practices. Washington, DC: USDA. Available online at *www.usda.gov/stream_restoration*.

Goforth, R. R. 1999. Local and landscape-scale relations between stream communities, stream habitat and terrestrial land cover properties. (Doctoral dissertation, Cornell University). *Dissertation Abstracts International*. AAT 9941190.

Hilsenhoff, W. L. 1988. Rapid field assessment of organic pollution with a family-level biotic index. *Journal of the North American Benthological Society* 7: 65–68.

Howarth, R., D. Anderson, J. Cloern, C. Elfring, C. Hopkinson, B. Lapointe, T. Malone, N. Marcus, K. McGlathery, A. Sharpley, and D. Walker. 2000. Nutrient pollution of coastal rivers, bays, and seas. *Issues in Ecology* (7). Available online at *www.esa.org/sbi/sbi_issues*.

Jackson, R. B., S. R. Carpenter, C. N. Dahm, D. M. McKnight, R. J. Naiman, S. L. Poster, and S. W. Running. 2001. Water in a changing world. *Issues in Ecology* (9). Available online at *www.esa.org/sbi/sbi_issues*.

Karr, J. R. 1981. Assessment of biotic integrity using fish communities. *Fisheries* 6: 21–27.

Vitousek, P. M., J. Aber, R. W. Howarth, G. E. Likens, P. A. Matson, D. W. Schindler, W. H. Schlesinger, and G. D. Tilman. 1997. Human alteration of the global nitrogen cycle: Cause and consequences. *Issues in Ecology* (1). Available online at *www.esa.org/sbi/sbi_issues*.

INQUIRY-BASED SCIENCE

Cothron, J. H., R. N. Giese, and R. J. Rezba. 1999. *Students and research*. 3d ed. Dubuque, IA: Kendall/Hunt.

Doran, R., F. Chan, P. Tamir, and C. Lenhardt. 2002. *Science educator's guide to laboratory assessment*. Arlington, VA: NSTA Press.

Driver, R., A. Squires, P. Rushworth, and V. Wood-Robinson. 1994. *Making sense of secondary science: Research into children's ideas*. London: Routledge.

National Research Council. 1996. *National science education standards*. Washington, DC: National Academy Press.

National Research Council. 2000. *Inquiry and the national science education standards*. Washington, DC: National Academy Press.

Thayer School of Engineering. 1996. *Engineering problem solving in the high school classroom*. Dartmouth College. Available online at *http://thayer.dartmouth.edu/~teps/classroom.html*.

OTHER BOOKS IN THE CORNELL SCIENTIFIC INQUIRY SERIES

Krasny, M. E., and the Environmental Inquiry Team. 2002. *Invasion Ecology, student edition and teacher's guide*. Arlington, VA: NSTA Press.

Trautmann, N. M., and the Environmental Inquiry Team. 2001. *Assessing Toxic Risk, student edition and teacher's guide*. Arlington, VA: NSTA Press.

Trautmann, N. M., and the Environmental Inquiry Team. 2003. *Decay and Renewal, student edition and teacher edition*. Arlington, VA: NSTA Press.

INTERNET RESOURCES

Invertebrate Identification

Web-based photographic key from the New York State Department of Environmental Conservation:

www.dec.state.ny.us/website/dow/stream/index.htm

U.S. Environmental Protection Agency links to resources for using invertebrates as indicators:

www.epa.gov/bioindicators/html/invertebrate.html

U.S. Geological Survey Protocols for the National Water-Quality Assessment Program:

http://water.usgs.gov/nawqa/protocols/doc_list.html

Impervious Surface Information

www.epa.gov/watertrain/protection

Urban Flow Information

www.epa.gov/watertrain/agents

SOURCES OF AIRPHOTOS, MAPS, AND SUPPLIES

Please note that the URLs, availability, and coverages of geospatial information may change. In addition to the following links, we will post updates at the EI Web site: *http://ei.cornell.edu/watersheds.*

AIRPHOTOS

▶ Center for Advanced Spatial Technologies

"Guide to mostly on-line and mostly free U.S. geospatial and attribute data."

www.cast.uark.edu/local/hunt/index.html

This terrific site is organized by both resource type and U.S. states. Many states now have regional geospatial data centers.

▶ Terraserver

http://terraserver-usa.com

USGS airphotos are available here for free and can be displayed on-screen at various resolutions or can be printed.

▶ EarthExplorer by the U.S. Geological Survey

http://earthexplorer.usgs.gov

This is an easy-to-use resource for locating satellite images, airphotos, and other cartographic products. Photos from the National Aerial Photography Program can be located by entering place names or zip codes, or by using clickable maps.

LAND USE MAPS

The U.S. Geological Survey provides Land Use/Land Cover (LULC) maps online, free of charge. These maps were produced using land use and land cover data from airphotos taken in the 1970s and 1980s.

http://edc.usgs.gov/products/landcover/lulc.html

ADDITIONAL RESOURCES

▶ How To Teach With Topographic Maps

This NSTA published "how-to" booklet for middle level science teachers features two sections: background information for teachers and classroom activities for teaching topographic maps to students. Includes a topographic map produced by the United States Geologic Survey (USGS), a glossary of terms, a detailed key of topographic mapping symbols, and a bibliography. Available for purchase from the science store at *www.nsta.org*.

ARTIFICIAL SUBSTRATES FOR AQUATIC INVERTEBRATES

Instructions for building Hester-Dendy multiplate samplers are available online in the Appendix of the *Hoosier Riverwatch's Volunteer Training Manual* at *www.ai.org/dnr/soilcons/ riverwatch/vsm/manual.html*.

They also can be purchased from:

▶ Water Monitoring Equipment & Supply

P.O. Box 344

Seal Harbor, ME 04675

Phone: 207-276-5746

http://watermonitoringequip.com

▶ Wildlife Supply Company

95 Botsford Place

Buffalo NY 14216

1-800-799-8301

http://wildco.com

▶ Forestry Suppliers, Inc.

205 West Rankin Street

P.O. Box 8379

Jackson, MS 39284-8397

http://forestry-suppliers.com

WATER CHEMISTRY TEST KITS AND PROBES

▶ Hach Company

www.hach.com

800-227-4224

▶ LaMotte Company

www.lamotte.com

800-344-3100

▶ See also the companies listed above, under "Artificial Substrates for Aquatic Invertebrates."

NOTES

NOTES

NOTES

CORNELL SCIENTIFIC INQUIRY SERIES

STUDENT EDITION

Watershed
Dynamics

NSTApress®

NATIONAL SCIENCE TEACHERS ASSOCIATION

CORNELL SCIENTIFIC INQUIRY SERIES

STUDENT EDITION

Watershed Dynamics

BY THE ENVIRONMENTAL INQUIRY LEADERSHIP TEAM
WILLIAM S. CARLSEN
NANCY M. TRAUTMANN
CHRISTINE M. CUNNINGHAM
MARIANNE E. KRASNY
ADAM WELMAN

WITH TEACHERS
HARRIET BECK (WELLSVILLE HIGH SCHOOL)
HARRY CANNING (NEWARK VALLEY HIGH SCHOOL)
MARK JOHNSON (ITHACA HIGH SCHOOL)

AND CORNELL SCIENTISTS
EUGENIA BARNABA
REUBEN GOFORTH
SUSAN HOSKINS

NSTApress®
NATIONAL SCIENCE TEACHERS ASSOCIATION
Arlington, Virginia

NATIONAL SCIENCE TEACHERS ASSOCIATION

Claire Reinburg, Director
Andrew Cocke, Associate Editor
Judy Cusick, Associate Editor
Betty Smith, Associate Editor

ART AND DESIGN Linda Olliver, Director
PRINTING AND PRODUCTION Catherine Lorrain-Hale, Director
    Nguyet Tran, Assistant Production Manager
    Jack Parker, Desktop Publishing Specialist
*sci*LINKS Tyson Brown, Manager
    David Anderson, Web and Development Coordinator

NATIONAL SCIENCE TEACHERS ASSOCIATION
Gerald F. Wheeler, Executive Director
David Beacom, Publisher

Copyright © 2004 by the National Science Teachers Association.
All rights reserved. Printed in the United States of America.
07 06 05   4 3 2

Library of Congress Cataloging-in-Publication Data
Watershed dynamics / by the Environmental Inquiry Leadership Team, William S. Carlsen ... [et al.].— Student ed.
    p. cm. — (Cornell scientific inquiry series)
  ISBN 0-87355-213-X
 1. Watersheds—Study and teaching (Secondary)—Activity programs. 2. Watershed ecology—Study and teaching
(Secondary)—Activity programs. 3. Water quality—Study and teaching (Secondary)—Activity programs. I. Carlsen,
William S. II. Series.
  GB1002.25.W28 2004
  551.48—dc22
                    2004002042

*Featuring sci*LINKS®—*a way to connect text and the Internet. Up-to-the-minute online content, classroom
ideas, and other materials are just a click away. Go to page xiii to learn more about this educational resource.*

This material is based on work supported by the National Science Foundation under Grant No.
96-18142. Any opinions, findings, conclusions, or recommendations expressed in this material are those of the
authors and do not necessarily reflect the views of the National Science Foundation.

Contents

STUDENT EDITION

SECTION 1: UNDERSTANDING WATERSHED DYNAMICS

SECTION 2. PROTOCOLS: INTRODUCTION TO RESEARCH

SECTION 3. INTERACTIVE RESEARCH: FIELD STUDIES AND EXPERIMENTS

Section 4. Interactive Research: Stormwater Treatment Design Challenge

FIGURES AND TABLES IN THE *STUDENT EDITION*

FIGURES

SECTION 1

SECTION 2

TABLES

Section 1

Section 2

SECTION 3

PREFACE

WHY STUDY WATERSHED DYNAMICS?

Water is an important issue for every community, whether that community is a bustling urban neighborhood crowded with people, or a pristine marsh crowded with ducks, amphibians, and fish.

The water resource concerns of human communities vary greatly. In some regions, fresh water for drinking and similar uses is in very short supply. The conservation of water, the identification of new sources of water, and the protection of drinking water reserves are high on the policy agenda in such places. In other regions, water is *too* abundant, and flooding after large storms is inconvenient and expensive at best, deadly at worst. In still other places, water supplies may be contaminated by improper chemical disposal, or may serve as battlegrounds pitting farmers against recreational river runners, or developers against environmental activists. There are few places where water is not an important issue. The details may vary, but everyone needs enough—but not too much—clean, fresh water. Natural communities also need enough, but not too much, clean, fresh water. Such communities include the plants and animal assemblages living in lakes, rivers, ponds, and streams; less obviously, they include terrestrial communities. Many insect species and most amphibians, for example, spend a significant part of their lives underwater. As adults, they disperse widely, where they contribute energy and ecological function. For example, they may eat other insects (dragonflies) or serve as food for birds (mayflies).

Public participation in water resource management requires public understanding about how water functions in natural communities, and how human activities affect the distribution and quality of this precious resource. One challenge—a fascinating one—is that just as watersheds do not respect political boundaries, watershed science does not respect disciplinary boundaries. Understanding watersheds from a policy perspective requires understanding biology, chemistry, Earth sciences, mathematics, sociology, economics, politics ... the list goes on and on. For that reason, the interdisciplinary study of watersheds is often considered an "advanced" topic. We believe, however, that if it is approached as a *foundational* topic, it can provide wonderful opportunities for original research—research that matters to communities of all kinds.

CARRYING OUT YOUR OWN RESEARCH

This book is part of the Environmental Inquiry series developed at Cornell University to enable you to conduct environmental science research on topics that relate to you and your community. Using the research protocols in this book, you will learn to carry out experiments and field studies related to remote sensing, land use, pollution assessment, and hydrology. You will use computer modeling to predict the effects of storms and to manage a simulated watershed. You will also work with other students to engineer a model system for managing stormwater.

We hope that your research and engineering experiences will lead to some interesting discoveries. You may find yourself coming up with new questions and uncertainties rather than with concrete answers. Don't worry—that is the way science works! One of the things that make science exciting is that it is a continuous process of discovery, and there is always more to be learned.

HOW TO USE THIS BOOK

This book is designed to help you design and conduct your own field studies and experiments and to experience some of the ways in which scientists work together to discuss ideas, exchange feedback, and collaborate on joint projects.

Section 1 provides background information about aquatic systems and watershed science. The next section presents 10 research protocols. Using one or more of these protocols, you will be able to design and carry out your own field studies, experiments, and computer simulations. Section 3 provides advice to help you choose from a wide range of ideas for research projects, and a series of worksheets designed to guide your progress through the various steps of designing and carrying out an experiment, presenting your results, and exchanging feedback with fellow students. Section 4 gives step-by-step directions for an engineering design challenge related to flood control.

As you make your way through your research and engineering design projects, we encourage you to visit our Web site (*http://ei.cornell.edu*) to find online resources and to share your experiences, observations, and questions with other participating students. Have fun, and good luck with your research!

—Bill Carlsen
Lead Author

How can you avoid searching hundreds of science Web sites to locate the best sources of information on a given topic? SciLinks, created and maintained by the National Science Teachers Association (NSTA), has the answer.

In a SciLinked text, such as this one, you'll find a logo and keyword near a concept your class is studying, a URL (*www.scilinks.org*), and a keyword code. Simply go to the SciLinks Web site, type in the code, and receive an annotated listing of as many as 15 Web pages—all of which have gone through an extensive review process conducted by a team of science educators. SciLinks is your best source of pertinent, trustworthy Internet links on subjects from astronomy to zoology.

Need more information? Take a tour—*www.scilinks.org/tour*

UNDERSTANDING WATERSHED DYNAMICS

CHAPTER 1

INTRODUCTION TO WATERSHED DYNAMICS

The title of this book, *Watershed Dynamics,* refers to the idea that streams, rivers, lakes, and other water bodies are dynamic systems, continuously changing in many ways—physically, chemically, and biologically. Have you ever wondered why some streams dry up during the summer while others continue to flow? Or where the water in a river comes from when the weather has been dry for several months? Have you wondered what sorts of organisms live in water, and why different varieties live in ponds vs. streams? Or how the fish and invertebrates you find in a stream during periods of low flow could possibly have survived the muddy, raging currents during spring runoff?

These are examples of the dynamic relationships that take place in water and the surrounding landscape. Every body of water interacts with the atmosphere, receiving precipitation and exchanging gases between water and air. Every water body also interacts with the surrounding landscape, receiving runoff along with sediments and dissolved materials that get carried along during rainfall or snowmelt events. Humans of course are an integral part of these dynamic systems, both affecting and being affected by water in all aspects of our lives.

When you turn on a kitchen faucet in New Orleans, Louisiana, some of the water that comes out has already been through several sets of human kidneys. The reason: New Orleans draws its drinking water from the Mississippi River, which extends 2350 miles upstream and gets used in many ways before making its way south to New Orleans. The river begins with rainfall and snowmelt draining into Lake Itasca, Minnesota. As it works its way downstream from Minnesota to Louisiana, Mississippi River water is used for drinking, bathing, washing, agriculture, and industry in over 70 communities along the way. In each city or town, some water drains directly

Topic: watershed
Go to: *www.sciLINKS.org*
Code: WD01

back into the river after use, but much is routed through wastewater treatment plants. There, excess organic matter and other contaminants are removed before the water returns to the river and continues its journey downstream.

It may seem distasteful to think of drinking water that has been "treated" by kidneys and sewage treatment plants. Perhaps you'd rather drink "pure" water—say, the water melting from a 10,000-year old glacier or a prehistoric, deep underground aquifer. Unless you live in a very unusual place, this probably isn't possible. The water that we all drink *has* been recycled through natural processes, human-engineered systems, or both. All of our water, whether it comes from a reservoir, a well, or even a bottle, is affected by how people use the land through which that water once flowed.

Protection of water resources is vital but also complicated. People have wide-ranging interests and concerns about land use and water resources, and management decisions are made based on combinations of science, politics, and values. For some people, the top priority is economic development, with the goal of creating jobs and encouraging commercial, industrial, and residential growth. In this case, abundant, inexpensive water is a high priority. Other people focus on preserving wild spaces and natural ecosystems, or protecting the purity of drinking water. These people are likely to want to restrict rather than promote construction of new development projects. The goal of watershed management is to balance multiple, competing demands, using scientific studies in combination with human judgment to make decisions about various watershed management options.

WHAT IS A WATERSHED?

A *watershed* is the region of land that contributes water to a stream, river, pond, lake, or other body of water. The boundary around a watershed is called the *watershed divide*. This is the line that divides one watershed from the next. Rain that falls on one side of the divide will drain into a stream in one watershed, and rain falling on the other side will drain into a different watershed.

> A *watershed* is the region of land draining into a stream, river, pond, lake, or other body of water.

One way to think of a watershed is to imagine a bowl. The body of water—such as a pond—is at the bottom of the bowl. The sides of the bowl represent the land draining into the pond, and the top edge is the divide that defines the boundaries of the pond's watershed. Of course, actual watersheds are not circular. Instead, they have irregular boundaries that follow the topography of the land. Using Protocol 3 (p. 57), you will learn how to delineate watershed boundaries by connecting the points of highest elevation in the land surrounding a stream or other water body.

Every land area, regardless of its location, is part of a watershed. As you might imagine, watersheds vary widely. Some are hilly and others are relatively flat. Some are forested and others contain cities. Some cover vast areas of land, and others are much smaller. The headwaters of a small stream near the top of a mountain may have a watershed the size of several football fields.

In contrast, the watershed of the Mississippi River covers about 40 percent of the lower 48 states! Of course, the Mississippi River is supplied by thousands of tributary streams and rivers, each of which has its own watershed. When considering huge watersheds such as that of the Mississippi River, the numerous smaller watersheds within it are called *sub-watersheds* (see Figure 1.1).

FIGURE 1.1.
The Mississippi River watershed is made up of many smaller sub-watersheds.

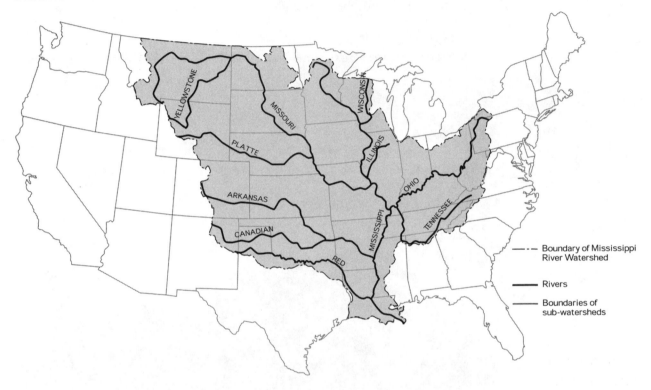

No two watersheds are exactly alike. The boundaries and characteristics of a watershed depend on many factors, including the geology of the region. What type of bedrock lies under the soils? Is the terrain steep and hilly, or broad and flat? Are there volcanoes in the area? Have glaciers covered the land in the distant past, leaving behind vast deposits of sand and gravel?

Climate also plays a major role in defining watershed characteristics. How much precipitation occurs per year? Does it occur primarily during a few wet months, or is it evenly distributed throughout the year? How warm are the summers, and how extreme are the winters? How strong are the winds? What types of vegetation are able to survive?

Vegetation is another key characteristic of watersheds. Because roots absorb water and anchor soil, the types of plants growing in a watershed determine how much—and how quickly—water runs off after storms or spring snowmelt. The vegetation in a watershed also affects the types of habitat available for animals and other organisms.

THE WATER CYCLE

On Earth, water shifts continuously between gaseous, liquid, and solid forms—between water vapor in the atmosphere and rain or other forms of precipitation falling on land or into the sea (Figure 1.2). When precipitation falls onto land, it can return to the atmosphere, percolate into the soil, or run off into surface water bodies such as streams, rivers, lakes, or wetlands. Water flows downhill through watersheds, emptying into larger bodies of water and eventually into an ocean. At all stages along the way, water vapor returns to the atmosphere through evaporation from land and water surfaces.

FIGURE 1.2.
Water cycles between land, water, and the atmosphere.

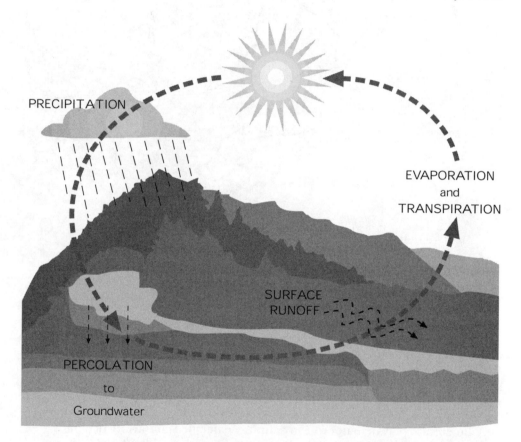

Some of the water that soaks into the ground percolates downward to become groundwater. Groundwater trickles in a general downhill direction through layers of crushed rock, gravel, soil, or other permeable material. Depending on factors such as soil type, geologic conditions, and precipitation patterns, the velocity of groundwater flow can range from several meters per day to only a few meters over the course of an entire year. Groundwater is the source of water for wells and springs, and it also slowly feeds into lakes, streams, and rivers. During periods with no rainfall, streams that receive groundwater are less likely to dry up than those fed solely through surface runoff.

Not all of the water that soaks into the ground becomes groundwater. Plants take up the water they need to sustain life. Through a process called *transpiration,* plants release water vapor back into the atmosphere. Gradually clouds form and grow, and the water cycle continues as precipitation once again falls to the Earth.

Of all the water on Earth, 97 percent is in the oceans and only 3 percent is fresh water. Of the fresh water, less than one percent is found in lakes, rivers, and other surface water bodies. Most fresh water is stored in ice caps and glaciers, or underground in the form of groundwater (Table 1.1). Nevertheless, the tiny fraction of the Earth's water that actively circulates as fresh water plays an incredibly important and dynamic role in life on Earth, sustaining human life and the lives of all other land-dwelling and fresh-water species.

Transpiration is the process through which plants release water to the atmosphere.

TABLE 1.1
Distribution of Fresh Water on Earth

Water Source	% of Fresh Water on Earth
Ice caps, glaciers, permanent snow, and permafrost	69.6%
Groundwater	30.1%
Lakes, rivers, wetlands, and other surface water	0.30%
Soil moisture	0.05%
Atmosphere	0.04%

Source: Gleick, P. H., 1996: Water resources. In *Encyclopedia of climate and weather,* ed. by S. H. Schneider, New York: Oxford University Press, (2) 817–23.

Although wetlands contain only a tiny fraction of the fresh water on Earth, they represent an important component of the water cycle. Marshes, swamps, bogs, and other wetlands are heavily vegetated areas that are saturated with water for at least part of the year. They cover approximately 6 percent of the Earth's surface, ranging from tropical mangrove swamps in Panama to peat bogs in the United Kingdom.

Wetlands play vital roles in physical, chemical, and biological processes in the Earth's water cycle. Physically, wetlands help to reduce flooding by storing great volumes of water, slowly releasing it to downstream waters in the weeks and months after each storm. Because wetlands release water slowly over time, they help to maintain flow in streams and rivers during dry periods of the year. Wetlands also help to purify the water that flows through them. Sediments settle out and some dissolved pollutants get broken down or taken up by plants as water trickles slowly through wetlands. And finally, wetlands provide a rich variety of habitats that support a diverse system of living things. Migrating birds take advantage of the abundant food supplies they find in wetlands, as do many other forms of wildlife.

Topic: properties of water
Go to: *www.sciLINKS.org*
Code: WD03

COMPETING NEEDS FOR WATER

Although the Earth contains vast amounts of water, supplies are not always sufficient in any particular location to meet the needs of various competing uses. Humans use water to irrigate crops, generate power, and support a wide range of industrial, commercial, and agricultural applications. We also rely on it for recreational activities such as fishing, boating, and swimming.

In our homes, each of us uses an average of 300 to 400 liters of water per day for household uses (Table 1.2). This doesn't include all the water it takes to produce the food we eat and the products we use. For example, a cow drinks roughly four liters of water for each liter of milk produced. To manufacture a new car requires over 8,500 liters of water, much of which is used in making the tires.

TABLE 1.2
Typical Water Use in American Homes

Type of Use	Typical Water Use
Tap water (hand washing, tooth brushing, etc.)	up to 5 liters per minute
Dripping faucet	up to 55 liters per day
Toilet (installed before 1992)	14 liters per flush
Toilet (low-flow)	6 liters per flush
Shower	8–20 liters per minute
Bath	100–200 liters per bath
Clothes washer	90–150 liters per load
Dishwasher	20–60 liters per load
Lawn watering	20–40 liters per minute

Source: www.h2ouse.org, developed by the California Urban Water Conservation Council.

Competing with all of these water uses is our desire to protect habitats for a wide range of aquatic organisms. We choose to protect some species because of their value for human uses such as sport fishing. Others are targeted for protection because they are endangered or are particularly important in maintaining healthy ecosystems. To help meet critical habitat needs, many states have passed legislation specifying minimum allowable flow rates in designated rivers or streams. In some cases this means that water must be released from a reservoir to maintain downstream flows during dry seasons. In other cases, irrigation or other uses might need to be reduced in order to maintain critical levels of flow needed for survival of fish and other aquatic organisms.

Water policies often are controversial because they deal with conflicting needs and values. Which is more important—Irrigating crops or providing high flows for recreational uses such as whitewater rafting? Which should take precedence—providing water for new residential development, or maintaining critical flows needed to preserve a valued wetland? Issues such as these are particularly difficult because the times when water is in shortest supply also are the times of greatest need for habitat protection as well as for residential, commercial, and industrial water uses.

DISCUSSION QUESTIONS

▶ What would you say if someone told you that you were drinking recycled water that had already passed through several wastewater treatment systems?

▶ What is the source of water for your school or home? Does it come from surface or groundwater? Do you know the name of the watershed you live in?

▶ Historically, wetlands have often been considered "wasted" land that can be drained, filled, and used as "new" land for development and construction. What are some possible ecological consequences of this type of development strategy?

▶ Consider the water use data in Table 1.2. If your community were experiencing a water shortage, what water use restrictions would be most worth exploring, and why?

Topic: groundwater contaminants
Go to: www.sciLINKS.org
Code: WD04

CHAPTER 2

WHAT'S IN A WATERSHED?

Think about how land is used in your community. If you live in a rural town, there may be many farms or forests. In cities, the land is more likely to be covered with buildings, highways, and parking lots, with parks and open areas scattered between. The types of land uses in a watershed affect the quantity and quality of water draining from the land. Using Protocol 1 (p. 51), you will visit your study watershed and conduct a field survey to make observations about land uses, water resources, and possible sources of pollution.

CLASSIFYING LAND USES

When scientists and land managers study watershed land use, they classify the land into categories such as urban, agriculture, wetland, or forest. Depending on the level of detail needed, each of these categories can be broken down into more specific land uses. For example, urban land is likely to include a combination of land in commercial, industrial, residential, and transportation uses.

Land uses can be organized into categories such as urban, agriculture, wetland, and forest.

You may be wondering why classifying land uses into categories is worth the time and effort. One reason is that land use affects the quantity and quality of water that drains from a watershed. By studying the effects of specific land uses, scientists and watershed managers gain information that is useful in protecting water resources for drinking water, recreation, and wildlife habitat.

One way to classify land use in a watershed is to go into the field and measure the areas of land devoted to uses such as agriculture, housing, or forests. Another approach is to work from your home or school using data gathered through *remote sensing*. Remote sensing refers to collecting data from a distance, for example using aerial photographs of the land taken from a plane. Aerial photographs, also called "airphotos," provide a bird's-eye view of land uses, management practices, drainage patterns, and potential sources of surface and groundwater contamination. In Protocol 4 (p. 62), you will learn how to use airphotos to estimate water quality in the streams draining a watershed. Although these estimates may not be as accurate as fieldwork in determining stream water quality, they do enable researchers to assess large watersheds in a limited amount of time.

Remote sensing **means gathering data from a distance, such as by satellite or aircraft.**

Airphotos also provide the possibility of investigating changes in land use over time. Many parts of the country have been repeatedly photographed over the years since the 1920s. By comparing airphotos taken at various dates, you may find former landfills, dump sites, lagoons, pits, and above-ground storage tanks that currently are hidden by development or vegetation. Analysis of changes in land use over time also provides insights into general trends in water quantity and quality, as discussed below.

EFFECTS OF LAND USE ON RUNOFF QUANTITY

After a rainstorm, some precipitation evaporates and some seeps into the soil, where it may be taken up by plants or may percolate downward to become groundwater. The rest drains into ditches, streams, wetlands, lakes, and other surface water bodies. Watershed land uses affect how water is distributed among these various routes.

Impervious surfaces do not allow rainfall to soak through and seep into the ground.

In wooded areas, vegetation tends to slow the flow of surface drainage. As runoff makes its way past tree trunks and through brush and other vegetation, much of the water is likely to soak into the ground rather than draining into streams. This changes when land is converted into highways, shopping centers, houses, schools, and other structures because more area gets covered with *impervious surfaces* such as roofs, sidewalks, and blacktop. Water cannot soak through impervious surfaces, so precipitation runs off rather than seeping into the soil. As a result, cities and suburbs tend to create more surface runoff than forested land, and to have less water percolating downward into the ground (Figure 1.3).

FIGURE 1.3
The impervious surfaces in cities create more surface runoff than in suburbs or forests and allow less water to percolate into the ground.

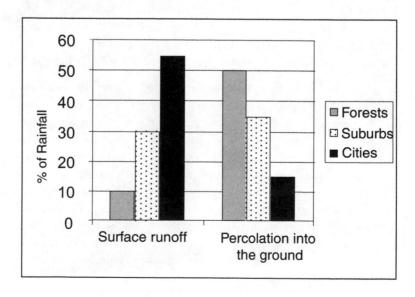

You may be wondering why it matters whether rainfall soaks into the ground or runs off into streams and rivers. One reason is that it affects flooding. As you might expect, increases in surface runoff lead to greater flooding risks in downstream areas. The greater the amount of impervious surface in a watershed, the more severe the floods tend to be, and the sooner flood peaks occur after each storm. This is discussed in greater detail in Chapter 4.

EFFECTS OF LAND USE ON WATER QUALITY

One of the steps in studying land uses and management practices in a watershed is to inventory point sources and non-point sources of pollution. *Point sources* are wastes or pollutants that come from a single source such as a pipe or smokestack. They include water that empties into a river from a factory, a wastewater treatment plant, or the cooling tower of a power plant. Point sources also include pollution events that can be traced to a single source, such as the Exxon Valdez oil spill caused by a tanker crash off the coast of Alaska in 1989. Point source pollutants can generally be tracked to a specific, localized source.

In contrast, *non-point sources* are those that cannot be traced to a single pipe or source of pollution. Water that drains from city streets after a storm is considered a non-point source of pollution, as is runoff from barnyards, agricultural fields, and fertilized lawns or golf courses.

EFFECTS OF LAND USE ON HABITAT

Every type of organism has certain requirements for sustaining life. These requirements differ from one species to another, and collectively they make up the *habitat* for each species. Sonoran Desert Toads are adapted to life in harsh, dry desert lands. They spend most of the year underground, surfacing only when summer rains moisten the earth and signal the beginning of their brief breeding season. Clearly, these desert toads are adapted to a different sort of habitat than most other types of amphibians, for whom constant moisture is a requirement to sustain life.

When land uses change, some types of habitat are destroyed and others are created. Some organisms can thrive in a variety of settings and therefore have broad habitat requirements. Other species survive only under a very limited range of conditions and therefore have much more narrowly defined habitats. Species with narrowly defined habitat requirements are vulnerable to environmental changes such as clearing of forests or filling of wetlands. Protection of habitat for sensitive species is one of the goals of watershed management, especially in *riparian zones*, the areas of land bordering the edges of streams and rivers.

Riparian Zones

Riparian zones are ecologically very important because they provide habitat for a diverse range of land-dwelling species and also help determine the habitats available for organisms living in the water. For example, trees lining a

Point source pollutants can be traced to a single source such as a pipe or smokestack.

Non-point source pollutants come from many sources, such as runoff from highways or farm fields.

The *habitat* for a species includes its specific needs related to shelter, food, water, and reproduction.

Riparian zones are the land areas along the banks of rivers and streams.

riverbank provide shade that keeps the water cool on a sunny day. Without shade, the water might become too warm in summer months to support sensitive fish such as salmon and trout.

The vegetation in riparian zones also helps to maintain water quality by controlling erosion and filtering runoff water. Sediments and some types of chemical pollutants get removed before water drains into the river or stream. In areas without adequate riparian zones, aquatic habitats are more vulnerable to degradation by sediments and other contaminants that drain from construction sites, logging operations, plowed fields, and other land uses with bare soils.

Because riparian zones influence aquatic habitats, they can be used to predict what types of organisms are likely to live in a river or stream. This approach is used in the Watershed Habitat Evaluation and Biotic Integrity Protocol (WHEBIP) model presented in Protocol 4 (p. 62). First, you estimate the percentages of your watershed that are devoted to various land uses. Then, using the WHEBIP model, you will be able to predict the quality of stream segments in terms of the habitat that they provide for aquatic organisms. Sites that receive "Excellent" WHEBIP ratings are the ones that would be most likely to support highly sensitive species of fish and invertebrates.

You may be wondering why you would want to use a model like WHEBIP, rather than going out in the field and collecting samples of stream life. Actually both approaches are valuable. Using field techniques such as those described in Protocols 5–7 (pp. 78–91), you can collect samples of aquatic invertebrates and interpret them to draw conclusions about the biological health of your study stream. Using the WHEBIP model will allow you to carry out a different sort of analysis, integrating information about watershed land uses in order to make predictions about the quality of life you would be likely to find in various sections of a river or stream. Although this may be less accurate than field sampling, it allows you to quickly analyze many stream sections and identify potential problem areas and stream segments especially worthy of protection.

When scientists and land use planners draw up watershed management plans, they use both field tests and modeling in order to take advantage of the different benefits of these two approaches. Models are developed based on field data. Once a model has been demonstrated to effectively represent watershed processes, it then becomes a valuable tool for prediction of the impacts of various land use management scenarios.

DISCUSSION QUESTIONS

▶ Describe different types of land use in your community. How has this changed over the past few years?

▶ Discuss how land use practices in your community may affect local rivers and streams.

▶ What are some of the advantages of remote sensing compared with field sampling?

SCILINKS.
THE WORLD'S A CLICK AWAY
Topic: water pollution
Go to: *www.sciLINKS.org*
Code: WD05

CHAPTER 3

BIOLOGICAL COMMUNITIES IN STREAMS

Have you ever walked through a stream, stirring up rocks along the way? If so, chances are good you have seen tiny fish, crayfish, and other organisms scurrying for cover. If you have picked up rocks and flipped them over, you may have seen aquatic invertebrates such as mayfly nymphs clinging to the wet, slippery surfaces. These organisms are examples of the wide range of living things that are adapted to life in flowing water. Their adaptations include various techniques for gathering food and staying in place while currents rush past.

Because aquatic organisms differ in their adaptations, they also have different habitat requirements. Some species of fish can survive only in cold, rapidly flowing streams with high concentrations of dissolved oxygen. Others need warm, slowly moving currents with warmer temperatures, and they can tolerate lower oxygen levels. The same variation is found among the aquatic invertebrates that these fish use as food. Some types of invertebrates cling to rocks in fast-moving currents, while others burrow into muddy sediments in slower-moving waters. Water temperature, velocity, the concentration of dissolved oxygen, and many other variables affect the types of organisms living in any particular section of a river or stream. Within any of these aquatic environments, the organisms are linked together through food chains and webs that define what they eat.

Mayfly Nymph

FOOD CHAINS AND WEBS

Life on Earth depends mainly on the work of *producers* such as green plants and algae. Through photosynthesis, most producers use energy from the sun to create their own food from carbon dioxide and water.

Animals and other organisms that cannot produce their own food are called *consumers*. Instead of absorbing carbon dioxide from the atmosphere and converting it into sugars, starches, and other organic matter, consumers obtain their energy and nutrients by eating other organisms or their wastes.

Producers use energy from the sun to make their own food.

Consumers get energy by eating other organisms or their wastes.

Food chains show simple relationships between producers and consumers.

A *food chain* illustrates a sequence of organisms and their food sources. Every food chain begins with a producer, which gets eaten by a consumer, which in turn becomes food for another consumer, and so on. *Food webs* combine more than one food chain into a more complex network of feeding relationships (Figure 1.4).

FIGURE 1.4S
Food webs combine food chains into complex networks of feeding relationships.

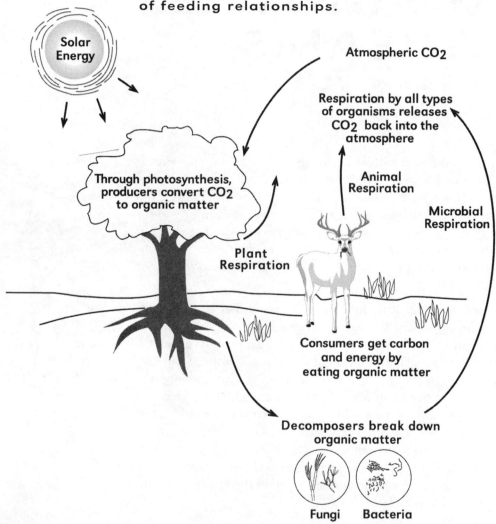

In streams, producers such as algae and aquatic plants form the basis for some food webs. Perhaps surprisingly, the producers for many stream food webs also include the trees and other vegetation growing along the shorelines. Many types of stream invertebrates are scavengers, adapted to eating the leaves, twigs, and other organic materials that fall into the water or wash in along with runoff or snowmelt from surrounding land. Some of these invertebrates shred leaves, and others catch particles from the current as the water flows by. Still others feed by scraping bacteria and algae off the surfaces of rocks. All of these types of invertebrates become food for fish and other higher-level consumers in aquatic food webs.

Decomposers are an often-overlooked part of food webs. When plants and animals die, fungi and bacteria break down the dead materials. While digesting wastes to meet their own nutritional needs, these decomposers also convert the organic matter into chemical forms that are usable as nutrients by other types of organisms, including the stream invertebrates that shred and eat leaves and other decaying vegetation.

STREAM INVERTEBRATES

Mayflies, blackflies, dragonflies, mosquitoes—these and many other familiar types of insects spend part of their life cycle in streams, rivers, or other water bodies, and make up important components of aquatic food webs. Many live in water during their immature stages, then emerge as adults to mate, reproduce, and die. Some live only a few hours after mating and don't even have mouthparts for eating. Others spend several months in adult form.

When aquatic insects emerge from a stream as adults, they mate and then deposit their eggs back in the water. When the eggs hatch, aquatic larvae or nymphs emerge. You may be wondering why some of these immature organisms are called "larvae" and others are called "nymphs." The answer has to do with the type of metamorphosis (complete or incomplete) they undergo to become adults.

Insects that go through complete metamorphosis have four life stages: egg, larva, pupa, and adult. Figure 1.5 illustrates these four stages in the life of a riffle beetle. Unlike the organisms discussed above, this species spends its entire life in streams, and the adults do not emerge from the water to mate and lay eggs.

SCi
LINKS.
THE WORLD'S A CLICK AWAY

Topic: invertebrates
Go to: *www.sciLINKS.org*
Code: WD07

FIGURE 1.5
Complete metamorphosis includes a pupal stage.

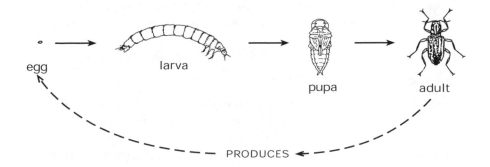

egg   larva   pupa   adult

PRODUCES

For insects that undergo complete metamorphosis, the larvae grow, shedding their exoskeletons (hard outer coatings) several times as they get bigger. After going through this series of small changes, each larva undergoes a dramatic change that requires a special resting and non-feeding stage called a pupa. The adults emerge from their pupae looking quite different than they did as larvae.

Insects that undergo incomplete metamorphosis go through only three life stages and do not form pupae. Their immature forms are called nymphs rather than larvae. Figure 1.6 illustrates the three stages in the life of a dragonfly.

FIGURE 1.6
Incomplete metamorphosis has no pupal stage.

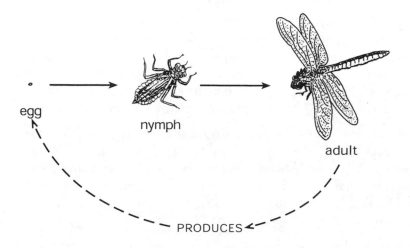

egg

nymph

adult

PRODUCES

As nymphs grow, they go through a series of gradual changes, at each stage looking a bit more like an adult. When dragonfly nymphs are fully grown, their wings have matured. They climb from the water, shed their exoskeleton one last time, dry their newly formed wings, and fly away as adults.

Many other types of invertebrates also inhabit rivers and streams. These include crayfish (crustaceans), mussels (mollusks), and snails (gastropods). Some live in riffles, where water tumbles over rocks and stones, and others live in pools, where stream water is deeper and moves more slowly.

USING INVERTEBRATES TO ASSESS STREAM QUALITY

Because of their sensitivity to environmental conditions, aquatic invertebrates commonly are used as indicators of stream water quality. Some types, such as stonefly nymphs, require cold, swift currents with rocky stream bottoms. Others, such as aquatic worms, prefer warm, slow-moving waters with muddy sediments. Protocols 5–7 provide techniques for collecting stream invertebrates and using these collections to assess water quality at your study site.

The concentration of dissolved oxygen is a critical factor determining habitat suitability for aquatic organisms. Organisms such as stonefly nymphs that live in quickly flowing currents tend to require high oxygen levels. Through evolution, other types of organisms have developed adaptations that enable them to live in ponds or other low-oxygen waters. For example, mosquito larvae use breathing tubes to connect with the atmosphere as they hang down from the water surface. Diving beetles carry bubbles of air on their backs as they swim into the depths. Other species have developed highly efficient techniques for extracting oxygen from the water, or of carrying out life functions using relatively small amounts of oxygen. Organisms adapted to life in cold, swiftly moving streams and rivers do not have these adaptations and will die if the water becomes too low in dissolved oxygen.

In streams that have become polluted with manure or inadequately treated sewage, drastic changes in stream life take place. Problems occur because as decomposer bacteria work to break down organic wastes, they use up dissolved oxygen. As a result, oxygen levels may drop to levels that do not support sensitive fish such as salmon and trout, or invertebrates such as stonefly nymphs. Drainage of fertilizers from lawns, golf courses, and farm fields can cause similar problems by stimulating overgrowth of algae and aquatic plants. When these mats of vegetation die, their decay uses up dissolved oxygen supplies (see the discussion of eutrophication on p. 35 for further explanation of this problem).

DISCUSSION QUESTIONS

▶ Why would it matter if input of untreated sewage or manure killed all of the pollution-sensitive invertebrates in a stream?

▶ Why does it make sense to use aquatic invertebrate populations to assess streamwater quality?

▶ What are some possible limitations of assessing streamwater quality using invertebrate sampling?

CHAPTER 4

PHYSICAL CHARACTERISTICS OF STREAMS

Streams are dynamic systems, changing from day to day in physical characteristics such as water temperature, turbidity, and the amount and velocity of flow. These changes affect the chemistry of the water and the types of biological life it can support.

TEMPERATURE

Stream temperature varies with the season, and also with the time of day and the extent to which sunlight warms the water. It also can be affected by land uses and management practices. If shoreline trees are removed, stream temperatures are likely to go up because of the reduced amount of shade. Warming of stream temperatures also can result from urbanization of the watershed. Runoff that drains from roofs and blacktop gets warmed more than water running off vegetated land surfaces.

Temperature is a physical characteristic of water that affects chemical and biological processes, including the rate of metabolism of aquatic organisms. For organisms that are adapted to life in cold water, warming of the water is likely to cause problems due to shortages of dissolved oxygen. This occurs for two reasons. First, the metabolic rates of organisms go up as the water warms, and this means that the organisms need increased amounts of oxygen to stay alive. Second, the concentrations of dissolved oxygen decrease as the water warms, meaning that less oxygen is available when more is needed.

TURBIDITY

Turbidity measures the amount of suspended material in water such as the sediments carried in muddy runoff after a storm. High turbidity can be caused by erosion of stream banks or watershed soils, or by stirring up of stream sediments during periods of high streamflow. In nutrient-rich waters, single-celled algae suspended in the water also contribute to high turbidity.

High turbidity levels and suspended sediments can harm stream organisms, for example by clogging the gills of fish and aquatic invertebrates and reducing the amount of oxygen they can take up from the water. This problem is compounded by the fact that suspended sediments absorb sunlight and cause stream water to become warmer, which decreases the amount of dissolved oxygen the water can hold.

Sediments also can impair fish spawning. A study in Carnation Creek, British Columbia, showed that nearby logging operations increased the amount of fine suspended sediments in the creek by about 5 percent, causing 50 percent reduction in the number of fish eggs that successfully developed into juveniles.

The high turbidity caused by suspended sediments also can reduce stream productivity by decreasing the amount of light available for photosynthesis by submerged aquatic vegetation.

STREAM ORDER

Streams drain watersheds following the path of least resistance as they make their way into larger streams, rivers, lakes, and oceans. Some streams flow year-round, others dry up during summer or winter months, and some flow for only brief periods after rainfall or snowmelt.

FIGURE 1.7
Stream order classification system

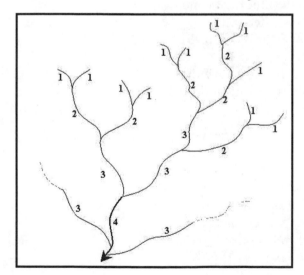

Stream order, a common stream classification system, refers to the size of a stream and its tributaries (see Figure 1.7). First-order streams have no tributaries; typically they are short and drain small areas at the high points of watersheds. Although first-order streams are small, collectively they make up about 75 percent of the total stream and river mileage in the U.S.

When two first-order streams come together, they form a second-order stream. Two second-order streams come together to form a third-order stream, and so on. Note that if a second order and first order stream merge, the resulting stream still is referred to as a second order stream.

Why is stream order important? It provides a useful classification of the characteristics of the stream segment. First-order streams are more likely than higher-order streams to dry up during summer months. They also tend to have steeper slopes and faster currents, which carve out v-shaped stream channels lined with boulders, rocks, and gravel. Higher-order streams are found farther downstream. They are likely to have flatter slopes and slower flows, resulting in u-shaped channels lined with smaller materials such as gravel, sand, and silt. These physical characteristics determine what types of life each stream segment can support. Organisms that are adapted to living in cold, clear, quickly flowing water are more commonly found in first order streams, while those that burrow in silty sediments are more likely to be found in slower moving downstream waters.

RATES OF FLOW

The volume of water flowing past a certain point over a designated period of time is called *streamflow* or *discharge*. In metric units, it is reported in terms of cubic meters per second (m³/sec). In small mountain streams, the rate of flow may be under 1 m³/sec, compared with 17,000 m³/sec for the Mississippi River. The world's largest river, the Amazon River in Brazil, averages just over 200,000 m³/sec.

Topic: stream deposition
Go to: *www.sciLINKS.org*
Code: WD08

Streamflow is measured in a variety of ways. Protocol 8 (p. 92) gives instructions for calculating discharge based on measurements you have made of water depth and flow velocity in your study stream. By taking depth measurements at regular intervals across the stream, you will be able to calculate the cross-sectional area of the stream at that particular time. Once you measure the velocity of the flow, you will be able to multiple the area (m²) times the velocity (m/sec), to calculate the discharge (m³/sec).

The U.S. Geological Survey monitors streamflow, using thousands of stream-gaging stations throughout the country. At these stations, a slightly different approach is used, called the "stage-discharge method." A mathematical equation is developed at each site that relates water height (stage) to streamflow volume (discharge). Once the formula has been developed, simple measurements of water height can be used to calculate discharge rates. The stage-discharge equation is different for each gaging station because it depends on the width of the stream and the depth and velocity of flow at various points across the stream channel. Stream channels are continuously changing, with sediments eroding in some places and depositing in others. Stage-discharge equations must periodically be revised to correct for these site-specific changes.

Streamflow Changes over Time

Have you noticed the changes that occur in streamflow after a large rainstorm? After the storm, the flow probably was higher, faster, and muddier than during drier periods? The stream may also have been carrying leaves, branches, or even tree trunks and other debris washed in with the storm runoff.

Clearly, streamflow varies over time, increasing after a rainstorm or snowmelt, and dropping or possibly even drying up completely during dry spells. Scientists and watershed managers use graphs called *hydrographs* to illustrate these changes in streamflow over time (Figure 1.8).

FIGURE 1.8
A hydrograph shows changes in streamflow following a heavy rainstorm.

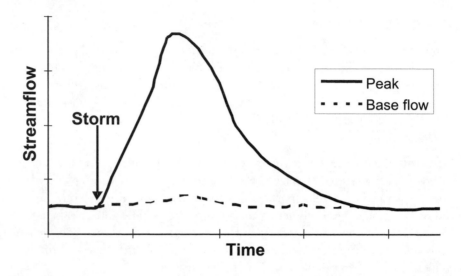

Base flow is the slow, steady flow of groundwater into streams.

During periods when a watershed receives no precipitation, its streams may still continue to flow due to input of groundwater. Just as groundwater bubbles to the ground surface in springs, it also seeps into streams. This steady input, called *base flow,* helps to maintain a relatively low and constant rate of streamflow during dry weather. After a storm, surface runoff increases rapidly, causing streamflow to go up. Within a few hours or days after a storm, streamflow reaches a peak, and then gradually declines to base flow level until another storm occurs (Figure 1.8).

Impact of Impervious Surfaces

Imagine a stream flowing through a forest. As rain falls, some of the water that reaches the forest floor seeps into the ground and the rest trickles overland and drains into a stream. Gradually the streamflow increases, reaches a peak, and then drops back down to baseflow over the next few days. Now imagine the same stream running through an area covered with parking lots, buildings, and roads. Given the same amount of rainfall, more water would drain into the stream and less would percolate downward through the soil to become groundwater (Figure 1.9).

FIGURE 1.9
Increase in impervious surface In a watershed causes increased surface runoff and decreased percolation of water into the ground.

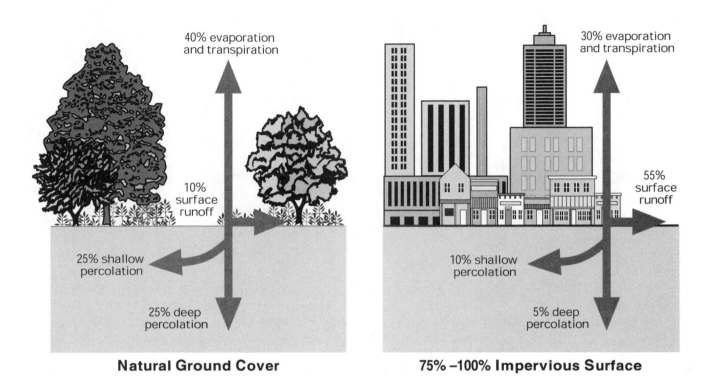

(Adapted from: Federal Interagency Stream Restoration Working Group. 1998. *Stream corridor restoration: Principles, processes, and practices.* Washington, DC: USDA.)

Increases in impervious surfaces within a watershed result in more surface runoff. As a result, floods become larger and more frequent. This is illustrated in Figure 1.10, which compares typical hydrographs for urban vs. forested watersheds. Streamflow in the urban watershed reaches a higher peak, indicating higher flood levels. Because less water seeps into the ground to recharge groundwater supplies, base flow during dry periods tends to be lower in urban watersheds than in forested ones.

FIGURE 1.10
Streamflows following storms rise more quickly and reach higher peaks in urban areas than in forested watersheds.

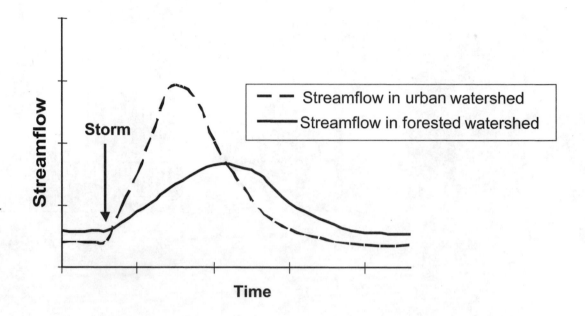

Flooding occurs naturally in rivers and streams, and aquatic organisms are adapted to these annual fluctuations in rates of flow. However, stream life is not necessarily adapted to the many other changes that occur as urbanization takes place. One of these changes is that increased surface runoff causes more erosion, both along the stream banks and from unprotected soils that the runoff flows across on its way to the stream. As eroded soils settle in streams, sedimentation destroys habitat for organisms that require rocky rather than silty stream bottoms. Increases in surface runoff also mean that less precipitation percolates downward through the soil to become groundwater. Less groundwater means decreased base flow in streams, causing habitats for fish and other stream dwellers to be degraded or eliminated during dry periods.

DISCUSSION QUESTIONS

▶ Why do some streams flow year-round, and others dry up during the summer months?

▶ How would you expect streamflow to change over the years as more open land gets developed into buildings, parking lots, and roads?

▶ What steps could be taken to reduce the impact of this development on flood levels after large storms?

CHAPTER 5

STREAM CHEMISTRY

Water chemistry is one of the main factors determining what sorts of organisms can live in a stream. In this chapter, we will consider the chemical parameters most commonly measured in stream studies: dissolved oxygen, nitrate, phosphate, alkalinity, pH and chloride. Most of these are measured in terms of milligrams per liter (mg/L), which is the same as parts per million (ppm).

One ppm means one part out of a million parts. If the dissolved oxygen in a stream is 4 ppm, that means that there are approximately four oxygen molecules in every million molecules of water. This is easier to visualize in terms of smaller numbers. For example, think about slicing a pie. If you cut the pie into 10 pieces, one part per ten would be one out of the ten slices, or 10 percent of the pie.

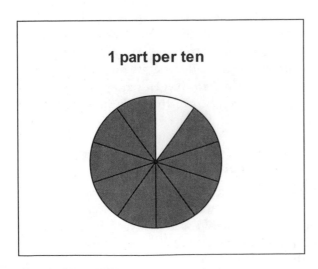

1 part per ten

Cutting the pie into a hundred slices would be more difficult, and a single slice would be almost too small to see. In this case, one slice would be 1 percent of the pie.

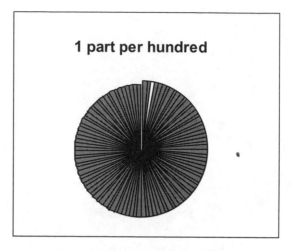

1 part per hundred

If the pie were cut into a million slices, each slice would represent only 0.000001 percent of the pie. Clearly, we can't illustrate one part per million this way, but you can get the idea that it is a tiny fraction of the whole. But just because the numbers are tiny doesn't mean they're not important! In terms of stream chemistry, the difference in a few parts per million of dissolved oxygen can mean the difference between life and death for aquatic organisms. Some species are more sensitive than others to dissolved oxygen and other chemical parameters, as discussed below.

DISSOLVED OXYGEN

**Topic: stream/ river pollution
Go to: www.sciLINKS.org
Code: WD09**

Humans and other land-dwelling organisms use lungs to breathe oxygen from air. In contrast, most stream organisms absorb dissolved oxygen through gills or directly through their skin. Although dissolved oxygen can range from 0 to 18 ppm in rivers and lakes, levels in the range of 7 to 11 ppm are required to support a diverse range of aquatic life. Warm water fish such as carp and catfish can tolerate oxygen concentrations as low as 4 ppm, but coldwater varieties such as salmon and trout do best at concentrations of 7 ppm or above. Invertebrates also differ in their oxygen requirements. Those that require high levels of dissolved oxygen can live only in cool, rapidly flowing streams, while other species with lower oxygen requirements can live in warmer, calmer waters.

Effect of Turbulence on Oxygen

Turbulence, the degree to which water mixes with air as stream water tumbles over rocks, is one of the factors affecting dissolved oxygen. Because oxygen concentrations are much higher in air than in water, oxygen molecules diffuse from the atmosphere into streams and other bodies of surface water. In a large, slow-moving river, this transfer of atmospheric oxygen into the water occurs slowly along the calm water surface. If wind and waves cause greater turbulence, this creates more mixing of water with air. Similarly, the turbulence in shallow streams allows more oxygen to enter water from the atmosphere as the water tumbles over rocks and mixes with air.

Effect of Temperature on Oxygen

Another physical factor determining dissolved oxygen concentration is water temperature. Have you ever noticed that warm soda tastes flat rather than bubbly? This is because colder liquids are capable of holding greater concentrations of dissolved gases. As soda gets warmer, it loses its bubbles. The same is true for dissolved oxygen in streams—if the water warms up, oxygen and other dissolved gases bubble out and are lost to the atmosphere. This occurs because water is saturated with oxygen at a lower concentration when the water is warm than when it is cooler. Saturation refers to the maximum concentration of oxygen that water can hold at any given temperature. As you can see in Figure 1.11, the saturation concentration of oxygen goes down as water temperature goes up.

FIGURE 1.11
Cold water can hold more dissolved oxygen than warm water.

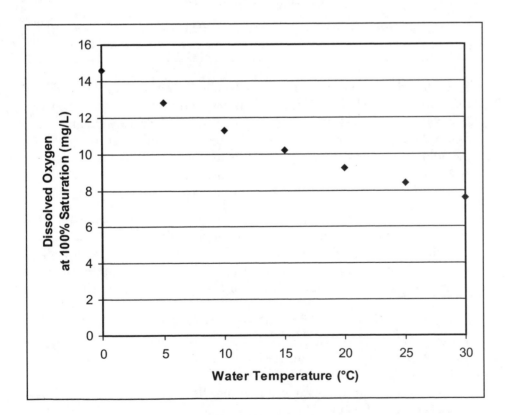

Effects of Living Things on Oxygen

When algae and green plants are exposed to light, they produce their own food through photosynthesis (Figure 1.12). Oxygen is given off as a waste product during this process. When photosynthesis takes place under water, oxygen is released into the water. This may cause dissolved oxygen levels to rise during daylight hours.

FIGURE 1.12
Through photosynthesis, green plants create organic matter and release oxygen.

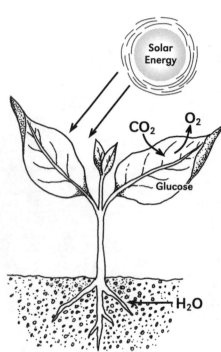

Photosynthesis:

carbon dioxide + water + solar energy → organic matter + oxygen

$6\ CO_2$ $6\ H_2O$ $C_6H_{12}O_6$ $6\ O_2$

(glucose)

Through a process that looks like the reverse of photosynthesis, plants and animals use oxygen to break down organic matter and release energy needed to sustain life. This process, called cellular respiration, uses dissolved oxygen and produces carbon dioxide.

Cellular Respiration:

organic matter + oxygen → carbon dioxide + water + energy

$C_6H_{12}O_6$ $6\ O_2$ $6\ CO_2$ $6\ H_2O$

Although photosynthesis takes place only during daylight hours, living things carry out cellular respiration both day and night. Many people think that plants use photosynthesis to create food and animals use cellular respiration to break it down. This is partly correct, but in fact all living things, including green plants, carry out cellular respiration. Throughout both day and night, plants and animals carry out cellular respiration to support growth, reproduction, and all of the day-to-day functions of life.

In streams and rivers with large populations of aquatic plants, oxygen levels increase during the day when photosynthesis is taking place. However, they drop in the night, when respiration is occurring but photosynthesis is not. Aquatic organisms that require high levels of dissolved oxygen may not be able to survive the low levels that occur during these nighttime hours.

Effects of Organic Pollution on Oxygen

Through the work of bacteria and other decomposer organisms, organic materials in rivers and streams break down and get recycled into nutrients and energy that support new forms of life. This sounds useful to humans— why not just dump our organic wastes into the water and let natural processes take care of them? Although this sounds like a reasonable idea, there is a limit to the capacity of natural waterways to break down organic wastes without suffering negative consequences.

For example, if too much manure or untreated sewage enters a stream, drastic changes in stream life will occur. Populations of decomposer bacteria will grow rapidly because of the increased food supply. As these bacteria work to break down the organic wastes, their cellular respiration uses up oxygen and produces carbon dioxide. As a result, dissolved oxygen levels may drop so low that sensitive species will not be able to survive.

pH

Topic: pH
Go to: *www.sciLINKS.org*
Code: WD11

Another variable that significantly affects stream life is pH, a measure of how acidic or basic the water is. The pH scale ranges from 0 (highly acidic), to 14 (highly basic). A pH of 7 is neutral (neither acidic nor basic). Unlike the other chemical parameters discussed in this chapter, pH is not represented in terms of milligrams per liter or parts per million. Instead, it has its own scale that represents the concentration of hydrogen ions (H^+) in solution. The pH scale is logarithmic, meaning that the drop from one pH level to the next represents a ten-fold increase in acidity, represented by hydrogen ion concentration (Table 1.3). For example, if the average pH of rainfall drops from 6 to 5, this means that the rain has become ten times more acidic. A small change in pH therefore can have large consequences to aquatic life.

TABLE 1.3
Relationship Between pH, Acidity, and H^+ Concentration

pH	Example Substances	Acidity	Concentration of H^+ Ions (moles/L)
1	Battery acid	highly	0.1
2	Lemon juice	acidic	0.01
3	Vinegar, soda pop	↑	0.001
4	Orange juice	↑	0.0001
5		↑	0.00001
6		↑	0.000001
7	Distilled water	neutral	0.0000001
8	Sea water	↓	0.00000001
9		↓	0.000000001
10		↓	0.0000000001
11	Ammonia	↓	0.00000000001
12		↓	0.000000000001
13	Bleach	highly	0.0000000000001
14	Household lye	basic	0.00000000000001

sciLINKS
THE WORLD'S A CLICK AWAY

Topic: acid water
Go to: *www.sciLINKS.org*
Code: WD12

Most streams typically have pH values ranging from 4 to 8. This is determined by the pH of the precipitation or other sources of water feeding each stream, and also by the alkalinity of the stream water (see p. 34).

Precipitation naturally is slightly acidic (pH of 5.6) because rainwater reacts with carbon dioxide in the atmosphere to form carbonic acid. Air pollution from cars, trucks, coal-burning power plants, and factories causes the pH of precipitation to drop even lower. Acid precipitation is defined to have a pH below 5.6. In northeastern states the average pH of rainfall is 4.0–4.5, and individual storms as low as 3.0 are not unusual. In sensitive regions of the country, acid rain can make lakes and streams so acidic that some species can no long survive.

Aquatic organisms are adapted to life within certain acceptable ranges of pH (Figure 1.13). In acidic water, the bones of many fish become soft, and females are unable to lay eggs. Most species do best at pH levels ranging from 6.5 to 8.2, and below 5.0 is deadly to many. Fathead minnows have a hard time surviving when the pH drops below 6.0, as do aquatic invertebrates such as mayfly, damselfly, and dragonfly nymphs. Yellow perch are more tolerant of acidic conditions and can survive in water with pH as low as 4.5.

Decomposer bacteria cannot thrive when the pH drops below about 5. This means that dead vegetation and other organic materials will build up in streams or lakes rather than breaking down and releasing nutrients that can be used by aquatic invertebrates and other forms of life.

FIGURE 1.13
Some types of aquatic life are more sensitive than others to acidic conditions.

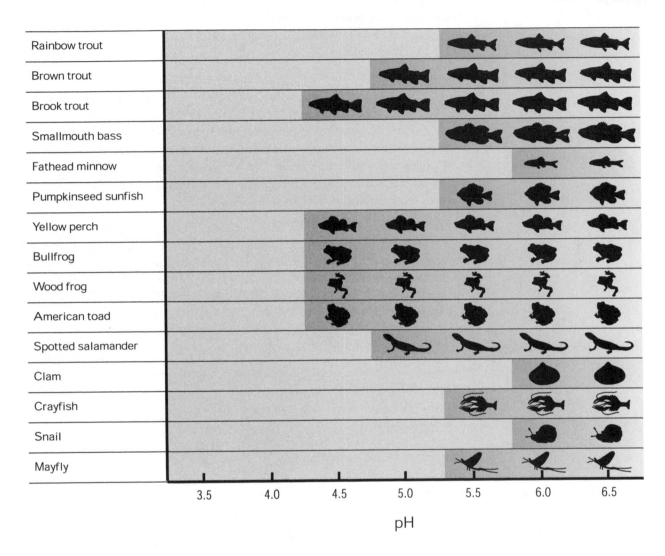

(Adapted from: Federal Interagency Stream Restoration Working Group.1998. *Stream corridor restoration: Principles, processes, and practices*. Washington, DC: USDA.)

ALKALINITY

Some lakes and streams are affected far less than others by acid rain or acidic drainage from mining operations. The reason for this difference is that some waters are better buffered, meaning that they are more capable of resisting change in pH. The buffering capacity of water is measured in terms of *alkalinity*. The higher the alkalinity, the greater the capacity of the water to neutralize acids.

Alkalinity is determined by the concentration of carbonate (CO_3^{2-}), bicarbonate (HCO_3^{-}), and hydroxide (OH^-) ions. These negative ions react with positive hydrogen ions (H^+), removing them from solution. As the concentration of H^+ ions goes down, the acidity of the solution gets neutralized. In watersheds containing limestone ($CaCO_3$) bedrock, streams and lakes tend to be well buffered because water picks up carbonate and bicarbonate ions as it passes over rocks and trickles through soil.

In watersheds without limestone bedrock, streams and other water bodies tend to have much lower alkalinity and therefore are more susceptible to damage by input of acidity from sources such as mine drainage or acid precipitation. When winds blow acidic clouds into regions with low alkalinity levels, the resulting acid precipitation can dramatically lower the pH of surface waters, making habitats unsuitable for many species of aquatic life.

PHOSPHORUS

Phosphorus is an important nutrient, used by plants and animals to build nucleic acids and ATP, a compound used to store energy in cells. As phosphorus cycles between living things and the environment, it takes a variety of chemical forms.

The Phosphorus Cycle

Unlike the water cycle and the nitrogen cycle, the phosphorus cycle does not have an atmospheric component. Phosphorus is a natural element found in rocks and soils. As rocks break down through physical and chemical weathering, phosphate ions (PO_4^{3-}) are released into surrounding soil, groundwater, and streams.

All organisms require phosphorus as a nutrient to support growth. Aquatic plants and algae take up phosphate from the water. Consumers such as insects and fish gain phosphorus by eating plants, algae, and each other, and they also excrete phosphate in their wastes. As plants and animals die, fungi and bacteria break down the dead materials, releasing phosphate and other nutrients back into the environment where they become available to support new life.

Some of the partially decomposed materials gradually settle out and become sediment in lakes, wetlands, and oceans. Over the course of millions of years, these sediments may transform into sedimentary rock, trapping phosphorus until it once again is released as the rock breaks down through weathering.

Topic: phosphorous
Go to: *www.sciLINKS.org*
Code: WD13

Effects of Excess Phosphate

When too much phosphate is added to a lake or pond, excessive plant growth is likely to occur. This is a fairly common problem. Phosphate is one of three essential plant nutrients included in most fertilizers, along with nitrogen and potassium. Just as these nutrients increase the growth of crops, lawns, golf courses, and gardens, they also stimulate growth of algae and other aquatic vegetation. When water bodies receive nutrient-rich runoff from fertilized land, the fertilizer may cause algae and other aquatic plants to grow out of balance with the natural forces of decay and renewal. This over-fertilization process is called *eutrophication,* derived from the Greek, meaning "well fed."

In fresh water, plant growth usually is limited by the amount of available phosphorus. If more phosphate is added, more growth occurs. In oceans and estuaries, nitrogen is more likely than phosphorus to be the nutrient in shortest supply. When extra nutrients are provided, they trigger faster growth of algae and other aquatic plants. Within certain limits, increased growth causes no harm. But if nutrient levels become too high, lakes, rivers, or coastal waters will become choked with mats of algae or beds of rooted vegetation.

Aquatic plants add oxygen to the water through photosynthesis, so you might think that the more they grow, the better. However, plants and animals also use oxygen through respiration. As a result, dissolved oxygen levels in eutrophic waters tend to fluctuate widely, with high levels during the day but low levels at night. Another problem is that photosynthesis occurs only in the surface layers where plants have access to sunlight. When the mats of algae and other plants and animals die, they sink. Oxygen gets used up in the deeper waters as all of this organic matter decomposes. As a result, the fish and other organisms that live in cool, deep waters may no longer be able to survive.

Manure and fertilizers are major non-point sources of phosphate that can be reduced through careful management practices. For example, paying close attention to the timing and amounts of fertilizer applications makes a difference in determining how much will be taken up by plants rather than lost to nearby waterways. If manure or chemical fertilizers are applied to fields too early in the season before crops are growing rapidly, the nutrients are likely to be washed away by rainfall before they can be taken up by plants. Similarly, if homeowners apply too much fertilizer to their lawns or gardens, or apply it too early in the spring, the nutrients are likely to end up getting washed away and fertilizing local waterways instead of the intended plants.

Point sources of phosphate include wastewater treatment effluent and industrial discharges. Much of the phosphorus in these sources comes from high-phosphate detergents used in automatic dishwashers and industrial cleaning solutions. Household laundry detergents also used to be high in phosphate but were reformulated in the 1990s after many states had imposed bans on phosphate in these products.

Eutrophic **bodies of water have high levels of nutrients and accompanying blooms of photosynthetic organisms.**

In order to protect lakes or streams that are in danger of becoming eutrophic, some wastewater treatment plants apply advanced treatment to remove phosphorus before releasing the water into the environment.

NITROGEN

Nitrogen is essential to life. An ingredient of proteins and DNA, nitrogen is a nutrient needed to support growth, reproduction, and metabolism of plants, animals, and microbes. All nitrogen compounds fall into one of two broad categories:

▶ Organic nitrogen compounds contain chains of carbon and hydrogen. Examples include proteins and amino acids.

▶ Inorganic nitrogen takes a variety of forms that do not contain carbon chains. Examples include nitrogen gas (N_2), ammonia gas (NH_3) ammonium (NH_4^+), nitrate (NO_3^-), and nitrite (NO_2^-).

Nitrogen continuously transforms back and forth between inorganic and organic forms as it cycles between air, water, land, and living things (Figure 1.14).

Through *nitrogen fixation*, bacteria convert N_2 to NH_4^+.

The Nitrogen Cycle

Most of the Earth's nitrogen appears in the form of N_2, a colorless, odorless gas that makes up 78 percent of our atmosphere. With this great abundance, you might think that nitrogen would be readily available to living things. However, only a few specialized types of bacteria can use N_2 directly. Through a process called *nitrogen fixation*, these microorganisms absorb N_2 and convert it into ammonium (NH_4^+). Nitrogen-fixing bacteria live in soil, fresh water, and oceans. Some species live in the roots of specialized plants called legumes. Smaller amounts of atmospheric nitrogen are "fixed" by the high pressure and energy generating by lightening during thunderstorms. In recent decades, humans have greatly accelerated the natural rate of nitrogen fixation by using N_2 to produce synthetic fertilizers.

Once ammonium is available, other types of bacteria transform it into nitrite (NO_2^-) and nitrate (NO_3^-) in a process called *nitrification*. Fixation and nitrification occur in soil and water, converting nitrogen into forms that are available for uptake by plants and algae. Plants take up nitrogen, usually in the form of nitrate or ammonium, and incorporate it into their tissues in the form of organic molecules such as proteins. Plants are the ultimate source of nitrogen for organisms higher in the food chain. For example, we humans obtain the nitrogen we need for metabolism, growth, and reproduction by eating plants and animals that in turn have fed on grasses, grains, or other plants or animals.

FIGURE 1.14
Nitrogen undergoes chemical changes as it cycles between land, water, air,
and living things.

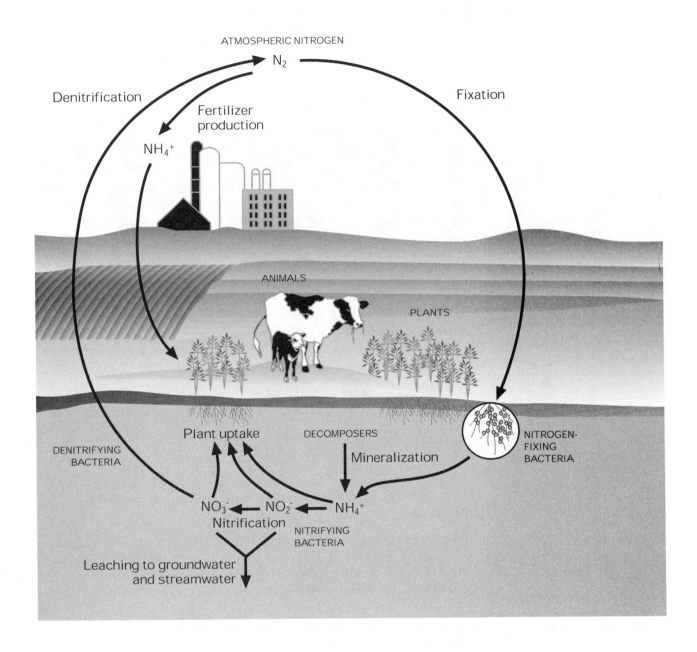

Nitrate that is not taken up by plants may transform through the work of *denitrifying* bacteria into gaseous N_2, which is either released back into the atmosphere or fixed again into ammonia.

When living things die and decompose, the nitrogen in their bodies returns to inorganic form through *mineralization*, a process in which bacteria convert nitrogen in organic compounds such as proteins into ammonium (NH_4^+). Plant roots absorb some of the ammonium, and some gets converted by nitrifying bacteria into nitrate and nitrite. The rest converts chemically into ammonia (NH_3), a gas that returns to the atmosphere.

Effects of Excess Nitrate

Although nitrogen is a nutrient that is needed by living things, in high concentrations it can be toxic to individuals and ecosystems. Through burning fossil fuels in our motor vehicles, homes, power plants and factories, humans add large quantities of nitrogen compounds to the atmosphere. As a result, increased concentrations of nitrate and ammonium return to Earth with precipitation and settling of dust particles. Depending on wind patterns, this can occur many miles from the source.

Another way in which humans impact the nitrogen cycle is through our land use and management practices, which affect the concentrations of nitrate draining into groundwater and surface water. Most of the nitrate that enters the nation's waterways comes from non-point sources of pollution, including runoff of fertilizers from golf courses, lawns, and agricultural lands. Drainage from septic systems is another source of excess nitrate in groundwater and surface water.

Unpolluted water typically has nitrate concentrations lower than 1 ppm. Higher concentrations may trigger excessive plant growth in estuaries and other coastal waters, leading to eutrophication problems similar to those in fresh water systems (see p. 35). You may have seen news stories about the "dead zone" in the Gulf of Mexico. Runoff of fertilizers and other nutrients carried into the Gulf by the Mississippi River have triggered eutrophication, causing oxygen levels to drop and fish, shrimp, crabs, and other sea life to die out.

Excessive nitrate also is a concern with regard to human health. The federal standard for nitrate in drinking water is 10 ppm because higher levels pose health hazards to humans, particularly bottle-fed infants. Babies are susceptible because bacteria in their digestive tracts convert nitrate to nitrite, which can hinder the blood's ability to carry oxygen. If their blood oxygen levels become too low, infants may develop blue-baby syndrome, leading in extreme cases to brain damage or even death.

CHLORIDE

Chloride (Cl⁻) is one of the major negatively charged ions found in saltwater, and to a lesser extent in freshwater. It is formed when salts dissolve in water. For example, sodium chloride (NaCl) dissolves to form Na⁺ and Cl⁻. Salts such as sodium chloride, calcium chloride, or magnesium chloride enter lakes and streams through weathering of minerals, runoff of highway de-icing compounds, industrial discharges, and runoff from irrigated farmlands. Treated wastewater tends to have high chloride concentrations because chlorination commonly is used to kill germs before the water is released to the environment.

As rivers empty into the sea, tidal waters cause mixing of saltwater and freshwater, causing elevated chloride concentrations to stretch many miles upstream from the river's mouth. This zone in which freshwater and seawater intermingle is called an estuary. The Hudson River flows 315 miles from its source in the New York's Adirondack Mountains to its mouth by New York City. The Hudson estuary stretches 153 miles upstream from the mouth, covering nearly half of the river's total length. Many types of organisms are adapted to the fluctuating salinity as the tide goes in and out, making estuaries highly productive ecological zones. However, in upstream reaches where organisms are adapted to living only in fresh water, inputs of chloride through sources such as runoff of highway salts can cause fish and other aquatic life to die off.

DISCUSSION QUESTIONS

▶ How do you think a watershed influences the chemistry of the streams flowing through it?

▶ What makes some lakes more susceptible than others to the effects of acid precipitation?

▶ What impacts would you expect to see in a lake if it received runoff containing high concentrations of fertilizer nutrients?

CHAPTER 6

MODELING AND MANAGEMENT

Suppose you were asked to manage a watershed, with the goal of preserving sensitive habitats while also protecting water quality for use by humans and wildlife. What factors would you need to consider, and how could you use these factors to come up with a useful watershed management plan? As you've seen in previous chapters, you could collect many types of data related to your watershed.

You might begin by going out in the field, traveling through your watershed to observe how the land is used, where the water flows, and what sources of pollution might be present. Back in your office, you could continue this investigation using maps and airphotos to estimate the areas of land covered in forest, agriculture, commercial development, and residential use.

Returning to the field, you could collect and classify aquatic invertebrates from one or more sites in your study stream. You also could measure physical characteristics of the stream water, including temperature, turbidity, and rates of flow, or chemical characteristics such as pH and concentrations of dissolved oxygen, nitrate, and phosphate.

Suppose that you have completed all of these studies. Now you are faced with what could be a bewildering array of data. How will you go about organizing these data, and interpreting them in ways that will help you to reach conclusions about your watershed? One way in which scientists and engineers handle tasks such as this is through modeling.

SCIENTIFIC MODELS

A model is a simplified representation of something that exists or occurs in the real world. For example, think about a single water molecule. We know that each water molecule is made up of one oxygen and two hydrogen atoms, held together with bonds created through sharing electrons. Nobody knows exactly what a water molecule looks like, but we can use illustrations like those in Figure 1.15 to represent the information we do know about what types of atoms come together and how they share their electrons. These pictures are examples of very simple scientific models.

FIGURE 1.15

Simple models of a water molecule illustrate bonds between hydrogen and oxygen atoms.

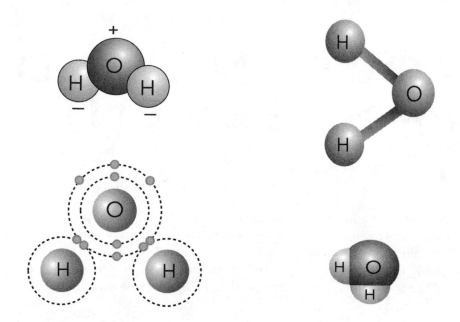

Bigger, more complicated models are used to represent properties of water and watersheds. Scientists build models to help them interpret their data and develop understandings about how the world works.

The WHEBIP stream habitat model presented in Protocol 4 (p. 62), for example, was created to better understand the relationships between land uses in a watershed and the types of organisms that will be able to live in its rivers or streams. The goal of this model is to make it possible to use land use data and other key watershed characteristics in order to predict the quality of its streams in terms of the habitat they provide to aquatic organisms.

Every model is a simplification of reality. One of the key steps in creating a model therefore is choosing which variables to include, and which can be left out because they are not likely to significantly influence the model results. The scientist who developed the WHEBIP model decided that forests and wooded wetlands have the greatest influence over stream habitat. Many other types of land users were lumped together or excluded from the model. This is an example of the type of simplification that must be made to make models manageable to build and to run.

Once a model has been built, the next step is to test the accuracy of its predictions. A Cornell University scientist created the WHEBIP model using data from a watershed in western New York State, and he invited school classes to test his model using data from other watersheds. In order to test the WHEBIP model in your study watershed, you could use the model to make predictions about suitability of stream habitat, then follow up by conducting field studies in which you collect and categorize the invertebrates living in your study stream (Protocols 5–7, pp. 78–91). This sort of testing helps in identifying whether the initial interpretations in the model are correct, and under what range of conditions these relationships hold true.

USING MODELS TO EVALUATE MANAGEMENT OPTIONS

Let's go back to the challenge presented at the beginning of this chapter. You are a watershed manager faced with the task of designing a management plan designed to preserve sensitive habitats and protect water quality for use by humans and wildlife. Confronted with complex sets of data, you need to figure out how to organize all these data to help you find answers to watershed management questions. For example, suppose you want to figure out what the impacts would be if wetlands were drained and filled to provide space for a new parking lot. Modeling is one way of addressing questions of this sort.

Protocol 10 (p. 106) provides instructions for writing your own model using a computer program called STELLA. First, you build a simple physical model to investigate factors important in regulating water flow. Then, you follow up by using the STELLA modeling software to write a computer model that predicts the rate at which water will drain out of a leaky bucket. Once you learn how to use STELLA, you will be able to design and build your own models to investigate a wide range of physical, biological, and chemical processes, and to evaluate various options for managing land and water resources.

Protocol 10 also includes two activities in which you use STELLA models to predict the effects of changes in land use practices on the quantity and quality of runoff water. In the first activity, you model expected changes in the patterns of water flow after a rainstorm. Variables in this model include the amount of rainfall and the percentages of land covered in farm, forest, suburban, and urban uses. Using the input values you provide for these variables, the model creates a graph of streamflow over time.

The second activity in Protocol 10 uses a model designed to predict effects of land management practices on rates of eutrophication in a simulated lake. Phosphorus is assumed to be the critical nutrient that limits growth of algae in this lake. By manipulating management practices related to agriculture and urbanization, you can investigate the impacts to the lake of increasing or decreasing the amount of phosphorus supplied in runoff from the watershed.

These STELLA activities provide examples of ways in which you can use models to simulate what might happen if you were to conduct an experiment in the field. When you're interested in changes that occur on the scale of an entire lake or watershed, you are unlikely to be able to set up a controlled scientific experiment in which you manipulate a variable and then measure the results. Instead, you could use data collected through smaller scale laboratory or field experiments.

For example, suppose you decided to investigate the impact of phosphorus on rate of growth of algae in lakes. You could start by measuring growth of algae in beakers containing water with various phosphate concentrations. In this laboratory experiment, only the phosphate concentration would vary from one beaker to the next. Light, temperature, other nutrient concentrations, and all other variables would be kept constant. Using the results of experiments such as these, you could develop a formula that relates phosphorus concentration to algal growth. This could become one piece of a larger model that also incorporates equations estimating factors such as how much phosphorus will drain from various types of land. Once a watershed model has been built and tested, it can provide a useful tool for running through many simulated experiments that might not be feasible to conduct in the field.

Managing a watershed to meet the needs of humans and wildlife is a balancing act that requires reliable scientific data and good models expressing various aspects of the relationships between living things and their environment. Using data and models, scientists and managers can look at an assortment of scenarios and predict the likely outcomes of various management strategies. The predictions that are generated through this process provide the framework for planning based on scientific understanding of the consequences of human land uses and management options. However, watershed management decisions rarely are easy, and they depend on far more than data collection and modeling. Human values play a key role in planning, and public land use decisions often are controversial because of the different values we all place on various aspects of our environment.

A CASE STUDY: MANAGING NEW YORK CITY'S WATER SUPPLY

New York City, one of the world's largest cities, obtains most of its water from a rural area located about 150 miles away. Three watersheds in upstate New York supply over six billion liters of water per day to the nine million people living in and near the city. With so many people depending on this large volume of water, watershed protection clearly is vital. However, protection of these watersheds also is complicated because it involves regulating land use and management practices on land that is owned and lived on by many rural residents.

You may be wondering who decides how clean New York City's drinking water should be, or who determines how to manage the watersheds that supply this water. Under the Safe Drinking Water Act, the Environmental Protection Agency is authorized to establish health-based standards to protect against naturally occurring and human-made contaminants in public drinking water supplies. To meet these standards, many cities and towns have built water treatment plants to purify water before delivering it to consumers. New York City chose a different route, deciding instead to protect the water at its source in the distant watersheds. This involved complex management decisions including upgrading of wastewater treatment plants, imposing restrictions on new septic systems near streams, and implementing agricultural management practices to reduce runoff of manure, fertilizers, and pesticides from farms.

Although New York City was willing to pay for most of these measures, watershed residents were concerned that the restrictions would reduce the value of their land by restricting the potential for development. In an attempt to resolve this problem, New York City has invested over a billion dollars to buy land or conservation easements in critical watershed areas. Conservation easements allow landowners to keep their land and pay reduced taxes, in exchange for legal limitations on the type and amount of development permitted. All of these watershed preservation and restoration measures are quite expensive but cost much less than the alternative option of building and maintaining a water filtration plant to treat the water instead of protecting it at its source.

Watershed management decisions such as those made by New York City involve compilation and assessment of a lot of scientific data, combined with evaluation of human values and priorities. In New York City's case, scientific studies were carried out to determine what types of management practices would best protect the city's water supplies from contamination by disease-causing organisms and chemical pollutants. Models were built and used to weigh the impacts of various management options. Citizens living in the watersheds participated in many meetings—some came to protest new regulations on the use of their land, and others came to help decide how their communities could better protect their natural resources. Of course, watersheds are dynamic, and New York City's watershed management did not end once their initial plan was developed. Studying, modeling, planning, and regulating will continue over the years as the city continues to work to maintain a clean and safe water supply through watershed management aimed at protecting the purity of the water at its source.

COMMUNITY ACTION: MAKING A DIFFERENCE IN YOUR OWN WATERSHED

Wherever you live, you live in a watershed. As you go through your watershed studies, think about ways in which you could help to protect and enhance your local environment, for human use and for the health of wildlife and ecosystems.

Do you know where your drinking water comes from? It might come from a well at your home, or you might be hooked into a municipal supply that comes from a lake, river, or deep groundwater source. What is your community doing to protect the quality of local water supplies? Are there ways in which you could participate? You might choose to engage in a campaign designed to teach residents not to dump motor oil or other contaminants into storm drains, which in many areas drain directly into lakes or streams without treatment. Another possibility is to think about water conservation measures. What could you do at home, at school, or elsewhere in your community to decrease the amount of water that goes to waste?

As you carry out your studies of local streams or other water bodies, think about ways in which you could make ecological improvements. For example, could you help your community to protect sensitive streams by restoring or enhancing the vegetation in riparian zones along the water's edge? Or could you work with a community organization to improve habitat in the stream itself, stabilizing the banks or providing cover for fish and invertebrates? The choice is yours—many options exist for ways in which you can use your watershed studies to make a difference in your community, helping to improve your local environment.

DISCUSSION QUESTIONS

▶ What can we do with models that we cannot accomplish through experiments in the lab or field?

▶ After we build a model, how do you think we could test it to evaluate the accuracy of its predictions?

▶ If you were a watershed manager, what is an example of a question you might need to answer? How would you go about getting the information you would need to address this question?

▶ What ideas do you have about projects we could carry out to improve the conditions in our study watershed?

▶ Watershed management requires balancing many competing needs and interests, such as balancing economic development with the need to protect water supplies. How would you establish this fine balance? Give specific examples to illustrate your ideas.

PROTOCOLS:
INTRODUCTION
TO RESEARCH

OVERVIEW

Protocols are techniques or methods used in conducting research. Once you have gained experience using one or more protocols, you will be able to use them in conducting your own research. This section includes protocols designed to enable you to study many aspects of watershed science in your community. Section 3 describes how you can use these protocols in research projects of your own design.

Protocol 1 – Watershed Field Survey is a field trip to a local watershed. During the field trip you will make observations about the watershed, either on foot or from a school bus. You will later use your field observations in the lab as you examine maps and airphotos of the same watershed.

Protocol 2 – Object Recognition Using Maps and Airphotos allows you to use topographic maps and/or airphotos to examine the watershed you visited in Protocol 1 or another one you or your teacher has selected.

Protocol 3 – Delineating a Watershed is another lab protocol involving the use of maps. In this protocol you draw the boundaries of the watershed that drains into your study stream .

Protocol 4 – Analyzing Stream Integrity Using Remote Sensing Data incorporates the Watershed Habitat Evaluation and Biotic Integrity Protocol (WHEBIP), a model that enables you to identify the quality of a stream segment based on the land surrounding it.

Protocol 5 – Collecting Aquatic Invertebrates is a field protocol in which you visit one or more stream segments and collect organisms living there. You will use the invertebrates collected with this protocol in Protocols 6 and 7.

Protocol 6 – Simplified Stream Biota Test (SSBT) uses organisms collected with Protocol 5 to quickly assess the quality of a stream segment.

Protocol 7 – Index of Biotic Integrity (IBI) Using Aquatic Invertebrates also uses organisms collected with Protocol 5 to assess the quality of a stream segment. This protocol is more complicated than Protocol 6, but yields a better stream quality assessment.

Protocol 8 – Measuring Stream Discharge is a field protocol that you can use to calculate the volume of streamflow based on measurements of water depth and flow velocity.

Protocol 9 – Aquatic Chemistry is a field and lab protocol in which you collect water samples from a study stream, analyze them using test kits or probes, and interpret your results.

Protocol 10 – Computer Modeling with STELLA is a lab protocol for creating a simple computer model using STELLA software. STELLA is also used in Activities 10.1 and 10.2.

TABLE 2.1
Example Uses of Watershed Protocols

Questions	Protocols	Examples
How has land use in the community changed over time?	Protocols 1–4: Watershed Surveys, in the field and through remote sensing	High school students investigated how a decided piece of land adjacent to their school has been used over the past 100 years.
How do current land use practices such as agriculture affect stream water quality?	Protocols 5–7: Stream assessment with aquatic invertebrates	Students suspected that the poor tilling and fertilizing practices of a local farm were having negative effects on adjacent streams.
How do different streams respond to precipitation events?	Protocol 8: Measuring stream discharge	Students were curious about the effects of parking lots on stream-flow, so they studied several different streams—both adjacent to and far from a nearby shopping mall—after significant rainstorms.
Are there differences in streamwater chemistry above and below potential pollution sources?	Protocol 9: Aquatic chemistry	Scientists and students began long-term moni-toring to examine effects of a new wastewater treatment plant on the chemistry of the dis-charge stream.
How will changes in rainfall, land use, and dis-charge affect streams?	Protocol 10: Computer modeling with STELLA (and additional STELLA activities)	Watershed managers and students helped construct a model that predicts how changes in community land use will affect streams.

PROTOCOLS

PROTOCOL 1. WATERSHED FIELD SURVEY

Objective

To conduct "ground truth" observations as part of a watershed analysis.

Background

You are going to make observations about a watershed while taking a field trip, either on foot or by school bus. These observations will help you become familiar with objects and features in the landscape that you will later see in airphotos. Some of these features – including the general terrain and how the land slopes—may have significant effects on water drainage patterns and water quality. In fact, surface topography provides good clues about the direction that water moves across (and under!) the landscape. Directly observing topography, objects, and other features is also known as making "ground truth" observations. By using ground truth observations, maps, and airphotos, you will develop interpretive skills and a better understanding of your study watershed.

Materials (per student group)

▶ Map of a local watershed, labeled with lettered observation points

▶ Sturdy footgear and clothing suitable for working outdoors

Procedure

1. Before your field trip, begin by inspecting your map. Then complete the top portion of the Watershed Field Survey Data Form.

2. Once you begin your field trip, consult your watershed map. It should be coded with letters indicating points where you will stop and observe the land use, land cover, natural features, and topography. You may locate those points on airphotos in subsequent protocols.

3. As you travel, record observations about each point on Table 2.2, noting how the land is being used. For example, do you see row crops, or a park, or perhaps a parking lot?

4. Look for possible sources of pollution such as storage tanks, houses and mobile homes, manure piles, factories, trash, discharge pipes, large parking lots, and farms or other places where nutrients and pesticides might be applied. Record your observations from steps 3 and 4 in Table 2.2.

WATERSHED FIELD SURVEY DATA FORM

Name _____   Date_____

Map Title _____   Map Scale _____

1. Describe in your own words the location of the watershed.

TABLE 2.2
Field Survey Observation Data

Map Point	**Observations** Notes about land use, slope, standing or running water, structures, vegetation, roads	**Possible Sources of Pollution** Note drain pipes, factories, fuel tanks, residences far from fire hydrants (these are likely to have septic systems), livestock, areas where nutrients or pesticides may be applied
A		
B		
C		
D		
E		
F		
G		
H		
I		
J		
K		
L		
M		
N		
O		
P		
Q		
R		

WATERSHED FIELD SURVEY: QUESTIONS

Name _____ Date _____

1. Based on your observations of the terrain, in what direction do you think water drains in this watershed? Why?

2. Describe the streams or rivers draining the watershed.

3. Before you went on the field trip, you may have looked at a map of your watershed. Compared to your map observations, did anything in the watershed surprise you? Could you have gotten all the information from the map, or was a field trip useful? Why?

4. What are the three major land uses in your watershed? Estimate, based on your trip, what percentage of the watershed is devoted to each land use.

5. Discuss any other thoughts you had or observations you made while exploring your watershed.

PROTOCOL 2. OBJECT RECOGNITION USING MAPS AND AIRPHOTOS

FIGURE 2.1
Example Airphoto

Photo courtesy of Cornell IRIS (Institute for Resource Information Systems).

Objective

To learn how to identify features and interpret map symbols on a topographic map and to identify objects on an airphoto.

Materials (per student group)

▶ An enlarged portion of a local topographic map

▶ Airphotos of the mapped area

▶ A key to map symbols

Procedure

1. Begin by familiarizing yourself with the map, using the symbol key. Concentrate on cultural features such as roads, railroads, structures, or cemeteries. Also note natural features such as streams and ponds, contour lines, and elevation. Record the title and scale on the Watershed Field Survey Data form.

2. Now turn to your airphoto(s). If available, compare recent and historical photos. Find structures or landscape features in the older photo that do not appear in the more recent photo, and vice versa. Record the dates and title on the Data form.

3. Observe the elevation changes and the contour lines on the map. Get a sense of what the landscape is like. If you took a field trip to the watershed on your map, see if you can match up the map with what you remember seeing.

4. If you did not complete Protocol 1 (Watershed Field Survey), complete Table 2.3. For each labeled point on the map, record descriptive, or "qualitative," observations you make using the airphotos.

5. If you did complete Protocol 1, first get out your field notes and locate each of the lettered "Map Points" where you made observations. Indicate whether the photos support your earlier identification of possible sources of pollution. Record this and other descriptive information in Table 2.3.

6. If you have airphotos from more than one year, note differences at the lettered points. For example, have drainage patterns been altered or streams been straightened? Have forests regrown? Are there new impervious surfaces, like paved parking lots? Record this information in Table 2.3.

WATERSHED FIELD SURVEY DATA FORM

Name _____ Date _____

Map Title _____ Map Scale _____

Airphoto Years(s), Title(s) _____

_____

TABLE 2.3
Qualitative Interpretation of Watershed Airphotos

MapPoint	Observations from Airphotos
A	
B	
C	
D	
E	
F	
G	
H	
I	
J	
K	
L	
M	
N	
O	
P	
Q	
R	

PROTOCOL 3. DELINEATING A WATERSHED

"...The new creek bed is ditched straight as a ruler; it has been 'uncurled' by the county engineer to hurry the runoff. On the hill in the background are contoured strip-crops; they have been 'curled' by the erosion engineer to retard the runoff. The water must be confused by so much advice."

—*A Sand County Almanac,* Aldo Leopold

Objectives

To develop and apply skills for reading maps and drawing ("delineating") watershed boundaries.

Background

Determining watershed boundaries is an important step in figuring out how land use affects streams. The skills you develop in this exercise will later help you estimate the quality of stream habitats, based on stream flow and nearby land use practices.

Ridges

On a topographic map, a ridge looks like a human nose. Think about a drop of water landing on your nose and running down either side. **Noses point downhill.**

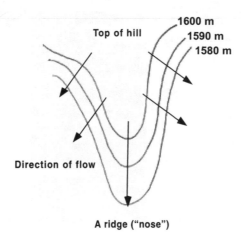

Ridges tend to divide watersheds. In other words, water runs down from the top of the ridge. Note the elevation of the contour lines.

Gullies

These features are depressions in the landscape. At first glance, they look a lot like the ridges, except that the topographic lines of **gullies point uphill**.

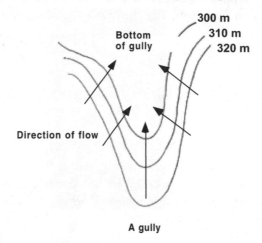

A gully

Whereas ridges divide watersheds, gullies channel water to a single point and may have streams running through them. Note that the contour lines show different elevations in this figure than in the preceding one.

Materials (per student group)

▶ USGS topographic map, preferably of the local watershed (7.5 minute quadrangle)

▶ A blank piece of transparency film

▶ Water soluble pens (two colors)

▶ An area-measuring grid (clear overlay)

▶ Erasable marker

Procedure

1. Take a few minutes to look over the topographic map and identify streams, rivers, wetlands, urban areas, high points in elevation, and any other unique features. Answer question 1 on the Delineating Watersheds Worksheet.

2. Place the blank transparency film over the map. Using an erasable marker, trace on the transparency all aquatic habitats (streams, tributaries, rivers, ponds, lakes, bogs, and wetlands) that are visible under the film.

3. Place small arrowheads on the streams to indicate the direction of flow. Here are two ways that may help you figure out which way the stream is flowing:

▶ Streams join as they flow downstream.

▶ As streams flow downstream, the elevation decreases. For example, if a stream crosses contour lines with values of 1900 and 1800, the direction of flow is from the 1900 line to the 1800 line.

4. Label the order number of your streams. Stream segments can be classified by **order**. Headwater streams are **Order 1**. When two Order 1 streams join, the section below the confluence is **Order 2**. When two Order 2 streams join, they form an **Order 3** stream. However, when an Order 1 and an Order 2 stream join, the resulting stream is still **Order 2**.

5. Using your second pen color, circle one ridge and label it, "Ridge." Circle one gully and label it, "Gully."

6. Find the stream segment labeled A–B on your map, and answer question 2 on the worksheet.

7. Find the peaks in the region around the A–B stream segment (peaks usually appear on topographic maps as circles). Place an "X" on the peaks near A–B.

8. Draw a line connecting the points of highest elevation (peaks) immediately around the A-B stream segment. You want the line to show the ridge separating the A–B watershed from the watersheds of other nearby streams.

   Figure 2.2 shows two examples of watersheds delineated in this fashion. Note that the only time that watershed boundaries cross streams is at a junction where streams drain.

   In the next step, we'll have you compare your answer with other students, but first give it your best effort. After you connect the peaks, "close" the basin by running lines down to point A from the nearest peaks. The area you have delineated is a small watershed. Rain falling anywhere in this region will make its way to point A.

9. Check your solution against the solutions of other students who have been analyzing the same A–B segment. Are they identical? Where do they differ? Evaluate your solution and make changes if you wish (your marker pen comes off with a damp paper towel). Answer question 3.

10. Now measure the area of your watershed in square kilometers, using either a method of your own design or a transparent grid overlay. Complete question 4. Describe your method to students in another group and see how your solutions compare.

FIGURE 2.2
Example Watershed Delineation

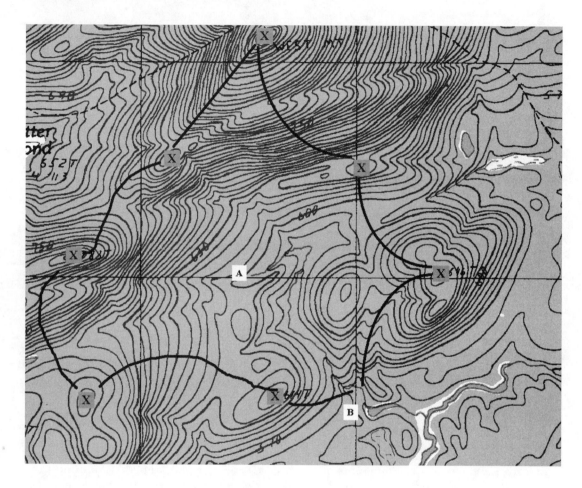

DELINEATING WATERSHEDS WORKSHEET

Name _____ Date _____

1. List three interesting features you found on the map:

2. Locate the stream segment labeled A–B on your map. Which is at a higher elevation, A or B? What are two ways you can tell?

3. In two or three sentences, describe how your solution compared with others you saw during Step 9 in the protocol.

4. Determine the area of your watershed in square kilometers.

   ▶ *Option 1:* a transparent grid (1/100 square kilometer grid). Some of the grid blocks lie completely within your watershed. Count them, as well as the blocks that are more than half-filled. Don't count blocks that are less than half-filled.

   Number of blocks in the watershed: _____ (A)

   Area of the A–B watershed ("A" divided by 100): _____ square kilometers

   ▶ *Option 2:* a method of your own design. What is the area of your watershed? Explain how you estimated its area:

PROTOCOL 4. ANALYZING STREAM INTEGRITY USING REMOTE SENSING DATA

Objective

To learn how to rate the quality of a stream section by assessing its riparian habitat using remote sensing data and the Watershed Habitat Evaluation and Biotic Integrity Protocol (WHEBIP).

Background

Determining the quality of a stream can be expensive and time consuming. Think about how long it takes to do fieldwork—a trained researcher has to visit the stream at a variety of sampling points, some of which may be inaccessible due to private property restrictions, dangerous topography, or distance from roads or other access points. To save time and avoid accessibility problems, scientists have long speculated that stream assessment might be done using airphotos or other *remote sensing* data.

A research protocol developed at Cornell University will enable *you* to do just that! The Watershed Habitat Evaluation and Biotic Integrity Protocol (WHEBIP) was developed by scientist Reuben Goforth, who used it to study the French Creek Watershed in Chautauqua County, New York State. Dr. Goforth developed WHEBIP to help scientists use models to predict aquatic biodiversity (the number of species in streams) in entire watersheds. In this protocol you will be calculating a WHEBIP Stream Integrity Rating for a section of stream. Stream integrity refers to streamwater and habitat quality, and higher integrity scores are associated with higher quality streams. Think of the WHEBIP Stream Integrity Rating as a *report card* for watersheds.

Materials (per student group)

▶ USGS topographic map of your watershed study area (7.5 minute quadrangle)

▶ Airphoto of your study site (may be recent or historical), with date

▶ Map showing land use in your study area (optional)

▶ Several small pieces of masking tape

▶ A piece of transparency film with the outline of the watershed that you created in Protocol 3, *or* a piece of blank transparency film

▶ A transparent area-measuring grid for use with the topographic map

▶ A colored transparency pen (erasable marker)

▶ WHEBIP Data form

Procedure

1. Gather the listed materials. If the topographic map does not lie flat, secure its corners to your desk using small pieces of tape. **Do not tape down the airphoto, because tape may damage the photo.** If the airphoto curls, place books on the corners.

2. Examine your airphoto and find its location on the topographic map. Determine the date of the photo and record it on the WHEBIP Data Form. The date may be on the back of the photo.

3. Some of the groups in the classroom may be using a photo of the same location, but from a different year. If they are, inspect their photo carefully and record its date on the Data Form.

4. Place your photo on your desk so that it is oriented North-South, like your map. Tape the transparency film to the topographic map using a small amount of masking tape. If the film has an outline on it (e.g., of the watershed you drew in Protocol 3), make sure that it is correctly positioned. If your transparency film is blank, position it so that it covers that part of the topographic map that is shown in your airphoto.

5. Identify the stream segment for which you will be calculating a WHEBIP score. It may be labeled with points "A" and "B" on your map. Use the erasable marker to trace the stream segment onto the transparency film.

6. Examine the categories listed on Table 2.4 ("WHEBIP Categories and Subscores"). For your stream segment you will assign a subscore for each of these categories. If you are not sure which of two subscores is appropriate, you may take the average. For example, if you cannot tell if an area is "wetland" (35 points) or "wooded wetland" (25 points), you could assign a subscore of 30 for Category 1.

7. Before getting into the details, make a preliminary prediction: Do you think your stream has "Excellent," "Very Good," "Good," "Fair," or "Poor" integrity? Explain your reasoning in an answer to Question 1 on the **WHEBIP Data Form**. Very high WHEBIP scores are associated with streams that have "Excellent" integrity.

8. Measure the area of your stream segment's watershed in square kilometers, using the measuring grid. Each cell on the grid is 1/100 square kilometer. Record this number at the top of the WHEBIP Data Form.

9. Use Table 2.5 ("Simplified Land Use Code Descriptions"), your map, and your airphoto(s) to estimate the percentage of your watershed that is devoted to different land uses. If you completed a watershed field survey (Protocol 1), review your notes from that trip as well. Record your results in Table 2.6 ("Land Use in Our Watershed").

There are several ways to estimate land use percentages. One quick method is to simply examine the airphoto and jot down your estimates of land uses in your watershed (e.g., "25% Forest"). Be sure that your estimates total 100%. Have your lab partner do the same thing independently, and then average your two estimates for each land use category.

For a more precise estimate, place your transparent grid onto the watershed outline, then calculate the percentage of table cells that cover each land use. Another approach would be to divide the watershed into polygons representing single land use types, and then compute the area of each of these polygons. For even greater precision, one might use a Geographic Information System (GIS): sophisticated computer software that can do such measurements automatically. For your purposes today, we suggest that you keep things simple.

10. In steps 10–21, you will be using Table 2.4 to determine your stream's subscores for each of the 12 categories. You will record each subscore in Table 2.7 ("WHEBIP Subscore Totals") in the WHEBIP Data Form. These instructions will walk you through the categories, step by step.

Begin with Category 1, **Land Use Along the Stream**. Examine the land uses along your stream segment and determine the stream's numeric score. If the stream runs through multiple land use categories, assign the lowest score. For example, if the stream flows through forest **and** row crops, use the row crops score of 5. Record your Category 1 subscore in Table 2.7 *Note: Category 1 refers to lands directly touching the stream segment.*

11. Category 2 in the WHEBIP is **Average Width of Riparian Belt**. To determine the average width of your stream segment's riparian belt, measure the width in several places and average your measurements. To convert your measurements to meters, you will need to know the scale of the enlarged airphoto. If you do not know the scale, find an object in the photo of known size, measure it, and divide the known length of the object by its measured length.

   For example, perhaps you have a football field on your map. A football field is about 91 meters long. If the field measures 20 mm on your airphoto, this would indicate that the photo's scale is 91 m/20 mm, or 4.55 m/mm. If the average-measured width of the riparian belt on your airphoto were 5 mm, then the actual width of your riparian belt would be

   $$5 \text{ mm} \times 4.55 \text{ m/mm} = 22.75 \text{ m, or approximately 23 m.}$$

   Record the Category 2 subscore in Table 2.7.

12. Category 3 is **Riparian Canopy Continuity**. Estimate how much of the stream has trees and brush along it, and record the appropriate subscore in Table 2.7.

13. Category 4 is **Presence of Wetlands**. What percentage of your stream length is in direct contact with wetlands? Assign the appropriate score.

14. Use the information you recorded in Table 2.6 to determine what percentage of the basin is **Active Agriculture** (Category 5), and **Forest or Brush** (Category 6). Record the subscores.

15. For Category 7, determine the dominant **Upstream Riparian Vegetation** and record the appropriate subscore. For Order 1 stream segments there is no "upstream"—so you should reenter the Category 1 subscore in Category 7. If your segment is Order 2 or higher, inspect your map and airphoto and determine what vegetation lines the banks of your segment's "feeder" streams. Refer to Protocol 3 or Section 4 for a discussion of stream order.

16. Category 8 in the WHEBIP is **Upstream Forest or Brush**. If your segment is an Order 1 stream, there is no upstream, so reenter your Category 6 subscore in Category 8. If your segment is Order 2 or higher, estimate the percentage of land in upstream watersheds that is Forest or Brush, and record the subscore.

17. Category 9 in the WHEBIP is **Watershed Land Gradient**. Examine the topography of your watershed and estimate how steep it is. To determine steepness, estimate how hard it would be to run uphill in your basin. If you visited your watershed as part of a watershed field survey, this may be easy to remember. If you did not visit the site, you'll need to interpret the topographic lines on your map—the closer the lines, the steeper the terrain.

To help you estimate steepness using only your stream segment's map, it may be useful to consult a topographic map of your own neighborhood. Find a few places on the map with varying gradients and note how close the topographic lines are. Then think about how hard it would be to run uphill in those places, and use this information to determine steepness on your stream segment map.

18. Category 10 in the WHEBIP is **Point Source Pollution**. Unlike runoff from a field or golf course, a pipe discharging waste chemicals from an industrial plant is considered a **point source**. Base your Category 10 subscore on information gained by observing your airphoto(s) and map, knowledge of your community, discussions with your classmates, or information gained from sources such as your library or the Internet.

19. Category 11 rates the **Presence of Roads**. Examine your topographic map and airphoto(s) and determine whether there are any roads in the watershed. If there are, note whether they cross the stream or approach to within 30 m. Record the subscore.

20. Category 12 in the WHEBIP is **Conservation Activity**. This may be visible from airphotos or maps, but you should also use your own knowledge of the community. Note that there is a special subscore for watersheds that are mostly forest and/or brush.

21. Total the subscores for the 12 categories in Table 2.7 Use Table 2.8 to determine the Stream Integrity Rating of your stream segment, and record it on the Data Form (p. 69).

Useful Web Sites:

Locations of Known U.S. Point Sources
www.epa.gov/enviro/html/em/index.html

Surf Your Watershed
cfpub.epa.gov/surf/locate/index.cfm

TABLE 2.4
WHEBIP Categories and Subscores

Category	Description	Subscore
1. Land Use Along the Stream	Forest or wooded wetland Brush, tall grass, wetland, bog Grazed grasses Row crops, construction, residential, commercial, or bare soil	35 25 5 1
2. Average Width of Riparian Belt If a riparian belt of trees or shrubs is present, estimate its average width.	> 30 m (or uninterrupted forest) 5–30 m < 5 m	35 25 1
3. Riparian Canopy Continuity Are there breaks in the tree/brush canopy along the stream?	No breaks in riparian canopy Trees & brush along >90% of the stream Trees & brush along 50–90% of the stream Trees & brush along <50% of the stream	35 25 10 1

4. Presence of Wetlands	Wetlands present along more than 50%
	  of streambanks
	Wetlands present along less than 50% of
	  streambanks
	No wetlands present
		
		20
		
		10
		5

5. Active Agriculture Estimated percent of the land *beyond the streambanks*	0–25% cropland or pasture 26–50% cropland or pasture 51–75% cropland or pasture 76–100% cropland or pasture	25 15 5 1
6. Forest or Brush Estimated percent of the land *beyond the streambanks*	76–100% forest or brush 51–75% forest or brush 26–50% forest or brush 0–25% forest or brush	35 20 10 I
7. Upstream Riparian Vegetation Dominant vegetation *along upstream segments* (for Order 1 streams, reenter the number from #1 above)	Forest Brush/tall grasses Grazed grasses Row crops or bare soil	50 40 10 I
8. Upstream Forest or Brush Estimated percent in all upstream watersheds combined	76–100% forest or brush 51–75% forest or brush 26–50% forest or brush 0–25% forest or brush	30 20 10 1
9. Watershed Land Gradient	Low or flat Moderate (difficult to sprint uphill) High (challenging to walk uphill)	20 15 10

10. Point Source Pollution (e.g., sewage treatment plants, factories, construction, barnyards)	No point source(s) likely Point source(s) likely within watershed Point source(s) likely along stream	25 10 1
11. Presence of Roads	No roads Roads pass within 30 m of stream or cross over bridges Roads cross through streambed, or construction	25 10 1
12. Conservation Activity Evidence of conservation measures (e.g., streambank fencing, rip-rap, soil conservation, set-asides)	Conservation actions for >10 yrs Conservation actions 5–10 yrs Conservation actions within < 5 yrs No conservation actions *Note: Subscore=25 if area is mostly forested or brush*	25 15 10 1

TABLE 2.5
Simplified Land Use Code Descriptions

Land Use Code	Description and Tips for Identification in Airphotos
A	**Active Agriculture.** Areas used for growing field crops, forage crops, and grains. Cropland is characterized by large open fields that are evenly planted or plowed. On a photo, the fields are identified by smooth textures, uniform gray tones, and patterns resulting from crop stages and tillage practices. Pasture is land used for grazing livestock. It usually consists of a mixture of uneven growth of grass, brush, and trees. On a photo, pasture appears rough in texture and mottled light gray.
C	**Commercial.** Facilities and areas associated with the sale of products and services. Included are urban centers, shopping centers, commercial strips, and individual businesses. In urban areas, commercial land use is indicated by multistory structures on main roads that have a higher density than surrounding homes. Suburban areas have commercial strips or shopping centers, indicated by large flat-roofed buildings with parking lots.
F	**Forest and Brushland.** Land with vegetative cover other than active agriculture. Included are woodlands of all types: deciduous, coniferous, mixed woods, and plantations. Also included are areas with shrub and brushcover not used for pasture. Mature woods are usually darker gray than agriculture on photos. Evergreen plantations are even in texture/shape and dark in tone. Deciduous woods are rougher in texture and lighter in tone. Brushlands are variable in texture and tone, depending on the variety of species, height, and density of vegetation.
I	**Industrial.** Facilities and areas devoted to product manufacturing. Examples: large structures or building complexes with truck access and parking; buildings or yards for storage of materials and finished goods. Appears similar to shopping centers and commercial areas, however, there will be less area devoted to parking.
OR	**Outdoor Recreation.** Includes golf courses, parks, and public gardens or any area developed for outdoor recreational uses. Smooth texture and even tone indicates mowed lawns. Dark spots and mottled gray areas indicate shrubs and trees of landscaped areas. Access roads, parking lots, and walking paths are often visible. Recognizable sports facilities include ball fields, tracks, tennis courts, and the unmistakable features of golf courses: fairways, greens, sand traps, and water hazards.
P	**Public.** Public and semi-public facilities oriented to providing a service to the public. Includes educational institutions, cemeteries, water and sewage treatment facilities, and highway equipment centers. This is a broad category and the features on the photos may be similar to other categories.
R	**Residential.** Housing: high density, single family and multiple-family units in urban areas; medium and low density neighborhoods in suburban and rural settings. Individual residences in rural areas should not be classified as Residential; instead use the underlying landscape classification (e.g., A or F).
W	**Water.** Water bodies, natural or man-made; they are very often dark but can be any gray tone.

WHEBIP DATA FORM

Name _____ Date _____

Date of airphoto _____ Date of Second Airphoto _____

Topographic Map Name _____

Stream Segment Watershed Size _____ km^2

1. Before you go through the WHEBIP protocol, predict the rating of your stream segment ("Excellent," "Very Good," "Good," "Fair," or "Poor"). Explain why you made this prediction.

2. Describe other land use data you used in this protocol.

3. Carefully describe the location of your stream segment.

TABLE 2.6
Land Use in Our Watershed. (See Table 2.5 for category explanation.)

Land Use Code	Category	Approx. % of Watershed
A	Active Agriculture	
C	Commercial	
F	Forest and Brushland	
I	Industrial	
OR	Outdoor Recreation	
P	Public	
R	Residential	
W	Water	
Total		100%

TABLE 2.7
WHEBIP Subscore Totals

Airphoto Date	WHEBIP Category and Subscores												Total of 12 Subscores
	1	2	3	4	5	6	7	8	9	10	11	12	

TABLE 2.8
Stream Integrity Rating

WHEBIP Total Score	WHEBIP Stream Integrity Rating	Check the Cell That Corresponds to Your Stream Segment
315-360	Excellent	
255-314	Very Good	
160-254	Good	
81-159	Fair	
<81	Poor	

4. What is the WHEBIP Stream Integrity Rating of your stream segment? _____

70

Date _____

…ntegrity Rating compare with your initial prediction?
…initial prediction.

…plying the WHEBIP to this stream segment.

…nent with the scores assigned by another student
…o different dates, compare your results with those of
…using an older or newer airphoto. How do you ac-
…scores, if any?

…stimates were? Do you think the accuracy affected
…e accuracy? Explain.

ACTIVITY 4.1—STREAM INTEGRITY AND AQUATIC COMMUNITIES

Objective

To assess the ability of WHEBIP scores to predict stream communities.

Background

Riparian habitats help determine streamwater quality, integrity, and the types of organisms that live in rivers and streams. To assess these variables, scientists usually rely on observations taken on the ground. An alternative to ground-based data collection is *remote sensing*, or observations made by using data collected from a distance. Remote sensing of riparian habitat and streams is useful for areas that cannot be reached on foot. It can also be done *historically*: if you have old airphotos, you can track changes in stream integrity over time. This may be a useful technique for understanding ecological changes in a region.

In Protocol 4 you evaluated a stream segment using remote sensing, with maps and airphotos serving as your primary data sources. By examining the maps and photos, you produced 12 subscores to calculate a "Watershed Habitat Evaluation and Biotic Integrity Protocol" (WHEBIP) score that evaluated a local stream segment. You then interpreted that score using Table 2.8 to rate the integrity of your stream segment, with possible ratings ranging from poor to excellent.

But how well do remote sensing stream assessment methods like WHEBIP actually predict what lives in streams? What does it mean for a stream to have "excellent" integrity? Is an "excellent" stream likely to have lots of fish? Does it matter if a stream has lots of fish all from the same species, compared to lots of fish from many different species?

This activity will explore questions like these, using data from the French Creek watershed. You will develop a better sense of the ecological concepts of *diversity*, *abundance*, and *biotic integrity*, and you will evaluate the usefulness of the WHEBIP protocol. If you are conducting local watershed studies, this activity may complement your analysis of water chemistry, stream organism diversity measurements, or other variables.

Testing WHEBIP

Cornell University scientist Reuben Goforth sampled aquatic organisms in 25 stream segments of the French Creek watershed in upstate New York. At each study site, he collected aquatic invertebrates using a standard sampling protocol. He also collected samples of fish using seines (nets). Using the invertebrate and fish population data, Dr. Goforth calculated *species diversity* for each site. Species diversity refers to the number of species in a certain area.

Using airphotos and other remote sensing data, Dr. Goforth also calculated WHEBIP scores for each of the 25 stream segments. He then compared the WHEBIP scores to his measurements of invertebrate and fish diversity. Finally, because the WHEBIP method was new and had not been extensively reviewed and tested by other scientists, Dr. Goforth conducted a second, ground-based, stream integrity assessment using a well-known method called the Riparian, Channel, and Environmental (RCE) Inventory. Part of his analysis involved comparing the results of the WHEBIP approach with the ground-based RCE method.

Although both the RCE and WHEBIP assess stream integrity, they are not identical methods. Both protocols include a subscore for the width of the riparian zone. However, the RCE includes a subscore related to the *stream substrate* (the size of stones on the bottom), which is something that cannot be assessed from an airphoto. And the WHEBIP includes subscores related to *upstream segments*, which are easy to see in an airphoto, but not from the ground. Like the WHEBIP, the RCE uses a 0–360 point scale, with low scores indicating poor stream integrity and high scores indicating excellent integrity.

In the data file you will use in this activity, each sample site will have WHEBIP, RCE, and several other indices. You will either create your own graphs or examine provided graphs of each of the indices against WHEBIP and make comparisons. First, you should become familiar with terms that will be used throughout the activity:

▶ **Species Richness**—the number of species in an area

▶ **Species Diversity**—this term is often used to refer to the number of species in an area (that is, its **species richness**). Mathematically, species diversity is calculated using *species richness* and the *relative abundance* of each species.

▶ **Biotic Integrity**—a weighted measure of species diversity: Species that indicate healthier systems are weighted more than species that are indicative of unhealthy systems. Streams with high biotic integrity have communities that are diverse and include organisms that do not tolerate pollution.

▶ **InvertBI**—a weighted measure of *invertebrate* species diversity. Stream segments with many species of aquatic invertebrates will tend to have higher scores than segments with few species. Species that require clean water to thrive (such as stonefly nymphs) are weighted more in the scale than pollution-tolerant species (like aquatic worms).

▶ **InvertPI**—the *percentage* of the invertebrates in a stream that are pollution intolerant. A high InvertPI score for a stream segment means that the stream has many organisms that live only in pristine, unpolluted areas.

▶ **Fish Species**—the number of fish species (fish "species richness") found at the site

▶ **FishBI**—a weighted measure of fish species diversity. High scores reflect more diverse communities with pollution-sensitive species present.

PROCEDURE

1. Before you begin, you should review the WHEBIP and consider the terms above. Read and answer questions 1–7 on the Stream Integrity and Aquatic Communities Worksheet.

2. In each of the next five steps, your teacher will instruct you to either create your own graph or examine the graph given to you.

3. Create/examine the graph comparing WHEBIP and RCE scores. Answer Question 8 on the worksheet.

4. Create/examine the graph comparing WHEBIP and InvertBI. Answer Question 9.

5. Create/examine the graph comparing WHEBIP and InvertPI. Answer Question 10.

6. Create/examine the graph comparing WHEBIP and Fish Species. Answer Question 11.

7. Create/examine the graph comparing WHEBIP and FishBI. Answer Question 12.

8. If instructed by your teacher, add linear trend lines to graphs of WHEBIP and RCE scores and WHEBIP and Fish Species scores. Linear trend lines are straight lines that best indicate the relationship between the two variables being graphed. Answer Questions 13–15.

ACTIVITY 4.1
WORKSHEET—STREAM INTEGRITY AND AQUATIC COMMUNITIES

Name _____ Date _____

1. Review the WHEBIP scoring method summarized in Table 2.8 (Protocol 4). Now consider hypothetical Streams 1 and 2. Stream 1 has a WHEBIP score of 248, and Stream 2 has a score of 175. Which is likely to be a healthier habitat for stream plants and animals? Why?

2. List three things you might find in a stream segment's watershed that would tend to *increase* the area's WHEBIP score.

3. Next, consider the term *diversity.* In the box below, draw ten small circles, eight small triangles, two small squares, and seven small lines. Imagine that each of the shapes represents a different organism living in a small area on the bottom of "Stream 3." For example, the triangles might represent mayfly nymphs.

> Stream 3 Community:

4. For "Stream 4," draw 30 small circles and 3 small triangles.

> Stream 4 Community:

5. Without using any actual numbers, describe the differences between the communities in these two streams. Which community do you think has greater diversity?

6. In any given region, greater diversity is generally indicative of a healthier system. In your own words, describe what you think *diversity* and *abundance* mean.

7. Look back to your diagram for Stream 4. Would it make a difference ecologically if the triangles represented stonefly nymphs—which require high levels of dissolved oxygen—instead of aquatic worms, which require very little dissolved oxygen? In your own words, describe differences between the terms *biotic integrity* and *diversity*.

8. After studying your graph of WHEBIP by RCE, does it appear that both methods rate the same stream similarly? For example, if the WHEBIP method rates one stream as excellent, does the RCE method rate it the same way, or very differently? Explain.

9. Describe what happens to InvertBI as WHEBIP scores *increase*. Explain why you think this is happening.

10. Describe what happens to InvertPI as WHEBIP scores *increase*. Explain why you think this is happening.

11. Describe what happens to the number of fish species in streams as the WHEBIP score *increases*. Explain why you think this is happening.

12. Describe what happens to FishBI in streams as the WHEBIP score *increases*.

13. If you completed Step 8 in the Procedure section, compare the trend lines you drew. One of these lines estimates the relationship between WHEBIP and RCE scores, and the other the relationship between WHEBIP scores and number of fish species. For which graph was it easier to draw a trend line? In other words, which graph seemed to show a stronger relationship between the two variables, and how can you tell?

14. Using these two graphs as examples, explain how useful you think linear trend lines can be in describing patterns in data series.

15. Finally, imagine that you are a member of a citizens' advisory group, charged with advising a watershed management task force. The task force plans to identify and protect sensitive regions of the local watershed. To do this, they are considering using either remote sensing (WHEBIP) or ground-based (RCE) stream integrity assessment, and they have determined that it would be cheaper and faster to use remote sensing. Based on the analysis you did today, which approach would you recommend, and why? Is it better to use remote sensing or ground-based stream assessment?

PROTOCOL 5. COLLECTING AQUATIC INVERTEBRATES

Objective

To safely collect, sort, and maintain samples of stream invertebrates prior to assessing biotic integrity.

Background

Topic: aquatic entomology
Go to: www.sciLINKS.org
Code: WD14

A healthy stream is a dynamic system and a home to many living organisms. One way to assess the health of a stream is to study the organisms living in it. Aquatic invertebrates, including insects that live part of their lives in water, are commonly used as indicators of stream health. Some, such as stonefly nymphs, are usually found only in very clean water because they require lots of dissolved oxygen. Others, such as some species of aquatic worms, may be able to survive in water that has very little oxygen. We call these organisms *biotic indicators* of water quality because their presence (or absence) gives us information about the quality of the stream.

Topic: freshwater ecosystems
Go to: www.sciLINKS.org
Code: WD15

Most streams—even polluted ones—contain a variety of organisms, and many invertebrate taxa (e.g., family or genus) include both pollution-tolerant and pollution-sensitive species. For example, most stoneflies are sensitive to pollution, but there are some exceptions. In other words, assessing the ecological health or *biotic integrity* of a stream is usually more involved that just looking for the stonefly order. Protocols 6 and 7 provide instructions for using aquatic invertebrates to assess the biotic integrity of streams, but before you can do that, you'll need to collect samples. This protocol guides you through the collection of aquatic invertebrate samples.

Materials (per student group)

- Waders, waterproof boots, or other non-slip footgear suitable for the conditions
- D-nets
- Collecting pans and 10–15 smaller containers
- Tweezers and plastic spoons for picking up animals
- Latex gloves (if the streamwater quality could be poor)
- Walking sticks to provide stability on slippery rocks
- Personal flotation devices (PFDs) if the stream is not uniformly shallow
- Stream Invertebrate Identification sheet (pp. 81–84) and other identification materials
- Hand lenses or plastic "bug boxes" with magnifying lids

Procedure

You will work in teams of three students to collect invertebrates. Because safety is very important while working in streams, your teacher will review precautions appropriate to your site.

Part 1. Collecting Macroinvertebrates

Topic: invertebrates
Go to: *www.sciLINKS.org*
Code: WD16

1. Sample an area of the stream that is shallow enough to wade but is moving fairly quickly. This type of microhabitat is called a *run*. All three of you should wade into the run: one carries a D-net, one carries a collecting pan, and one—the "shuffler"—needs both hands free.

2. Facing upstream into the current, the person with the D-net should hold the handle upright and place the net on the bottom of the stream. The shuffler should stand a foot or two upstream of the net and disturb the stream bottom by slowly shuffling his or her feet, dislodging stones. Many invertebrates will jump off into the current and be carried down to the waiting net (that's one reason you're sampling where there is a good current). If the water isn't too deep or cold, reach to the bottom and lift up and brush some rocks as well. Try not to kick up too much silt and sediment.

3. After a couple of minutes of shuffling, check the net. If there is a lot of mud in it, raise and lower it into the water a few times to rinse. Then empty the contents of the net into your pan, which should start with about an inch of water.

4. Look in the pan to see if you collected any animals. You may need to wait a minute or so for sediments to settle. Your goal is to collect about 100 macroinvertebrates, but chances are good that there are many more in the pan than you see at first.

5. Move a few feet from your original sampling site and repeat the shuffling-and-netting procedure. Unless your collecting pan is getting crowded with leaves, stones, and other debris, you will be able to add the contents of several nets to the pan before returning to shore.

Part 2. Preliminary Processing

1. Unless you are planning to preserve your sample in alcohol, do your best to keep alive the animals you collected. Two common physical problems with collected aquatic invertebrates are thermal shock (sudden temperature change) and insufficient dissolved oxygen. If it is a sunny day and the air is much warmer than the water, do your on-shore work in the shade. Periodically give the animals some fresh water, and don't crowd lots of larger animals into a small container. Cool water holds more dissolved oxygen than warm water, so keeping the water cool will reduce both types of mortality.

2. Now observe the animals you've collected. How do they move? How might they breathe? How do they appear adapted to the habitat in which you caught them? Take a look at the Stream Invertebrate Identification sheet and try to identify a few organisms from the drawings.

Part 3. Sorting

1. Put some fresh water into your smaller containers and begin sorting the invertebrates by appearance. You can pick them up gently with the forceps or use a plastic spoon or small container to scoop them. At this point, you are only estimating how many taxa and how many individuals you have, and do not need to specifically identify each one. A taxon (plural taxa) is a group of related individuals. Note that many aquatic invertebrates go through several similar-looking life stages that differ primarily in size. Individuals that look the same in every respect except size should be considered members of the same taxonomic group.

2. Examine your collected macroinvertebrates with a hand lens and look for differences in head and body shape, the appearance and placement of feathery external gills, coloration, and the number of tails. Put different types in different containers. If you run out of containers, you can combine the less common creatures in one container—but keep an eye on it to make sure they don't eat each other before you have a chance to record your results!

Part 4. Checking in

1. After doing a quick sorting and counting, check in with your teacher and report how many taxa and how many individuals you have. Bear in mind that you'll find more as you continue to pick over your sample. Your teacher may direct you to return to the water to do some more collecting, or may decide to combine the collections of more than one group of students. If you'll be doing Protocol 7 later, you'll probably need at least 100 individual invertebrates.

2. While you're on your feet, visit with some of the other student groups and see what they found. They may have some interesting and uncommon species that didn't show up in your sample. Ask them what they've identified and make sure that what they're calling, for example, a "mayfly" is what your group is calling a mayfly.

Part 5. Final Processing

1. Continue picking over your sample until you're pretty confident that you've found most individuals. Look hard for smaller and slower-moving creatures: they "count" as part of the biota, but are easy to miss. Also look on the surface of any stones in your sample, where some animals, such as water pennies, may be hanging on.

2. Once your sample is completely sorted, you are ready to process your samples. Processing your samples includes identifying and counting them, and is part of the separate biotic integrity protocol. When you're through with that protocol, you may want to return your animals to their native habitat. In the meantime, keep an eye on the containers and give your animals some fresh water if they appear distressed.

Analysis

Now that you have collected and identified invertebrates, you are ready to analyze the water quality of your stream section. You can use either Protocol 6 or 7 for this purpose, but there are important differences between them.

Protocol 6

The simplest method for assessing water quality is to look for invertebrates that are especially sensitive to pollution ("indicator species"). If these organisms are present in your stream, then the water is probably not very polluted. In contrast, if these organisms are missing, your stream section might be influenced by pollution. Protocol 6 allows you to assess the water quality of your stream by looking for specific types of invertebrates.

Protocol 7

Like Protocol 6, this protocol also considers what indicator species are present in your stream. However, Protocol 7 also considers how many species are present in the stream ("species richness") as well as how many individuals of each species are present ("dominance"). While Protocol 7 may take longer to complete, it will yield a more precise analysis of your stream.

STREAM INVERTEBRATE IDENTIFICATION SHEET

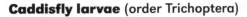

—Require high dissolved oxygen levels

Stonefly nymphs (order Plecoptera)

Description: 1–4 cm; six legs, each ending in double hooks; visible antennae; two tails (never three). No gills on abdomen.

Feeding: Most species gather and eat decaying plants or animals, but some eat bacteria and others are predators.

Habitat: Swiftly moving streams with high oxygen levels.

Mayfly nymphs (order Ephemeroptera)

Description: 0.5–3 cm; six legs, each ending in a single hook; visible antennae; three long tails (sometimes two). Plate-like or feathery gills along sides of abdomen.

Feeding: Grazers or gatherers; eat algae and organic matter.

Habitat: Some cling to rocks, some burrow in mud, and others are free swimmers. Diversity of mayfly species decreases with stream degradation.

Caddisfly larvae (order Trichoptera)

Description: <2.5 cm; six legs with hooked claws; two hooks at tail end. Some species build cases of small stones or sticks, and others are free-living or spin nets attached to rocks.

Feeding: Some graze algae, others filter-feed detritus, and a few free-living species are predators.

Net-spinner

Habitat: High-quality streams; some are tolerant of mild pollution.

Case-builder

Dobsonfly larvae (order Megaloptera)—also known as "Hellgrammites"

Description: 2–10 cm; six legs; large pinching jaws; pointed feelers with feathery gills along abdomen; two tail projections, each with two hooks.

Feeding: Predators with powerful chewing mouthparts. *Caution:* If they pinch you, it hurts!

Habitat: High-quality streams.

Beetle larvae and adults (order Coleoptera)

Water penny larvae

(top view)

Description: 0.5–1.25 cm; broad flat saucer-shaped body; six small legs underneath.

Feeding: Graze algae and other material attached to rocks.

Habitat: Cling to rocks in cold, fast-running, high-quality streams.

(side view)

Riffle beetle larvae and adults

Description: Larvae are <1.25 cm; worm-like but hard body; six legs and small tuft of white filaments at tail end. Adults are 1–2 cm, black, and look similar to many terrestrial beetles.

Feeding: Collect and gather algae, diatoms, and organic debris.

Habitat: Larvae cling to rocks in stream riffles. Adults walk slowly along stream bottom.

Notes: Unique in that larval and adult stages both are aquatic.

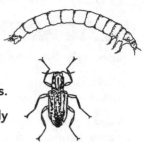

—Can survive with moderate oxygen levels

Fly larvae (order Diptera)

Watersnipe fly larvae

Description: <3 cm; cylindrical, slightly flattened; cone-shaped abdomen; many legs with suction tips; pale to green.

Feeding: Predators.

Habitat: Moderate quality streams and rivers.

Cranefly larvae

Description: 6 cm; large, fleshy, segmented, and worm-like, with four finger-like lobes at hind end; light brown, green, or milky color.

Feeding: Most graze on algae or are gatherers, but a few are predators.

Habitat: Can be found burrowing in mud.

Blackfly larvae

Description: <0.5 cm; head has feathery gills, tail end has suction pad. Shaped like a bowling pin.

Feeding: Filter small particles of organic matter from the current.

Habitat: Live attached to submerged rocks; require swiftly flowing water.

Damselfly and Dragonfly nymphs (order Odonata)

Damselfly nymphs

Description: 0.25–5 cm; large protruding eyes; six thin legs; long, thin, abdomen with no gills; three broad "tails" that actually are gills.

Feeding: Predators.

Habitat: Typically found in medium-quality, slowly moving water.

Dragonfly nymphs

Description: 1.25–5 cm; large protruding eyes; round to oval abdomen; six hooked legs.

Feeding: Predators; eat aquatic insects, tadpoles, and small fish.

Habitat: Slowly moving water.

Alderfly larvae (order Megaloptera)

Description: <3 cm; six legs and six to eight filaments on each side of abdomen; distinguished from Dobsonfly larvae by single-tail projection with hairs but no hooks.

Feeding: Aggressive predators.

Habitat: High- or medium-quality water.

Scuds (order Amphipoda)

Description: <1.25 cm; swim rapidly on their sides and resemble shrimp; flat sides, hump-shaped back, and several pairs of legs; white, gray, or pink.

Feeding: Gather dead and decaying matter.

Habitat: Some highly sensitive to pollution; others found in moderately polluted water.

Crayfish (order Decapoda)

Description: <15 cm; look like small lobsters, with two large claws and eight smaller legs.

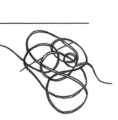

Feeding: Predators; use large claws to tear plant and animal prey into small chunks.

Habitat: Slow-moving streams, rivers, and ponds.

—Can live in streams with low dissolved oxygen levels

Midge larvae (order Diptera)

Description: <1.25 cm; have a worm-like body and distinct head; often C-shaped; sometimes bright red. 2 leg-like "prolegs" near the head

Feeding: Most filter-feed or gather detritus; a few prey on other insect larvae.

Habitat: Can survive in water with low oxygen concentrations.

Aquatic worms (class Oligochaeta)

Description: Usually <7.5 cm; long, thin, segmented worms with no legs.

Feeding: Ingest mud and filter out organic material.

Habitat: Tolerant of pollution; high numbers indicate poor water quality.

Leeches (order Hirudinea)

Description: <5–8 cm; worm-like, brown, and slimy; flattened, with sucker at each end.

Feeding: Some attach suckers to prey and drink blood; others gather detritus.

Habitat: Indicators of low dissolved oxygen.

Snails (class Gastropoda)

Description: 0.5–2 cm; flat or cone-shaped shell surrounding soft body.

Feeding: Scrape algae and bacteria from surfaces of submerged rocks.

Habitat: Some species have lungs and can live in waters with low oxygen levels, and others breathe with gills and require high oxygen concentrations.

Aquatic sow bugs (order Isopoda)

Description: 0.5–2 cm; relatively flat; have long antennae and seven pairs of legs.

Feeding: Scavenge both dead and live plants and animals.

Habitat: Can tolerate high levels of decaying organic matter; typically found in muddy, slow-moving water.

Notes: Sow bugs are crustaceans, not bugs as their name suggests.

PROTOCOL 6. SIMPLIFIED STREAM BIOTA TEST (SSBT)

Objective

To use the Simplified Stream Biota Test (SSBT) to assess water quality of a stream.

Background

A simple method of assessing the water quality in a stream is to look for pollution-sensitive indicator organisms. Three groups of aquatic invertebrates are common in clean water but are sensitive to pollution. For example, manure and other types of organic pollution can cause dissolved oxygen levels to become too low to support sensitive species. The Simplified Stream Biota Test (SSBT) rates the quality of a study site based on the presence or absence of these organisms. It is important to note that because factors other than water quality may also influence which organisms live in streams, tests like the SSBT are useful—but not perfect—tools for assessing water quality.

Materials (per student group)

▶ Stream Invertebrate Identification Sheet and other identification materials

▶ Macroinvertebrates collected with Protocol 5

▶ Table 2.10 from Protocol 7 (Optional)

Procedure

1. Identify the organisms that you collected in Protocol 5 by comparing them to the descriptions in your reference materials. Make sure that you can identify stoneflies, mayflies, and caddisflies.

2. Complete Table 2.9 on the Simplified Stream Biota Test (SSBT) Data Form. All the SSBT requires is that you note the presence or absence of stoneflies, mayflies, and caddisflies.

3. (Optional) You and your classmates should decide whether to tally a more detailed description of your collection. You can use Table 2.10 to do this. If there are organisms that you cannot identify, record their numbers in the "Unknown organisms" row and provide a brief description or a sketch. Although you don't need Table 2.10 to use the SSBT, you may later wish to combine the results of all groups for further analysis using another quantitative measure of biotic integrity.

SIMPLIFIED STREAM BIOTA TEST (SSBT) DATA FORM

Name _____ Sampling Date _____

Other Students in Your Group _____

Study Site Location_____ Teacher's Name _____

Weather Conditions on Sampling Date_____

_____

TABLE 2.9
Simplified Stream Biota Test (SSBT)

Organisms in Sample	Stream Quality (circle one)
Stoneflies and mayflies present	Excellent
Mayflies and caddisflies present, but no stoneflies	Good
Caddisflies present, but no stoneflies or mayflies	Fair
No stoneflies, mayflies, or caddisflies	Poor

Is your SSBT result different than what you would have predicted before you collected macroinvertebrates from your stream? Why? Explain.

PROTOCOL 7. INDEX OF BIOTIC INTEGRITY (IBI) USING AQUATIC INVERTEBRATES

Objective

To use the Index of Biotic Integrity (IBI) to rate the biological integrity of a stream.

Background

This protocol rates the biological integrity of streams by analyzing samples of aquatic invertebrates. The Index of Biotic Integrity (IBI) that you will calculate is affected by three things: *species richness* (the number of invertebrate species you found), *dominance* of one species, and the presence of certain *indicator species*: mayflies, stoneflies, and caddisflies. Each component is described below. It is important to note that because factors other than water quality may also influence which organisms live in streams, tests like the IBI are useful—but not perfect—tools for assessing water quality. Nonetheless, higher IBI scores are generally indicative of better water quality.

Species Richness

In many cases, a larger number of species indicates a more complex and balanced ecological system, where many different niches are available to a wide variety of organisms. A well-oxygenated stream with a rocky bottom and a mixture of sunny and shady stretches can support many invertebrate species: some will graze algae from rocks, some will filter their food from the water, and others will eat their fellow invertebrates. In turn, the presence of diverse invertebrate communities is likely to support diverse communities of higher organisms, including fish.

Dominance

Imagine two 100-invertebrate samples taken from different streams. Both samples contain five invertebrate species, but the first sample has 20 individuals of each species, and the second has 96 individuals of one species and one individual of each of the other four species. Our previous measure—species richness—would rate these two samples identical, but clearly they are ecologically distinct. Healthy stream ecosystems are rarely dominated by a single species of invertebrates, and the second component of the IBI reflects this.

Indicator Species

A simple, quick method of assessing the water quality in a stream is to look for pollution-sensitive indicator organisms. Three groups of aquatic invertebrates are common in clean water but are sensitive to pollution, especially organic pollution like fertilizers or other nutrients. These are mayflies (Ephemeroptera), stoneflies (Plecoptera), and caddisflies (Trichoptera). The third component of the IBI not only looks for these indicators, it reflects the diversity of these indicator taxa.

This protocol was adapted from one developed by Dr. Barbara Peckarsky, an aquatic entomology professor at Cornell University. The weightings associated with each component are based on research on streams in the northeastern United States.

Materials

▶ Stream Invertebrate Identification Sheet and other identification materials

▶ Macroinvertebrates collected with Protocol 5

Procedure

1. You will need approximately 100 organisms to calculate the IBI. If you have fewer than 75, you should collect some more animals or pool your data with another group. Identify the organisms that you've collected by comparing them to the descriptions on your reference sheet. Then fill out the top portion of the Index of Biotic Integrity Data Form.

2. If you haven't already done so, tally the results of your collection in Table 2.10.[1] If there are species that you were unable to identify, tally their numbers in the "Unknown organisms" row and provide a brief description or a sketch.

3. Copy the "number of different types" total from the bottom of Table 2.10 to the "number of species" column in the Species Richness Subscore table (Table 2.11) on your Data Form. Note: you sorted your invertebrates based upon their appearance, and you may have identified three "types" of mayflies in your sample. For our purposes here, we will consider these three types to be three different species. The number of species in your sample is the *species richness*.

4. Use the reference table accompanying Table 2.11 to determine your Species Richness Subscore.

5. Refer again to Table 2.10 to determine which was the most abundant invertebrate in your sample. Describe it in Column A of Table 2.12. For example, if you found three species of mayfly and one of them was your most common organism, write "Mayfly species" in Column A.

6. In Column B (Table 2.12), indicate how many individuals you found of the most abundant organism. In Column C, report how many individuals you counted of all species in your sample. In Column D, calculate the proportion of your most abundant species compared to all species (Column B ÷ Column C). Finally, use the accompanying reference table to look up the Dominance Subscore.

7. Record in Columns F, G, and H the number of species that you found of mayfly, stonefly, and caddisfly. You tallied this information in Table 2.10 in the column titled, "Number of different types."

8. In Table 2.13, enter the appropriate numbers into Columns F, G, and H. Record the sum of these three columns in Column I. Then look up the Indicator Species Subscore in the accompanying reference table.

9. Finally, sum the three subscores (species richness, dominance, and indicator species) to calculate your Index of Biotic Integrity. Use Table 2.14 to determine the Water Quality of your stream segment, and record it on the Data Sheet.

---

[1] Table 2.10 is included in the instructional materials for both Protocols 6 and 7, and therefore appears twice in this book. The two tables are identical.

TABLE 2.10
Aquatic Invertebrate Tally

A Invertebrate Group	Number of Different Types	Number of Individuals of Each Type (Use As You Have Types)					Total Individuals
Examplefly (Example)	4	3	1	5	1		10
Group One Taxa — Stonefly nymph							
Mayfly nymph							
Dobsonfly larva							
Water penny larva							
Riffle beetle larva or adult							
Caddisfly larva							
Group Two Taxa — Other beetle larva							
Cranefly larva							
Scuds							
Clams and mussels							
Crayfish							
Dragonfly nymph							
Damselfly nymph							
Blackfly larva							
Alderfly larva							
Watersnipe larva							
Group Three Taxa — Midge larva							
Snail							
Sowbug							
Leech							
Aquatic worm							
Unknown organisms (describe or sketch each on separate page)							
Totals							

INDEX OF BIOTIC INTEGRITY DATA FORM

Name _____ Sampling Date _____

Other Students in Your Group _____

Study Site Location _____ Teacher's Name _____

Weather Conditions on Sampling Date _____

_____

1. Did you pool your data with another group? If so, why?

TABLE 2.11
Species Richness Subscore

Number of Species	Species Richness Subscore

Reference Table	
If your "Number of Species" is	Then use this subscore
>26	12
19–26	9
11–18	6
<11	3

TABLE 2.12
Dominance Index Subscore

(A) Most abundant species	(B) # of individuals of most abundant species	(C) # of individuals of all species	(D) Proportion dominant (B÷C)	(E) Dominance subscore

Reference Table	
If (D) is	Then use this subscore
>.30	12
.30–.50	8
>.50	4

TABLE 2.13
Indicator Species

(F) Number of mayfly species	(G) Number of stonefly species	(H) Number of caddisfly species	(I) Sum of F+G+H	Indicator Species Subscore

Reference Table	
If (I) is	Then use this subscore
>10	12
6–10	9
2–5	6
0–1	3

2. Calculate the Biotic Index Score using the following formula:

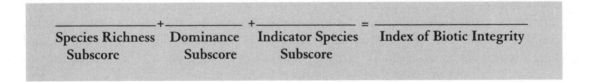

$$\underline{\hspace{2cm}} + \underline{\hspace{2cm}} + \underline{\hspace{2cm}} = \underline{\hspace{2cm}}$$

Species Richness Subscore   Dominance Subscore   Indicator Species Subscore   Index of Biotic Integrity

TABLE 2.14
Index of Biotic Integrity and Water Quality

Index of Biotic Integrity	Water Quality(circle one)
32–36	Excellent
23–31	Good
15–22	Fair
< 15	Poor

3. What is the water quality of your stream segment, as determined by the Index of Biotic Integrity? What local conditions do you think may be affecting water quality here?

PROTOCOL 8. MEASURING STREAM DISCHARGE

Objective

To measure the velocity and discharge of a stream.

Background

In this protocol you will measure the speed (velocity) of water flowing in a stream. You also will measure water depths at regular intervals across the stream, and then use this information to calculate the stream discharge. Stream discharge is a measurement of how much water flows past a certain point in a stream in a given time interval.

There are several reasons why you might want to measure velocity and calculate discharge. One might be to compare these variables from one sampling date to the next so that you can compare streamflow with weather patterns or land use changes. Another reason might be to investigate the effects of discharge volume on biological and chemical variables in streams. For example, during periods of low flow, concentrations of contaminants may increase because less water is available for dilution. During high flows, many aquatic invertebrates may get washed downstream, leaving lower populations in upstream reaches once the floodwaters recede.

In this protocol you will use a floating object (an orange) to measure stream velocity. The first step is to locate a straight section of your study stream with no large boulders, logs, or other debris that would affect motion of the orange as it floats downstream with the flowing water. With a meter stick, you will measure the cross sectional area of the stream and then use this information and velocity to calculate discharge. Because the orange travels slightly faster than the average velocity of the streamwater, you will apply a correction factor to obtain your final discharge value.

Materials (per student group)

▶ One orange (or a cork if your stream is very shallow)

▶ Measuring tape (metric)

▶ Meter stick

▶ Four sets of waders

▶ Personal flotation devices (PFDs) if the stream is not uniformly shallow

Procedure

Measuring Stream Velocity

1. Find a straight, ten- to thirty-meter-long section of stream. Water flow should be unobstructed by debris such as fallen trees and large boulders.

2. Measure the length of the section using a measuring tape, and record it on the Stream Discharge Worksheet.

3. In this activity, each student will be referred to as a tech. Tech A should have at least one orange. Tech C should have a stopwatch, and Tech D will catch the floating orange. All techs will need waders.

4. The four techs should enter the stream. Tech B should stand at the very beginning of the straight length of stream, and Tech C should stand downstream at the very end. Tech A stands about 2 meters upstream of Tech B, and Tech D stands about 2 meters downstream of Tech C (see Figure 2.3).

5. An alternate approach would be to tie a rope across the stream where Techs B and C *would be* standing (in this scenario these two techs would not enter the water) and have someone on shore start the stopwatch when the orange passes the first rope and stop it when it crosses the second. For this option, Techs A and D would perform the same tasks.

6. When everyone is in position, Tech A should drop an orange carefully into the stream, being careful to stand to one side and not directly upstream of the orange.

7. Tech B should call out "Start!" when the orange floats past him or her, and Tech C should start the stopwatch.

8. When the orange is even with Tech C, he or she should stop the stopwatch.

9. Tech D should retrieve the orange.

10. Record on the worksheet the time it took the orange to travel from Tech B to Tech C.

11. Repeat steps 6–11 a total of five times.

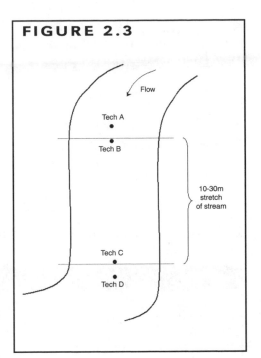

FIGURE 2.3

Measuring Stream Depth and Cross-Sectional Area

1. Find a portion of the stream section that has roughly the average width of the entire section.

2. Techs A and B hold the tape measure across the stream.

3. Divide the entire width of the stream into segments of equal width (e.g., 50 cm).

4. Using the meter stick, Tech C will measure the depth at each point, and Tech D will record the measurements on the worksheet. For example, if your stream is 4.5 meters wide and you divided the stream into 50 cm segments, Tech C will measure the depth at 0 cm, 50 cm, 100 cm, and so on across the stream (see Figure 2.4). Record the data on the worksheet.

FIGURE 2.4

0 cm   Meter stick   200 cm   400 cm   Tape measure

Cross section of stream

Record the depth from stream surface to stream bottom

Calculating Discharge

1. Use the formulas on the worksheet to calculate the corrected total stream discharge.

STREAM DISCHARGE WORKSHEET

Your Name(s) _____

Stream Name _____ Date _____ Time _____

Location _____

Current and Recent Weather _____

1. Record the length of the stream section in meters _____

   Distance Traveled (m)

2. Record the elapsed orange travel time in the table below.

Trial	Time Elapsed(seconds)
1	
2	
3	
4	
5	
Average Time	

_____
Average Time (sec)

3. To calculate the stream velocity, divide the distance the orange traveled (stream section length) by the average time.

   _____ ÷ _____ = _____

   Distance Traveled   Average Time   **Average Stream Velocity (m/sec)**

4. Record the depths and stream segment widths in the following table. For example, if you divided your stream into 50 cm segments, then the "Stream Segment Width" in the table will be 50 cm. Be sure to record your data in meters.

5. Multiply the depth by each segment width to get the segment area, and then total the segments' areas to get the Total Stream Cross-Section Area.

Section #	Depth (m)	Stream Segment Width (m)	Stream Segment Area (m²)
	Total Stream Cross-Section Area (m²)		

6. To calculate the "Total Stream Discharge," complete the following equation.

_____ x _____ = _____
Total Stream Cross-   Average Stream   **Total Stream**
Section Area (m²)   Velocity (m/sec)   **Discharge (m³/sec)**

7. To calculate the "Corrected Total Stream Discharge," multiply the Total Stream Discharge by the appropriate correction factor: 0.8 for sandy or muddy stream bottoms, and 0.9 for rocky stream bottoms.

_____ x _____ = _____
Total Stream   Correction Factor   **Corrected Total Stream**
Discharge (m³/sec)   (0.8 or 0.9)   **Discharge (m³/sec)**

STREAM DISCHARGE QUESTIONS

Your Name(s) _____

Name of Stream _____ Date _____ Time _____

1. Using your Corrected Total Stream Discharge, calculate the discharge for different time units.

Per Minute: _____ Per Hour: _____
       Corrected Total Stream   **Corrected Total Stream**
       Discharge (m^3/min)   **Discharge (m^3/hour)**

Per Day: _____ Per Month: _____
       Corrected Total Stream   **Corrected Total Stream**
       Discharge (m^3/day)   **Discharge (m^3/month)**

2. If you are studying the watershed that drains into the stream you just measured, find out how much rain has fallen on the watershed in the past month. You may need to contact local watershed managers, field research stations, or town officials, or you may need to measure it yourself. (Rainfall is commonly reported in inches. Multiply by .0254 to convert to meters.)

_____
Rainfall (m)

3. Locate or calculate the total area of your watershed.

_____
Watershed Area (m^2)

4. Using the watershed area and rainfall amount, calculate the *volume* of rain that fell on your watershed in the past month.

_____
Rainfall Volume (m^3)

5. Compare your monthly rainfall volume with your stream's monthly discharge rate. How do the two compare? Explain.

6. How would you expect the comparison in Question 5 to change if a greater percentage of your watershed was paved? Would the monthly stream discharge likely increase or decrease? Why? Explain.

7. Measuring your stream discharge using this protocol, and then using it to calculate the monthly discharge rate *may* lead to over- or underestimations of flow. Why is this? How could you make a more accurate measurement of your stream's monthly discharge? Explain.

8. How variable was the time it took for the orange to travel the length of the stream section? In terms of this variability, do you think the floating orange is a good method for measuring stream velocity? Discuss.

9. How would you expect your stream discharge rate (m^3/sec) to change after a slow, steady rainstorm? Would you expect the discharge rate to increase very quickly and then drop back to a lower level quickly? Or would you expect the rise and fall of the rate to take longer? Are there other possibilities? Discuss how you think your stream would respond and why.

10. Although estimates vary, an average American uses about 300–400 liters (0.3–0.4 m^3) per day. Using the daily stream discharge value you calculated, how many people could obtain their daily water needs from your study stream?

PROTOCOL 9. AQUATIC CHEMISTRY

Objective

To collect and analyze water samples and understand how aquatic chemistry affects organisms that live in streams and other bodies of water.

Background

Test kits and probes that measure streamwater chemistry variables such as pH, dissolved oxygen, or nitrate are widely available to students and teachers. These tools are useful because they provide quantitative information about how streams differ from each other, how upstream and downstream sections of the same stream vary, or how suitable a stream is for different types of aquatic organisms. In this protocol you will collect samples, measure them with test kits or probes, and analyze the resulting data.

To begin, you should choose a question you would like to answer about water in your study stream. For example, you may be interested in learning how acidic your stream is, or you may be curious about dissolved oxygen levels upstream and downstream of the wastewater treatment plant in your town. Your question may be determined in part by what test kits are available, and will likely fall into one of three categories: point measurement, time series, or site comparison. A *point measurement* refers to one or a few water samples taken from a single site at one time. Taking a point measurement can help answer simple questions such as, "How much nitrate is in the stream behind our school right now?"

If you were to measure the nitrate concentration in the same location over several days, weeks, or months, you would be taking a *time series*. Time series help answer questions that are more complex, such as, "How does the nitrate concentration in my stream change over time?" By comparing the nitrate concentration in the same stream with another one across town, you would be conducting a *site comparison*. Measuring nitrate in an upstream and downstream location in the same stream is also an example of a site comparison. As the name implies, site comparisons can help you determine how stream locations are different from each other. Finally, taking samples from several sites over a period of time is a combination of a time series and site comparison, and would allow you to answer more complicated questions.

After you have recorded your question, you will next make a final decision about what chemical test kits or probes you will need to use to answer it. Then you will collect samples from your study stream and measure them using instructions provided with your test kits or probes. Finally, after organizing or graphing your results, you will explore how the values you measured affect organisms that live in streams.

Materials (will vary with sample site)

- Waders, waterproof boots, or other non-slip footgear suitable for the conditions
- Latex gloves (if streamwater quality is poor)
- Walking sticks to provide stability on slippery rocks
- Personal flotation devices (PFDs) if the stream is not uniformly shallow
- Chemical test kits or probes (e.g., from LaMotte or Hach)
- Safety goggles

- Bucket with lid to collect chemical wastes
- Clipboard and pencil
- Clean sampling bottles
- Aquatic Chemistry Reference Sheet
- Aquatic Chemistry Data Form(s)
- Cooler (optional, for taking replicate samples to be analyzed at a later date)

Procedure

You will work in teams of about three students to collect water samples and analyze their chemical properties. There are many different techniques and technologies for water testing, and the specific methods you use will depend on what equipment your school has or what variables you would like to measure. The following are general instructions; for specific instructions consult your test kit.

Part 1. Before You Start Sampling

At School

1. Develop a question or series of questions about the streams you will be sampling. Then use this question to plan your sampling strategy.

2. Before leaving your school, make sure you have everything you need. Check your chemical test kits to ensure that sampling bottles are clean and that you have written instructions for each test and enough test chemicals or tablets. If your bottles are not clear, wash thoroughly and rinse thoroughly with distilled or deionized water.

In the Field

3. Establish a central rendezvous area in the field.

4. Consult with your teacher and classmates to coordinate who will sample, which tests they will conduct, and where. It is often easiest to split up into small groups, each with specific responsibilities.

5. Decide how many replicate tests you will conduct. Replicate tests involve taking more than one sample at each time and place so that you will be able to check for variability in your results. You might choose to test replicate samples in the field, or to keep them cool and bring them back to the lab to analyze when you have more time. Temperature, pH, and dissolved oxygen should be measured in the field because these values are likely to change when samples are stored.

Part 2. Collecting Water Samples

6. If you are wading into the water to collect samples, take your time. Moving slowly will help you keep your balance. It will also reduce the amount of sediment you kick up, which can affect your readings and the readings of anyone sampling downstream.

7. To collect a sample, face upstream and fill your sampling container with water flowing toward you. If you are sampling for dissolved oxygen, point the opening of the bottle toward you and lower it slowly into the water in order to minimize mixing of water and air.

8. If you are collecting from shore, a boat, or a bridge, you may be using a commercial sampling device, or perhaps one of your own design. If you collect a sample from a depth other than the surface, lower the sampler to a known depth, then open the sampler. Be sure to indicate the water depth in your written description of the sampling location on the Aquatic Chemistry Data Form.

Part 3. Analyzing Samples

9. Follow the instructions for your test kit or device. It is usually best to run each test twice for each sampling location, to check for errors in measurement or method. Alternatively, for tests other than dissolved gases, you can collect and label duplicate samples for each sampling location. Keep these samples cool until you and your classmates have had a chance to review the data. If any of your measurements look suspect, you can repeat the test later with the duplicates you have saved. (This won't work for dissolved gases, because gases bubble out of solution as the sample water warms).

10. Complete the Aquatic Chemistry Data Form. Sketch a map of your study area and indicate your sampling locations on the map. Include features that will be easy for others to find at a later date, such as bridges, docks, or culverts. If you have a GPS device or a topographic map, record the latitude and longitude as well.

Part 4. Checking in

11. After collecting and analyzing your samples, enter your data in Table 2.17. Then gather your gear and carry it to the rendezvous area. If you collected samples to take back to school, check that they are labeled and put them in the cooler. Pour processed samples into the waste bucket, for disposal at your school. Turn in clipboards and data sheets.

Interpreting Your Data

Once you have finished collecting and testing your samples, the next step is to organize, graph, and analyze your data.

Organizing Your Data

After filling out your Aquatic Chemistry Data Form, step back for a moment to consider how to organize your data to meet your needs. If you took a few samples or measured only one variable, you may decide that your results are already well organized on the Data Form. However, if your data are more complicated, you may want to create summary tables to help you evaluate your results. For example, suppose you are interested in comparing pH and dissolved oxygen for two replicate samples at each of two stream sites. Assembling these data into summary tables for upstream and downstream sites is one way of organizing the results (see Tables 2.15 and 2.16).

Graphing Your Data

You may be able to notice differences between sites and samples simply by looking at your data tables. For example, in Tables 2.15 and 2.16, it appears that the upstream site is more acidic and contains higher concentrations of dissolved oxygen. How-

TABLE 2.15
Downstream Chemistry Data

Site	pH	Dissolved Oxygen (mg/L)
Site A Sample 1	5.5	7.8 mg/L
Site A Sample 2	5.6	7.8 mg/L
Site B Sample 1	5.4	7.7 mg/L
Site B Sample 2	5.4	7.8 mg/L

TABLE 2.16
Upstream Chemistry Data

Site	pH	Dissolved Oxygen (mg/L)
Site C Sample 1	6.6	5.9 mg/L
Site C Sample 2	6.6	5.7 mg/L
Site D Sample 1	6.4	5.5 mg/L
Site D Sample 2	6.6	5.9 mg/L

ever, if you had a larger number of samples or replicates, you might find it easier to make sense of your data if you first create graphs. If you have replicates, you could graph each as a separate point, or you could calculate mean values among replicates and then graph the means.

You'll need to choose the appropriate type of graph. One possibility is a *line graph* (Figure 2.5), which is useful for showing patterns over time. For example, if you sampled the pH of a certain section of stream every day for two weeks, a line graph would be a good way to portray these data. *Bar graphs* (Figure 2.6) show differences between the means of two different treatments. For example, if you took temperature measurements from two different locations in the same stream, you could use a bar graph to show the difference between their means.

Interpreting Your Results

Once you have organized and graphed your data, then the Aquatic Chemistry Reference Sheet will help you to interpret your results in terms of water quality. Think back to the question you prepared before beginning the protocol. Have you answered your question? You might also consider using Protocol 5 to collect aquatic macroinvertebrates, allowing you to compare chemical and biological measures of water quality.

Keep in mind that each water sample provides limited information about your stream. If you took one or a few point measurements, think of them as "snapshots" of the stream at the moment you sampled. Like real snapshots, point measurements reflect only what is happening in the stream at the exact moment they are taken. In fact, point measurements can be highly variable due to environmental effects like season, discharge rate, or temperature or recent events such as forest fire, land clearing, agricultural activities, or construction.

FIGURE 2.5
Example Line Graph

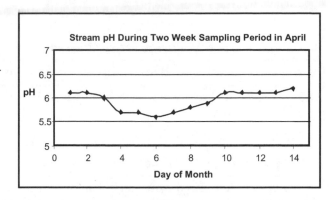

FIGURE 2.6
Example Bar Graph

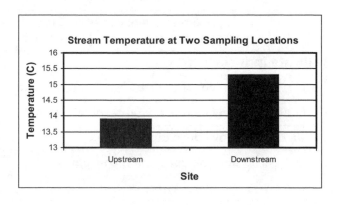

If you sampled a single stream over a long period of time, look for variability—are the results from all your samples very similar, or do they vary over time? What could be responsible for the variation? If you sampled from more than one site on the same stream, or from more than one stream, examine your data to see if there are differences between sites. Are the differences constant (e.g., does one stream always have higher phosphate levels than the other)? Or do they vary? Discuss why the sites have different results, or why they are similar. If you decide to use this protocol again in your watershed research, consider how different types of questions might provide you with more information about your study stream(s).

Useful Web Sites:

▶ The Volunteer Monitoring Project: *www.epa.gov/owow/monitoring/volunteer/issues.htm*

▶ Volunteer Stream Monitoring: A Methods Manual *www.epa.gov/volunteer/stream/index.html*

AQUATIC CHEMISTRY REFERENCE SHEET

pH		
0–4.0	Aquatic life is severely stressed	
4–4.5	Few fish and invertebrates can survive	pH (measured in pH units) indicates the concentration of H^+ ions in a solution, measured on a logarithmic scale. A solution with a pH of 4 is ten times more acidic than one with a pH of 5. Most aquatic organisms favor relatively stable, neutral streams, though some tolerate or thrive in moderately acidic or variable streams. The median pH of US streams and rivers is about 8.
4.5–6.5	Acid-tolerant invertebrates and fish can survive	
6.5–8.5	Suitable for most aquatic animals	
6.5–13.0	Suitable for most aquatic plants	
5.0–9.0	Suitable for human consumption	
Phosphate (ppm or mg/L)		
0.005–0.05	Typical of undisturbed forest streams	Phosphate typically limits plant growth in rivers and streams, and phosphate levels above 0.1 ppm can result in algal blooms. The presence and extent of blooms will vary according to other variables such as temperature and nitrate levels. Stream phosphate levels may be too low to detect. Consult your test kit or probe to determine appropriate range. Most US streams and rivers have 0.05 to 0.3 ppm phosphate.
<0.5	Suitable for human consumption	
0.05–0.1	May increase aquatic plant growth	
>0.1	Likely to cause algal blooms	
1.0	Approximate ideal upper limit for wastewater treatment plant effluent	
Nitrate (ppm or mg/L)		
0.1	Typical of undisturbed forest streams	Nitrogen is an important nutrient for plant growth, and nitrate levels above 0.1 ppm can result in algal blooms if sufficient phosphate and other nutrients are present. High nitrate concentrations indicate pollution from fertilizers or runoff from agricultural or urban sources. Most rivers and streams in the US have levels between 0.2 and 0.9 ppm.
0.1–1.0	May increase aquatic plant growth	
>1.0	May cause algal blooms	
<10	Suitable for human consumption	
<90	No *direct* effect on fish	
Dissolved oxygen (ppm or mg/L)		
0–3	Few organisms can survive	Because it is a gas, oxygen diffusion into water is limited by temperature. Colder water can hold more oxygen than warmer water. Using the nomograph in Figure 2.7, you can determine the percent saturation for each sample. Percent saturation levels lower than 80 percent may indicate presence of decomposing organic matter such as untreated sewage or manure. Most US streams have dissolved oxygen levels from 8.5 to 10.5 ppm.
3–4	Only a few fish and invertebrates can survive	
4–7	Most non-trout, warm-water fish species can survive	
5	EPA's suggested lower limit for maintenance of healthy aquatic biota	
> 7	Necessary for trout, salmon, and many invertebrates. Neither low nor high dissolved oxygen levels are *directly* harmful to humans	

Alkalinity (mg/L CaCO₃)		
20	FPA's suggested lower limit for maintenance of healthy aquatic biota	Alkalinity is typically expressed as mg/L CaCO₃. It is a measure of a stream's ability to buffer inputs of acidity, for example by acid precipitation. The higher the alkalinity, the higher the buffering capacity. Highly buffered streams are better able to support organisms sensitive to acidity. Most US streams range from 25 to 150 mg/L CaCO₃.
<25	Poorly buffered	
25–75	Moderately buffered	
>75	Highly buffered	
Chloride (ppm or mg/L)		
<12	Typical of undisturbed forest streams	Chloride is a component of salt (NaCl). Road salt runoff can raise streamwater chloride levels to over 10,000 ppm and harm stream organisms. Note that chloride is an ion (Cl⁻), and should not be confused with the chlorine (Cl₂) that is found in bleach and used to disinfect swimming pools.
0–200	Suitable for most fish and invertebrates	
200–1000	Suitability varies by species	
<500	Suitability for human consumption	
>1000	Most aquatic invertebrates are negatively affected	
Temperature (°C)		
<13	Suitable for cold-water species such as trout, salmon, mayflies, caddisfiles, and stoneflies	Temperature is important because aquatic organisms are adapted to life within certain temperature ranges, and also because it affects the concentrations of dissolved oxygen. Salmon and trout require high dissolved oxygen levels that can be found only in cold streams. As water gets warmer, concentrations of dissolved oxygen decrease at the same time that the need for oxygen goes up because of increases in metabolic rates of cold-blooded organisms.
13–20	Suitable for some salmon, mayflies, caddisflies, stoneflies, and beetles	
20–25	Suitable for most other fish, invertebrates, and warm-water species	
>25	Lethal to trout, salmon, many aquatic insects, and most cold-water species	

FIGURE 2.7
Dissolved Oxygen Nomograph

You can use this dissolved oxygen nomograph to estimate the percent saturation of dissolved oxygen in your samples. For each sample, line up a ruler or other straightedge with the temperature of the water on the top scale and the dissolved oxygen concentration on the bottom scale. Where the straightedge crosses the middle scale is the percent saturation value for this sample.

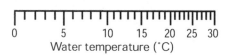

Water temperature (°C)

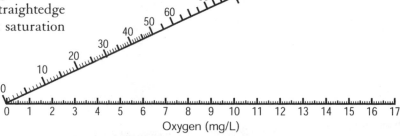

% Saturation

Oxygen (mg/L)

AQUATIC CHEMISTRY DATA FORM

Name(s) _____

Time: _____ Date _____

Stream Name: _____ Watershed Name: _____

County: _____ State: _____

Latitude: _____ Longitude: _____

Site Description: _____

_____

Weather in Past 24 Hours: _____

Weather When Samples Were Taken: _____

Sketch a site map below, labeling your sampling locations.

AQUATIC CHEMISTRY DATA FORM, PAGE 2

TABLE 2.17
Chemical Measurements

Sampling Site	Sample ID No.	Chemical Test (e.g., pH, D.O.)	Value and Units (e.g., 8.4 ppm)	Replicate Average (indicate which rows were averaged)

PROTOCOL 10. COMPUTER MODELING WITH STELLA

Objective

To become familiar with STELLA computer models by observing and modeling how water flows out of a container.

Background

STELLA is a computer program designed to help scientists, natural resource managers, and others make predictions about watersheds or other natural systems. To develop a STELLA model, scientists and planners first collect basic data. Then they use these data to make and test simple predictions about their systems. After running these tests, the data and results are used to design a more complicated STELLA model. By then running the model with different, updated, or unusual data, scientists and planners are able to make predictions about a variety of conditions in their systems.

So what are models, and how are they used in the real world? Models are simplified versions of objects or events, and they are used to help us better understand and predict relationships. Predicting floods is one example of model use. If you live in an area with streams that are prone to flooding during at least some portion of the year, you have probably heard weather forecasters give very specific flood warnings. For example, forecasters might predict exactly how many feet water would rise above a river's bank. To make these specific predictions, forecasters rely on computer models. Flood prediction models are developed using data from previous rainstorms, snowstorms, or hurricanes, and the floods that resulted from them. By entering this historical information into modeling software such as STELLA, forecasters are able to construct models that help them to predict future flooding events. In other words, models are a way to use computers to make predictions about the future based on knowledge about the present or the past.

In this protocol, you begin by making observations about how water flows out of a container. After experimenting with your container, you will predict its outflow rate for a given starting volume. Finally, you will use STELLA modeling software to create a model that predicts the rate at which water flows out of a leaky bucket.

Materials (per student group)

Part 1

▶ Ring stands

▶ Plastic soda bottles with caps (preferably 1-liter or 2-liter bottles)

▶ Drill with various sized bits (to drill holes in bottle tops)

▶ Large beaker to collect water

▶ Graduated cylinders (between 100 mL and 500 mL) to collect and measure water volumes

▶ Stopwatches to time measurements

▶ Scissors or knife (to remove bottoms of soda bottles).

▶ Graph paper

Parts 2 and 3

▶ Computer with STELLA modeling software installed

Procedure

Part 1. Exploring Flow Using a Physical Model

Your setup for Part 1 will be an upside-down soda bottle on a ring stand. The bottom will be cut out of the bottle and a hole will be drilled in the cap. The water will flow out of the cap and into a beaker (see Figure 2.8).

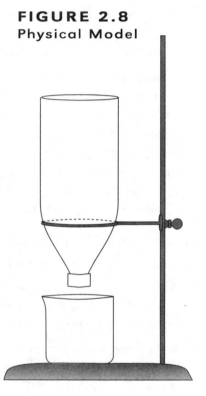

FIGURE 2.8
Physical Model

1. Choose the size bottle you would like to use, and then cut the bottom off. Decide what size and shape hole you want in the bottle cap and use the drill to make it.

2. Put the bottle in the ring stand. Hold your finger over the hole in the cap, and fill the bottle with a known amount of water.

3. Release the hole and allow the water to drain for 10 seconds.

4. Record how much water you started with and how much water flowed out of the container in 10 seconds. Use a graduated cylinder to measure the volume collected in the beaker.

5. Repeat filling and pouring, each time starting with different amounts of water and draining for 10 seconds. When doing this, think about what range of volumes and how many trials you should use in order to see a trend. Record the results in a table.

6. Graph your results by plotting the starting volume of water in the container (x-axis) versus the volume of water that drained in 10 seconds (y-axis).

7. Use your graph to predict the flow rate (in mL/10 sec) for a volume you did not try.

8. Run one more trial to test this prediction. Answer question 1 on the STELLA Worksheet.

Part 2. Developing a Simple STELLA Model

Now that you have experience with how initial water volume affects the outflow rate of a container, you will design a computer model that will predict how different leak rates (equivalent to the hole in your container) relate to how much water is in a bucket, and how quickly the bucket gets refilled.

Opening STELLA and Navigating Between Layers

1. Open the STELLA software.

2. Locate the "Navigation Arrow" (Figure 2.9) near the upper left side of the screen.

3. STELLA has three views, or "layers." Click on either the up or down arrow to move between layers.

FIGURE 2.9
Navigation Arrow

Using the Construction Layer

4. Navigate into the Model layer. Because it is the "middle" layer, it is the only one that shows navigation arrows pointing both up and down.

5. The icons below the title bar are grouped according to their function, and will allow you to perform different STELLA functions. Moving your mouse over each icon will display its name.

Creating a "Bucket" Stock

6. Position the cursor on the rectangular Stock icon and click once. Note that the cursor now takes the rectangular form of a Stock.

7. Position the cursor towards the middle of the empty page. Click once to "deposit" the Stock. The cursor should now appear as the Hand tool again, and there should be a square with a label in the middle of the page. This is an unnamed Stock.

8. The Stock's "Noname" label should be highlighted. Type "Bucket" and press enter to name the Stock. You can rename objects by clicking on their labels. You may also move objects by clicking and dragging with the Hand tool. Finally, you can delete objects by clicking on them with the Dynamite tool.

Putting a Leak in the Bucket

9. Choose the Flow tool by clicking once on the Flow icon.

10. Position the cursor inside the Bucket Stock, click and hold down the mouse button as you drag the cursor to the right about 5 cm, and release. As you do so, a Flow will appear, coming out of the Bucket Stock.

11. Notice that there is an unnamed circle on the Flow icon. This represents the regulator on the amount of flow out of the Stock, and you should label it "Leak."

Setting Initial Values

12. Next, you will set the initial value of the bucket to 800 units of water (e.g., gallons, liters, etc). To do this, first locate the Toggle icon near the upper left border of the page that either has "X^2" or an image of a globe on it.

13. If the icon has the globe image on it, click it once to change it to the X^2 icon. If the icon already appears as X^2, do not click it. Notice that question marks appear in the Bucket and Leak icons.

14. The X^2 icon indicates that you are in STELLA's modeling mode, which allows you to define mathematical relationships. Double click on the Bucket stock. A dialog box containing two blank fields and other features will appears. Type in 800 in the lower text field, and click the OK button.

Defining Leak Rate

15. Double click on the Leak circle icon, and then type in 50 in the lower text field. By completing this step, you have set the initial bucket leak rate to 50 units. This means that for every unit of time, 50 units of water will leak out of the bucket.

FIGURE 2.10
Stock Icon

FIGURE 2.11
Unnamed Stock

FIGURE 2.12
Dynamite Tool

FIGURE 2.13
Flow Icon

FIGURE 2.14
Flow from Bucket

FIGURE 2.15
Toggle Icon

Creating a Graph

16. In the next several steps you will design a STELLA graph. Graphs in STELLA allow you to see what's happening in your model. First, choose the graph tool and then click anywhere below the Bucket icon. A blank graph will automatically appear.

17. Double click anywhere on the graph to bring up the dialog box that controls what is displayed on the graph.

18. The "Allowable" column on the left contains those quantities in your model that may be used in the graph. The "Selected" column on the right contains the quantities that actually are being used in the graph. Double click on Bucket, and then double click on Leak. Both the Bucket and Leak should now appear in the Selected field. You may return to this dialog box later to adjust the scale of the axes or make other changes to your graph.

19. Click on the OK button to close the dialog box and return to the graph.

Running the Model

20. Select "Run" from the Run pull-down menu at the top of the screen.

21. You should see two lines on the graph: one for the Bucket, and one for the Leak. The Bucket should drop at a steady rate until it hits zero, and the Leak should remain constant. *Note that the scales for the two lines are different.*

22. Close the graph to return to the Model layout.

Refilling the Bucket

23. This section will guide you through the steps that direct STELLA to refill the bucket during the model. First, select the Flow tool again.

24. Click and hold the mouse button down about 5 cm to the left of the Bucket stock, drag the mouse pointer to the right so that it is over the Bucket stock, and release. A Flow should form going into the Bucket stock.

25. Label the new Flow "Flow In," and set its value to 30.

26. Answer Question 2 on the worksheet.

27. Now, add the Flow In rate to the graph. Double click on the graph icon to open the graph, and then double click on the graph to open the dialog box. As you did with Leak and Bucket, add Flow In to the selected column.

28. Close the dialog box.

29. Run the model.

Changing the Scales of the Graph Axes

30. Notice that on the graph the Flow In and Leak rates appear to be the same. To change the scale of the graph, return to the graph's dialog box, and find the double-headed scale arrow to the right of each of the three variables in the Selected column.

FIGURE 2.16
Graph Tool

FIGURE 2.17
Flows In and Out

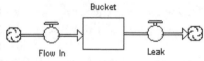

FIGURE 2.18
Scale Arrow

31. Click on Flow In rate and then the double-headed arrow next to it. Boxes will form around the range values, indicating that they can be edited.

32. Set the range from 0 to 50, and click on "Set". Notice that the double-headed arrow now has straight lines on the ends.

33. Set the Leak range to the same values.

34. Close the dialog box, and note the change in the graph.

FIGURE 2.19
Connector Tool

35. Go back to the model and experiment with different values for Leak, including values that are both higher and lower than the Flow In rate.

36. Answer Question 3 on the worksheet.

Making the Leak Rate Depend on the Bucket

FIGURE 2.20
Leak Connector

37. Next, you will adjust the Leak so that it is not a simple, constant value. As you noticed in Part 1 of this protocol, the amount of water flowing out of a container can depend on the amount of water in the container itself. In other words, the Leak rate will depend on how much water is in the Bucket.

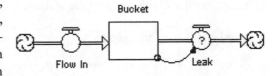

38. Select the Connector tool.

39. Click on the Bucket Stock and drag to the Leak flow. As you do this, an arrow will form, and the Leak will again have a question mark indicating the need to edit something.

40. Double click on the Leak to open the dialog box. Notice that Bucket is not in the "Required Inputs" box.

41. Click on Bucket to put the value of the Bucket stock in the equation.

42. Type or use the screen keypad to enter "*.1". This tells STELLA to make the Leak rate 10 percent of the contents of the Bucket. Click OK.

Running the Model Again

43. Return to the graph and run the model again, noticing that its behavior is very different than it was before you modified the Leak rate.

44. Also notice that by changing the graph's time axis, you might get a better picture of what is happening.

45. Choose "Time Specs" or "Run Specs" from the Run pull-down menu.

46. Replace 12 with 30.

47. Return to the graph and run the model again.

48. Answer Question 4 on the worksheet.

Part 3. Further Development of the Model

This section is a continuation of Part 2, and will introduce you to additional features of STELLA modeling software.

Creating a Slider for the Flow In Rate

49. Flow In and Leak can be manipulated using dialog boxes, but in the next few steps you will create "Slider Bars" that will allow you to manipulate those variables directly and easily. First, click on the up arrow on the left side of the page until you reach the top layer.

50. Click on the "Slider" tool.

51. Click on the upper left area of the page to create a blank slider control.

52. Double click on the Slider box to bring up its dialog box. On the left side, there is a column containing the values you can choose to be controlled by this box.

53. Double click the Flow In rate, and notice that a range now appears. Make the range 0 to 5, and click OK to close the dialog box.

Using the Slider

54. Move the slider to choose a different value for Flow In rate, noticing how the number changes. Also notice that a "U" button appears. Clicking on this button will restore the Slider to its default value.

55. Recreate the graph is this mode, just like you did in Part 2.

56. Run the graph for several values of the Flow In rate. Use the slider bar to adjust the Flow In rate.

Creating a Slider for the Leak Rate

57. Follow the same steps as above to create a slider for the Leak rate. The range should be from 0 to 50. Notice that instead of a U button, there is a "~" button.

58. Click the ~ button, which will change the value to read "eqn on". This means that the model is using the equation designated in the modeling model, and not a constant value.

59. Click on the ~ button again, and change the value of the Leak.

60. Run the model and examine the graph. Notice that the Leak is once again a constant, and no longer depends directly on the bucket volume.

Creating a Variable Leak Factor

61. Now you will make it possible to control the Leak using the slider bar, but maintaining the equation that controls. In other words, the Leak will still depend on the volume in the Bucket, but you will be able to modify this with the slider bar. First, click on the down arrow to return to the Model layer.

62. Choose the Converter tool.

63. Click near the Leak flow to place the Converter.

64. Label the converter "Leak Factor". Double click on the converter, and give it a value of 0.

FIGURE 2.21
Slider Tool

FIGURE 2.22
Blank Slider Control

FIGURE 2.23
Flow In Slider Control

FIGURE 2.24
Converter Tool

FIGURE 2.25
Leak Factor Converter

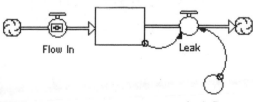

65. Choose the Connector tool. Make a connection from the Leak Factor to the Leak. Notice that the Leak now has a question mark again.

66. Double click on the leak flow. Highlight only the ".1" and then click on Leak Factor from the "Required Inputs" column. The equation should now read "Bucket * Leak_Factor".

67. Click OK.

Adding a Slider for Leak Factor

68. Click on the up arrow to return to the top layer. Choose the Dynamite tool and click on the Leak Slider to erase it.

69. Choose the Slider tool and create a slider for the Leak Factor. Make its range from 0 to 1, and click OK.

70. Run the model a few times, trying different values for the Leak Factor.

71. Answer Question 5 on the worksheet.

Exploring the Model

72. You now have a model that demonstrates how a bucket full of 800 units of water will empty given a certain Flow In rate and a Leak rate that depends on how full the bucket is. Run the model several times, each time with a different slider value for either the Leak Factor or Flow In rates. You may even want to change the Flow In slider to allow values from 0 to 30.

73. Answer Questions 6, 7, and 8 on the worksheet.

STELLA WORKSHEET

Name_____ Date_____

Part 1 Question

1. How did your results from Step 8 in Part 1 compare to your predictions? Explain.

Part 2 Questions

2. If the Flow In rate is 30 and the Leak rate is 50, what should happen to the amount of water in the bucket over time?

3. What happens when the Leak rate is less than the Flow In rate? What happens when they are equal?

4. What happens to the Leak rate as the volume in the bucket decreases?

Part 3 Questions

5. What happens as you increase the Leak factor?

6. Describe the overall relationships between the Bucket, the Flow In rate, and the Leak rate. Compare the model to results you obtained during Part 1 of this protocol. If necessary, run the model several more times before completing an answer to this question.

7. Do you think this model would accurately represent a real-life situation in which a water hose was filling a leaky bucket at a constant rate?

8. What natural or man-made feature in a watershed might be simulated with a "leaky bucket" model? What would Flow In represent? What would Leak represent?

9. Do you think simple models like this one could be useful in predicting changes in real-life situations? Why or why not? How has your experience with this protocol affected your answer?

ACTIVITY 10.1—MODELING LAND USE AND STREAMFLOW

Objective

To become familiar with how modeling software can be used to predict land use effects on streamflow.

Background

Imagine that you have moved to a new town and are concerned about the quality of the water you drink. You do some research and discover that your water comes from a watershed that provides water not only for you and your neighbors, but also for people living in a nearby city. Several housing and commercial developments are being considered for location in the watershed. You are concerned that the quality of water may decrease if development continues.

After you have lived in the town for several months, your mayor announces that volunteers are needed to serve as part of a Watershed Advisory Working Group. The purpose of this committee is to develop recommendations about land use planning for the watershed. You have been chosen to be on the committee and are trying to learn as much as you can about relevant issues. Another member of the committee—a high school science teacher—has given you an educational computer model to help you explore how changes in land use impact the flow of water into streams. Changes in land use influence how rainwater runs off the landscape or is absorbed into the ground, and how it eventually flows into streams and reservoirs.

In this activity you will use the model to look at changes in the patterns of water flow after a storm event occurs. You will be able to change the amount of water that falls on the watershed as well as how land is used in the watershed. You can change the percentages of land that are farm, forest, suburban, and urban. The model creates a graph of streamflow showing the volume of water in the stream due to the rainfall event over a period of time.

MODELING LAND USE AND STREAMFLOW WORKSHEET

Name_____ Date_____

1. Open the streamflow STELLA model. You should see a control panel that includes a graph and several smaller boxes.

2. The graph at the top of the screen will generate a "hydrograph" showing how streamflow responds to rainfall and land use in your model watershed over a 14-day period. The model is set up so that a 3" rain event will occur on Day 4 (you will change this later). Four "slider" controls set the land use in the watershed.

3. What initial conditions have been set for land use practices? In other words, what percent of the landscape in the model is farmland, forest, suburbs, and urban? Record your answer in the space below.

4. This initial setup—100% forest—reflects conditions found in much of North America at the time of European settlement. Without changing the settings on the slider controls, record your prediction for how streamflow will respond to a 3" rainfall event on Day 4:

    a. Double click on the Streamflow Prediction graph.

    b. Using your mouse, drag a graph line on the grid to show your prediction for streamflow. Remember, 3" of rain will fall on Day 4.

    c. Click OK to close the window.

5. Now select *Run* from the "Run" menu to run the model. Record your findings in Table 2.18. How did the prediction you made in Step 3 compare to the model run? Explain.

6. Use the slider controls to change the land use so that *Percent Urban* equals 100 and *Percent Forest* equals 0. To change land use in the model, click on the slider control bar and drag it to the appropriate position, or click on the number window, type in a new value, and press "Enter". As you did in Step 3, record your predictions on the Streamflow Prediction graph first, and then run the model. Record your findings in Table 2.18. How did your predictions compare to the model? Explain.

7. Click on the bottom left corner of the hydrograph to look at Page 2 of the graph. This page compares all the model runs you have performed so far. You can use it to compare the first model run with the second. How did the streamflow change when the land use was changed from 100% forest to 100% urban? What's different about the graphs? Explain below.

8. Clear Page 2 of the graph by clicking on the dynamite icon at the bottom of the graph.

9. Change the rainfall event by double-clicking on the "Rainfall" graph. To increase the amount of rain on Day 4 from 3 inches to 6 inches, click on the "Rainfall" column for Day 4 and type "6" in the "Edit Output" box.

10. Run the model three times using the 6" rainfall event and the land use percentages in the table below. This table contains the land use percentages for an upstate New York watershed. Alternatively, you may use your own local watershed land use data. Record your findings in Table 2.18.

Year	% Farm	% Forest	% Urban	% Suburban
1600	0	100	0	0
1910	75	21	4	0
1992	23	65	7	5

11. Look at Page 2 of the graph and compare the findings from the three simulations. How did streamflow change as land use changed over time? Explain.

12. As a member of the Watershed Advisory Working Group, what would you tell the mayor about the impact of different land uses on streamflow?

13. Now that you have experience with the streamflow model, you can begin to consider questions that might arise as you serve on the mayor's committee. Experiment with different combinations of land usage. Each time, before you run the model, enter a prediction for the streamflow and compare your predictions to your findings. Remember that you can clear a graph by selecting the dynamite tool and clicking on the graph.

14. Now consider a developer who wants to create a subdivision with many new houses in your town. Your town currently has land use percentages of: 23% farm, 65% forest, 7% urban, and 5% suburban. How would you change these percentages to model the impact the developer might have on streamflow? How do you think the streamflow will respond to these changes? Explain.

15. The city is buying some old buildings located next to a stream, bulldozing the buildings, and planting trees to create a forest. How do you predict streamflow will respond to these changes? Why? Explain.

16. Why do you think streamflow patterns matter in terms of water quality and quantity? Why would it matter to town residents if all the rainwater washed out of the watershed in streamflow very quickly or more slowly?

TABLE 2.18
Model Stream Flow

Use this table to record the model streamflow response to your land use and rainfall settings.

Land Use Settings				Rainfall	Response
% Farm	% Forest	% Urban	% Suburb	Describe the rainfall event(s)—how much fell on which days.	Record how the streamflow responded to the rainfall event. Did you see one peak or multiple peaks? Did the streamflow graph increase steeply or gradually? How did it decline?

ACTIVITY 10.2—MODELING THE MANAGEMENT OF A WATERSHED TO LIMIT EUTROPHICATION

FIGURE 2.26
A Watershed Landscape

Objective

To become familiar with how modeling software can be used to predict land use effects on eutrophication.

Background

Imagine that you have just been hired as the Watershed Manager for the Lake Tuscaloosa Watershed District in upstate New York. Your job will be to manage inputs into the lake in an effort to control eutrophication.

Lake Tuscaloosa has a surface area of one km², and an average depth of 10 m. It drains a watershed of about 2,500 km². The lake borders Tuscaville, a small city with a population of 10,000. Twenty percent of the land in the watershed is urban. The remaining area is a mix of agricultural and forested land. Most of Tuscaville's sewage flows to a local sewage treatment plant, and treated water is discharged into Tuscaloosa Lake. A few small creeks and rivers run into the lake, which is drained by a larger stream.

In past summers, residents have complained about large blooms of algae on Lake Tuscaloosa. As Watershed Manager, you know that lake eutrophication and algal blooms are usually caused by a high inflow of phosphorus. It is your job to keep the lake from becoming eutrophic by reducing the inflow of phosphorus.

To help understand the factors that contribute to phosphorus inflow and the eutrophication problem, you have decided to use a STELLA eutrophication model to predict the effects of different management scenarios. This model will let you investigate the impact of some human behaviors on the inflow of phosphorus into Lake Tuscaloosa.

Specifically, you will use the model to determine how the following **Watershed Factors** affect eutrophication of Lake Tuscaloosa:

▶ **Agricultural Practice**—agricultural management may be rated on a scale of 1 to 9, where 1 represents poorest management (high phosphorus runoff) and 9 represents best management practices (low phosphorus runoff). Management may include such practices as crop rotations, harvesting schedules, timing and concentration of fertilizer applications, and the construction of manure holding ponds.

▶ **Percent of Watershed in Agricultural Use**—the percent of land in the watershed used for agriculture. The urban zone is held constant at 20% of the watershed area. The forested area equals the area of watershed not occupied by agricultural or urban land.

▶ **Population Served**—the number of people living in the watershed.

▶ **Wastewater Treatment Plant Efficiency**—the efficiency of the sewage treatment plant. At 35% treatment efficiency, 35% of the phosphorus in incoming sewage would be removed before discharge to the lake.

The model then predicts how the watershed factors affect eutrophication and the following three variables:

▶ **Algal Density**—the number of algae cells per milliliter of water.

▶ **Secchi Depth** (meters)—the maximum water depth at which a black and white 30 cm diameter disc (a Secchi disc) is still visible. Oligotrophic lakes usually have Secchi depths of more than 5 meters. Eutrophic lakes usually have Secchi depths of less than 2 meters.

▶ **Dissolved Oxygen on Bottom** (mg/Liter)—the concentration of dissolved oxygen in water near the bottom of the lake.

Procedure

1. Open the STELLA Eutrophication model. You should see a control panel that is labeled, "Watershed Management," and includes a few boxes, tables, and buttons.

2. Near the top of the control panel are four "slider" controls that will be used to adjust the **Watershed Factors** described above.

3. To the right is a graph that depicts the response of three variables to changes in the Watershed Factors: Secchi Depth, Dissolved Oxygen on Bottom, and Algal Density. Next to each variable at the top of the graph is a number that corresponds to one of the lines on the graph. For example, the graph line labeled "1" refers to Secchi Depth. After you have located the slider controls and the graph, you are ready to use the model.

4. Note that the initial watershed conditions are: 80% agricultural land, 20% urban land, 0% forest, level 2 agricultural practice, 25% sewage treatment efficiency, and a population of 10,000. In the next part of the activity you will use the model to predict the impacts of three different scenarios on Lake Tuscaloosa. After you complete a scenario, be sure to reset the initial conditions by clicking on the slider control "Restore" buttons, which are labeled "U".

MODELING WATERSHED MANAGEMENT SCENARIO I

—Population Growth in Tuscaville

Name_____ Date_____

1. Tuscaville expects significant population growth in the next decade. You know that more people mean more sewage, and that more sewage means more phosphorus discharged into Lake Tuscaloosa. What do you predict will happen to **Algal Density** in the lake as the population of Tuscaville increases? Why? Explain.

2. First use the STELLA model to run a simulation using the initial Watershed Factor values. To run the model, press the "Run" button. Then record the approximate Algal Density values as they appear on your graph. Draw a sketch of what happens to **Algal Density** over time. "Day 0" refers to the day in the spring when the ice covering Lake Tuscaloosa melts and algae living in the lake can begin photosynthesizing and multiplying in earnest.

Day	Algal Density (cells/mL)
0	
30	
60	
90	
120	

3. Run the model three more times, using population values of 40,000, 60,000, and 100,000. To change the population value, either slide the "population served" control bar to the appropriate number or click on the slide bar's number window, type in a new value, and press "Enter". For each population value, record the day on which the Algal Density reaches 50 cells/mL.

4. As **Algal Density** increases, what changes do you think you might observe in Lake Tuscaloosa's appearance? Why?

Population	Day Algal Density Reaches 50 Cells/mL
10,000	
40,000	
70,000	
100,000	

5. Set the human **Population** to 70,000 and run the model again. As **Algal Density** increases, what happens to **Secchi Depth** and **Dissolved Oxygen on Bottom**? Draw a sketch of each and label the minimum and maximum values with units.

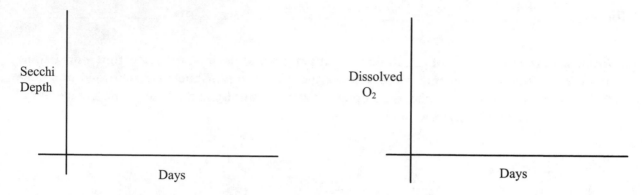

6. As a lake becomes less clear, the Secchi Depth decreases. Recall that a Secchi Depth of less than 2 m indicates a eutrophic lake, while a Secchi Depth of more than 5 m indicates an oligotrophic lake (between 2 m and 5 m Secchi Depths, lakes are known as "mesotrophic"). Based on the Secchi Depth line, as the population in Tuscaville increases, does the lake become more or less eutrophic?

7. What could be done to the treatment plant to offset the increased level of phosphorus from more sewage? Explain.

8. Based on your answer above, try to reduce the rate at which **Secchi Depth** declines. With a population of 70,000, how efficient must the wastewater treatment plant be to preserve a Secchi Depth of at least 10 m 90 days after ice-out? Run the model each time you use the Plant Efficiency slider control bar to make a change.

9. As Watershed Manager, what would you tell the townspeople of Tuscaloosa about the effect of population on the lake? Explain.

MODELING WATERSHED MANAGEMENT SCENARIO II

—Agriculture Land Use Increases

Name_____ Date_____

1. As agriculture increases in Tuscaville, increasing amounts of phosphorus from fertilizer are draining into Lake Tuscaloosa. As Watershed Manager in this scenario, you will use the STELLA model to make predictions and help you with management decisions. Before you begin, what do you predict will happen to Lake Tuscaloosa as agricultural land use increases? Will it become more or less eutrophic? Why? Explain.

2. What will happen to forested land as agricultural land increases?

3. Run four simulations with Percent of Watershed in Agricultural Use equal to 20%, 40%, 60%, and 80%, and keep all other variables constant. To change the Percent of Watershed in Agricultural Use value, either slide the "Percent of Watershed" control bar to the appropriate number or click on the slide bar's number window, type in a new value, and press "Enter".

4. In the chart below, record the day Secchi Depth falls below 10 m. Was your prediction correct? Did the lake become more or less eutrophic? Explain.

Agricultural Land Use %	Day Secchi Depth Falls Below 10 M
20%	
40%	
60%	
80%	

5. What generally happens to **Dissolved Oxygen on the Bottom** as **Algal Density** increases?

6. What causes this general pattern in **Dissolved Oxygen on the Bottom** of the lake?

7. Set the **Percent of Watershed** in agricultural land use to 65%, and use the model to observe what happens to **Secchi Depth** as Agricultural Practice changes. Run the model four times using Agricultural Practice values of 2, 4, 6, and 9. Record the results in the chart below.

Agricultural Practice	Day Secchi Depth Reaches 10 M
2	
4	
6	
9	

8. As Watershed Manager, what general recommendations would you make to the town of Tuscaloosa about Agricultural Practices and Land Use? Explain.

MODELING WATERSHED MANAGEMENT SCENARIO III

—Budget Cutbacks

Name_____ Date_____

1. In this scenario you have submitted a watershed management plan to the Town Board. Your plan calls for improvements in efficiency to be made to the wastewater treatment plant and for the town to give agricultural management seminars. Because of necessary budget cuts, the Town Board informs you that they can only afford to spend $200,000 on improvements and seminars.

2. You discover that it costs $40,000 to increase the efficiency of the wastewater treatment plant by 10%. Currently the efficiency is 25% and the town population stands at 16,000.

3. You calculate that seminars leading to one point of improved agricultural management practices cost $20,000. The current agricultural practice is 4, and 65% of the watershed is used for agriculture.

Watershed Factor	Current Condition
Plant Efficiency	25%
Agricultural Practice	4
Percent of Watershed in Agriculture	65%
Population Served	16,000

Remedy	Cost
Plant Efficiency	$40,000 per 10% increase
Agricultural Practice	$20,000 per 1 point increase

4. Set the Watershed Factors to the current conditions above, and then use the model to determine the best way to allocate the $200,000 in your budget. What mix of increased wastewater treatment efficiency and agricultural practices will maximize your goal of keeping Lake Tuscaloosa from becoming eutrophic while minimizing costs? First record your predictions in the space below, and then record the Watershed Factors and Secchi Depth results from each model run in the table below.

Plant Efficiency	Cost to Improve	Agriculture Practice	Cost to Increase	Total Cost	Day That Secchi Depth Reaches 10 M

5. Given your limited budget, what did you find to be the best mix of remedies to keep Lake Tuscaloosa from becoming eutrophic? Were you able to find a "solution" to this problem? Will it be necessary for the Town Board to spend more money? Explain your reasoning.

WORKSHEETS FOR PLANNING PROTOCOLS

PROTOCOL PLANNING FORM

Name _____ Date _____

1. What is the name of the protocol you will be using?

2. What is the purpose of this protocol?

___ To monitor existing conditions.

___ To compare conditions in two or more different habitats or ecosystems.

___ To perform an experiment in the laboratory.

___ To perform an experiment in the field.

___ To build and test a model.

___ Other.

Explain the purpose:

3. What question are you hoping to answer using this protocol?

4. What type of samples will you be using?

5. Describe the field sites or lab setup you will be using:

DATA ANALYSIS PEER REVIEW FORM

Name _____ Date _____

Are the data presented clearly?

Very clear	❏	Comments about what was done well:
Mostly clear	❏	
Somewhat clear	❏	Suggestions for improvement:
Largely unclear	❏	

Are the conclusions clearly stated?

Very clear	❏	Comments about what was done well:
Mostly clear	❏	
Somewhat clear	❏	Suggestions for improvement:
Largely unclear	❏	

Do the data clearly support the conclusions?

Very clear	❏	Comments about what was done well:
Mostly clear	❏	
Somewhat clear	❏	Suggestions for improvement:
Largely unclear	❏	

INTERACTIVE RESEARCH:
FIELD STUDIES AND EXPERIMENTS

IDEAS FOR WATERSHED DYNAMICS RESEARCH

Watersheds are complex and dynamic ecological communities, affected by human activities as well as by other chemical, physical, and biological factors. Because of this complexity, many different types of watershed-related research are possible, and in fact necessary in order to get an integrated picture of water quality and watershed health.

The protocols in this book provide techniques for studying land uses, stream invertebrate populations, water chemistry, and streamflow volumes. You could choose one, or combine several of these topics in your studies. The topics and ideas presented below are meant to stimulate your thinking as you work to develop your own research questions and plan of study.

The following discussion is designed to help you plan an interesting research project. You may find it overwhelming to read all the topics. We suggest that you start by filling out the **Choosing a Research Topic** worksheet (p. 144), and then read the sections below that cover topics you are interested in investigating.

Before you begin your watershed studies, start by developing basic goals. What are you interested in learning about your watershed? Would you like to investigate more than one watershed? Why? Are there others in your community already studying these or other watersheds? Does it make sense to collaborate with them? Can anyone in your community use the data you will be collecting?

After you have a basic plan, determine how you will carry out the monitoring. Who will be responsible for measuring which variables? If different people will be measuring the same thing, how will you ensure that everyone uses consistent techniques? How often will you take measurements? How will you present your data? Who will use your results? How can your results be used to guide future decision-making in the watershed? Once you begin your monitoring program, be sure to document the protocols you use, any changes you make in these protocols, and any unusual events that occur over the course of your study. This will help you to interpret your data and make your results more useful to others who follow after you with similar monitoring studies.

WATERSHED SURVEYS

Watershed surveys are critical early components of most watershed research. Before scientists or watershed planners can determine how watersheds should be managed or how they are affected by environmental variables, they must first explore the watersheds, delineate their boundaries, and determine how the land is being used.

Land Use

Protocols 1–3 provide techniques you can use to address questions related to land use. For example, you may be curious about how land use in your watershed has changed over time. Or you may be interested in how changes in land use in one watershed compare to those in an adjacent watershed. Perhaps you are curious about the history of land use in the area surrounding your school.

Airphotos provide a wealth of information on current and historical land uses. You could start by making predictions. For example, what percentage of land in the watershed do you think was used for agriculture 50 years ago, compared with a more recent date? After making your predictions and explaining the basis for them, obtain airphotos from the period of time in which you are interested. Use watershed survey protocols to compare your predictions with the actual patterns of land use. Were your predictions correct? How has land use in your watershed changed over time? Has change been relatively constant, or was there a period of time when land use changed very quickly? How have *riparian* land use practices changed over time?

Because riparian land use directly affects streamwater quality, you also may be interested in examining the effects of local land management practices on your study stream. To address this question, you could start by using Protocol 2 to catalog current land use practices in your study watershed. Then you could use this information to make predictions about streamwater quality above and below areas being managed in different ways. You could test your predictions using biological and chemical stream assessment techniques (Protocols 5–7 and Protocol 9). Your results may lead you to make conclusions about how local land management practices are affecting streamwater quality, or about how future changes in land use could affect streams. You may even consider presenting your results and predictions to local watershed planning officials.

WHEBIP

Another way to assess historical riparian habitat and streamwater quality is by using the WHEBIP model (Protocol 4) to analyze airphotos from several different time periods. For example, if you have access to several historical airphotos of your watershed you could explore how WHEBIP scores changed over time. Do these scores suggest that the quality of riparian habitat in your study watershed is improving, getting worse, or staying about the same? You also could use this information to make predictions about how future land use management decisions would be likely to affect the streams in your watershed.

Invasive Species

If you are familiar with invasive species, you may be interested in conducting surveys to see if any have become established in your study watershed. For more information on invasive species, visit the EI Web site (*http://ei.cornell.edu*) or EI publication *Invasion Ecology*.

STREAM ASSESSMENT WITH AQUATIC MACROINVERTEBRATES

Watershed scientists collect and examine aquatic macroinvertebrates to assess the water quality of streams. You can use the same techniques (Protocols 5–7) to answer questions about the quality of streamwater flowing through your study watershed. Monitoring aquatic macroinvertebrates will also help you learn more about the basic ecology of these organisms and the streams in which they live.

Comparing Assessment Protocols

This book includes two protocols that can help you assess water quality by collecting and analyzing samples of macroinvertebrates. Protocol 6 is simple and designed for quick analyses. Protocol 7 takes longer but provides more detailed results. Scientists and watershed monitors often have to make decisions about what types of protocols to use, weighing time and resources against the need for accuracy. You may be interested in comparing Protocols 6 and 7 to see if they yield similar results for your study stream.

There are other variables to consider as well. For example, if several groups of students analyze the same stream section, do they get consistent results? Does one protocol achieve more consistent results than the other? Do protocols from disturbed areas show the effects of disturbance? Which protocol do you think more accurately reflects the water quality in your study stream? Do protocols from disturbed areas show the effects of disturbance? By completing both protocols in several streams, you may be able to make conclusions about when it is appropriate to use one or the other, and which protocol might be generally better suited to the needs of you and your classmates.

Effects of Land Use by People

If you have made predictions about how land use management practices affect stream water quality, you could collect and examine macroinvertebrates to test your predictions. For example, perhaps you are curious about the effect of a new mall—and runoff from its parking lots—on macroinvertebrates in your study streams. To test this you could sample and compare invertebrates from several sites above and below the parking lots.

Field studies (Protocols 5–7) and modeling (Protocol 4) provide different approaches to assessing the quality of stream habitats. You could compare the results obtained through these two approaches. After sampling and identifying macroinvertebrates in your study stream, you will be able to calculate a water quality rating (Protocol 5–7). After assessing riparian habitat using airphotos (Protocol 4), you can calculate a similar rating using a different sort of data. How well do these two methods compare?

Another option is to compare biological and chemical measures of water quality. What can you conclude after analyzing the abundance, diversity, and types of stream invertebrates found at your study site? How does this compare with conclusions you reach through analyzing chemical parameters such as dissolved oxygen, pH, and nutrient concentrations? For example, if your dissolved oxygen readings suggest that your study site is contaminated with organic pollution, do invertebrate community samples also indicate poor water quality?

Aquatic Invertebrate Ecology

Invertebrate sampling (Protocols 5–7) may also be used for basic ecological research. You might want to investigate whether different types of stream habitat support different invertebrate communities. You could compare macroinvertebrate communities from headwater and downstream reaches, or between pool and riffle areas. Before you sample, make predictions about what you expect to find. After analyzing your results, think about what further studies you could carry out to help explain the patterns you observe.

Another basic ecological research topic is how aquatic invertebrate communities change over time. Although answering this question could take much of the school year, it would allow you to gain experience with long-term monitoring. Your teacher may be interested in beginning a study that can be continued for several years by subsequent classes. To examine how invertebrate communities change over time, you could first sample and identify invertebrates from one or more streams. Then, make predictions about how you might expect the communities to change over the next several months or year. Remember that aquatic insects live much of their lives in streams, and then emerge to live as terrestrial adults. Many types emerge in summer, but others are adapted to emerging during winter months. After making predictions, collect and identify invertebrates at regular intervals, and then compare the results to your predictions.

You may find you have access to invertebrate data collected by other students or watershed monitoring groups. If so, you could compare your data with the broader sample. Do similar types of organisms appear throughout the year, or do the populations seem to vary by season? Consider possible explanations or additional research projects you could conduct to explain any differences you observe.

Topic: precipitation
Go to: www.sciLINKS.org
Code: WD17

FLOW

By calculating stream discharge (Protocol 8), you will be able to compare stream flows under various conditions in your study watershed, or to evaluate the effects of flow rates on other variables such as chemical concentrations or biological life.

Precipitation and Impervious Surfaces

You might begin by examining how your study stream responds to rainstorms. Do flow rates or discharge volumes increase very quickly after a rainstorm, indicating that rainwater drains rapidly into streams? Or do flow and discharge increase slowly, indicating that much of the water seeps into the ground? To answer these questions you could measure discharge of your stream several times before and after a variety of storm events.

The amount of impervious surface in a watershed is a major factor determining the amount of runoff and how quickly the flood peak occurs after a storm. You might be interested in how roads, houses, parking lots, and other impervious surfaces affect streamflow in your study watershed. For example, how will the construction of a new parking lot affect the amount of water flowing into the nearby stream? You could make a prediction, and then test it by monitoring streamflow following rainstorms both before and after the parking lot is constructed. With this type of question it is important to take frequent measurements or to use a stream gage that provides constant monitoring of streamflow.

Another way to examine the effects of impervious surfaces on streamflow is to monitor flow rates before and after rainstorms in similar watersheds or subwatersheds that contain varying amounts of development and impervious surfaces. For example, your school may be located in an area with a lot of impervious surfaces, while your home or apartment or a nearby forest preserve might be in an area with greater proportions of grassy or wooded land. By comparing changes in streamflow rates after storm events in streams from these different areas, you may be able to make general conclusions about the effects of impervious surfaces on streams. However, you will need to keep in mind that streamflow also is affected by other variables such as slope, soil type, and location within the watershed.

Snowmelt

In regions that receive acid precipitation and have cold winters, acidic snow accumulates during the winter. When the snow pack melts in the spring, the runoff forms an acidic "pulse" draining into streams and lakes. To determine if this is affecting streams in your watershed, you could measure discharge and pH over time. Examine these data to see if pH values are lower during periods of high spring discharge.

Invertebrates

Streamflow affects what types of organisms live in streams. Some aquatic macroinvertebrates live in fast currents, while others prefer lower rates of flow. One way to examine this is to measure flow rates in several different areas of the same stream. Then sample invertebrates from areas with different flow rates and compare the samples. As you make these comparisons, be sure to consider possible effects of other variables such as differences in sunlight, stream substrate, or stream chemistry from one site to the next.

Online Flow Data

One way of studying streamflow is to take your own measurements using Protocol 8. Another way is to use data that are available online from automated stream-gaging stations. The United States Geological Survey's (USGS) Web site (*www.usgs.gov*) provides access to real-time data from thousands of monitoring stations, as well as historical stream discharge data, and related data about lakes, other surface waters, and groundwater. If you have a gaging station in your watershed, you will be able to analyze long-term trends using these data. In your watershed, you might see a water level scale painted on the edge of a bridge or weir. If so, you could contact local officials to ask whether they have a stage-discharge graph that would allow you to calculate discharge simply by reading the water level.

STREAM CHEMISTRY

Through monitoring and interpreting stream chemistry data, you will be able to answer a variety of research questions related to stream water quality and impacts of various human activities.

Point and Non-point Sources

One common question about streams is how potential point or non-point sources of pollution affect stream chemistry. For example, are fertilizers from the new golf course increasing stream nitrate or phosphate levels? How does the wastewater treatment plant in your community affect dissolved oxygen levels in the discharge stream? To answer these and related questions you could measure streamwater chemistry above and below the potential source of pollution. Before taking samples, determine which parameters (such as dissolved oxygen, pH, or nutrients) are important, and make predictions about how these parameters could be affected by the potential source of pollution. After collecting and analyzing your samples, compare your results to your predictions. Are there other protocols or research projects that you could conduct to help explain any unexpected results?

Another question is how nutrient concentrations vary over the course of a year. For example, are phosphate or nitrate levels higher in one season compared to another? Do these differences correspond with any land use activities in your watershed?

Nutrient Load

You may also be interested in examining how the nutrient *load* of your study stream varies seasonally. The nutrient load carried by a stream is calculated by multiplying the concentration and the discharge. When discharge volume goes up, the concentration of nitrate might go down through dilution. However, the total amount of nitrate being carried by the stream might actually go up because of the increased amount of water being transported. Nutrient loads are important because nitrate and phosphate may end up in a lake that is vulnerable to *cultural eutrophication*—that is, human-induced acceleration of aquatic plant growth. To monitor nutrient loads in your watershed over time, you need to pay attention to both nutrient concentrations and stream discharge.

Dissolved Oxygen

You may be interested in studying the levels of dissolved oxygen in your streams—what determines these levels, and how do they affect stream organisms? Are oxygen concentrations affected by discharge? Do oxygen levels approach saturation during periods of maximum flow, when the water is being aerated most? To answer this question, measure flow and dissolved oxygen over time, being sure to include periods of both high and low flow. If oxygen levels do not increase with flow, it could be because runoff carrying organic pollution is increasing biological oxygen demand, thereby lowering oxygen levels.

As you are setting up your study design, remember that streams are complex and variable systems. Temperature, flow, nutrient concentrations, pH, temperature, aquatic organisms, and other variables can be quite different in sections of stream that are very close to each other. It's best to take plenty of samples to account for this variability. Watershed scientists and managers take as many samples as their schedules and budgets allow, over as long a time as possible. While you will not be able to take hundreds of samples over the course of several years, you should plan to take replicate samples so that you will be able to take a look at the degree of variability in your results.

MODELING

Professional watershed managers and scientists use models to help them understand and predict how different land use management practices, runoff, pollution, and other variables could affect watersheds, streams, and downstream communities. The models described in this book (Protocol 10, Activities 10.1 and 10.2) may help you to make some general predictions about your own watersheds.

The streamflow model provided in Activity 10.1 allows you to determine relationships between land use, rainfall, and streamflow in a simulated stream. If you want to investigate the relationship between impervious surfaces and streamflow volumes, you could run the model several times, changing the percentages of land uses such as "forest" or "urban" for each run. Comparing the outputs, you could look for trends and make predictions, then test your predictions by resetting the input parameters and running the model again.

sci LINKS.
THE WORLD'S A CLICK AWAY

Topic: nutrient load
Go to: *www.sciLINKS.org*
Code: WD18

Another possibility would be to compare the relationships in the model to those observed in your study stream. Although this model is not tailored to conditions specific to your watershed, you could use the model to make predictions about your stream, and then test your predictions using actual measurements. This would allow you to determine whether your stream responds in the same way as the model to precipitation events, or whether the model would need to be adjusted in order to accurately reflect the conditions specific to your watershed.

Similarly, the STELLA Eutrophication model in Protocol 10 is a simplified version of reality and is not tailored to lakes in your community. However, you could use the model to make general predictions about the effects of changes in nutrient concentrations on lakes. You also could carry out laboratory experiments to test the effects of nutrient concentrations on growth rates of algae, then compare these results with your predictions.

ONLINE RESOURCES AND LONG-TERM DATA

Many online sources provide data related to streamflow quantity and quality. For example, the USGS posts streamflow data for many rivers and streams. If these data are available for your study site, you could conduct research on streamflow without regularly measuring it yourself. Historical data can also be very useful in putting your own data into perspective. How often, for example, does your stream reach flood stage?

Another useful online resource is the Environmental Protection Agency's (EPA) Web site (*www.epa.gov*). In addition to its "Surf Your Watershed" program, the EPA maintains an online national database of all registered point sources. This database includes wastewater treatment plants, and it is likely to have information on plants serving populations in your area. You may find it useful to browse this Web site as you consider conducting research on effects of potential point source pollution. The EPA, USGS, and other useful Web sites are all listed on the "Watersheds" section of EI's Web site (*http://ei.cornell.edu/watersheds*).

In many watersheds, data related to land use and water quality are available online or through local community organizations. If you find that you have access to long-term data, you will get a better picture of your watershed's health by interpreting your data within the context of longer-term trends.

FORMS FOR INTERACTIVE RESEARCH

See Table 4 (p. 15) in the *Teacher Edition* for a description of where each of these forms fits in the Environmental Inquiry research process.

PLANNING RESEARCH

CHOOSING A RESEARCH TOPIC

Name _____ Date _____

How has the land use in my town changed over the past fifty years?

How does streamwater chemistry affect invertebrate populations?

Are the aquatic invertebrate communities upstream of a new highway bridge similar to communities downstream?

Do models help determine relationships between land use, rainfall, and streamflow? How do they compare with trends observed in my study streams?

Do changes in riparian habitats (e.g., from forest to farm) have immediate effects on aquatic invertebrate populations?

How does streamwater quality relate to watershed land use practices?

1. Make a list here of questions that you would be interested in investigating using *Watershed Dynamics* protocols.

   Example: How does the benthic invertebrate community and stream quality differ upstream and downstream of a potential source of pollution (e.g., wastewater treatment plant, agricultural field, golf course)?

2. Of these questions, which seem the most important and interesting? Pick three:

a.

b.

c.

3. For each of the three questions you have chosen, think of how you might design an experiment. Then fill out Table 3.1

TABLE 3.1
Potential Research Questions

Question	Brief description of an experiment you might do to address this question	What equipment and supplies would you need?	How long would it take to carry out this project?	Would fieldwork or travel to field sites be required?
Example: Do stream invertebrate communities differ up-stream vs. downstream of the school's parking lot?	*Collect stream invertebrates several times, upstream and downstream of drainage from the parking lot.*	*Water, D-nets collecting pans, tweezers, magnifying glass, ID sheet.*	*3 double periods for collecting and identifying invertebrates on 3 different dates.*	*Fieldwork is required, and travel time would take 10 minutes each way for each trip.*
Question 1:				
Question 2:				
Question 3:				

4. Looking over Table 3.1, consider whether each project would be feasible for you to carry out. Are the equipment and supplies available? Do you have enough time? Will you be able to do whatever fieldwork is needed? Eliminate any questions that do not seem feasible based on logistics such as these.

	Would this project be feasible?	Why or why not?
Example Project	<u>Yes</u> No	*There is easy access to the stream that runs by our school. We will be able to sample both upstream and downstream of the parking lot.*
Project 1	Yes No	
Project 2	Yes No	
Project 3	Yes No	

5. Choose a project you have decided is feasible and interesting, then continue on to **Interactive Research Planning Form 1** or **2.**

INTERACTIVE RESEARCH PLANNING FORM 1

(for exploratory-level experiments)

Name _____ Date _____

1. **What question have you chosen to investigate, and why?**

    Example: Do WHEBIP and macroinvertebrate protocols yield similar results about stream and riparian habitat quality?

2. **Briefly describe a project you would like to do to address this question.**

    Example: First we will select two sections of a stream flowing near our school. Then we will obtain airphotos and conduct the WHEBIP protocol on all sections. Next, we will collect macroinvertebrates from each stream section and use Protocol 7 to assess water quality. Finally, we will compare results.

3. **What supplies will you need? How will you get any that are not already available in our classroom?**

    Example: We will need airphotos and materials listed in Protocol 5. We have all the equipment except waders, which we will borrow from the nearby university.

INTERACTIVE RESEARCH PLANNING FORM 1 *(continued)*

4. **How do you plan to schedule your project?**

   Example: We will need two class periods to conduct the WHEBIP protocol on the two stream sections. Then we will need two double class periods to sample and identify invertebrates. Finally, we will need one or two class periods to complete Protocol 7 and compare results with the WHEBIP protocol.

5. **Can you find reports by other students or professional scientists on this topic? If so, what can you learn from what has already been done?**

6. **Meet with another student or group to discuss these plans using the Experimental Design Peer Review Form** (p. 158). **Then describe any changes you've decided to make based on this discussion.**

INTERACTIVE RESEARCH PLANNING FORM 2

(for rigorously designed experiments)

Name_____ Date_____

1. **What question do you plan to investigate?**

   Example: "Will a new horse paddock adjacent to the stream near our school have an effect on streamwater quality and/or benthic macroinvertebrate communities?"

2. **Why is this question important or relevant to environmental issues?**

   Example: Riparian habitat can have significant effects on streams. Therefore, changing the land use practices in these areas may have consequences for streamwater quality and macroinvertebrate populations. Removing trees to build a horse paddock is a change in riparian land use.

3. **Can you find reports by other students or professional scientists on this topic? If so, what can you learn from what has already been done?**

4. **What is your hypothesis (the prediction of what you think will happen, stated in a way that can be tested by doing an experiment)? Why did you choose this prediction?**

   Example: Our hypothesis is that the macroinvertebrate population downstream of the proposed paddock will shift from one that is indicative of "excellent" water quality to "good" water quality, and that streamwater nitrate, phosphate, and turbidity levels will increase and dissolved oxygen levels will decrease.

INTERACTIVE RESEARCH PLANNING FORM 2 *(continued)*

5. What is your **independent variable** (the factor that that you will change to make one treatment different from another)?

Example: The independent variable is the construction of the paddock, including how much time has passed since construction began. We will sample upstream and downstream of the paddock before it is built and after construction begins. We will sample again after horses begin using it.

6. What is your **dependent variable?** (This is the factor you will measure to determine the results of the experiment—it is called "dependent" because the results depend on changes in the independent variable from one treatment to the next.)

Example: The dependent variables are the water chemistry and invertebrate populations of the stream above and below the paddock.

> If you are confused about the independent and dependent variables, it may help to think back to your research question and then think about how you might want to present the results of your experiment.
>
> On the x-axis is your independent variable. These are the numbers that you decide in advance, to create your various treatments.
>
> On the y-axis is your dependent variable. This is the factor you will be measuring in your experiment.

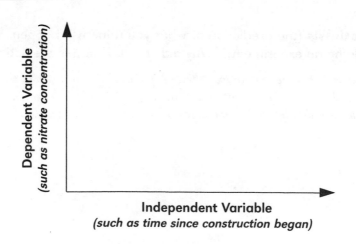

INTERACTIVE RESEARCH PLANNING FORM 2 *(continued)*

7. What **treatments** do you plan? (Each level of your independent variable is a treatment. You should plan to change only the independent variable from one treatment to the next, keeping all other conditions constant.)

   Example: Our only treatment is the construction and subsequent occupation of the horse paddock. Owners suggest it will take about a month to build, and horses will be using it in about a month after it is finished.

8. How many **replicates** will you have for each treatment? (The more replicates you can manage, the better, but you will have to figure out how many are feasible for your experiment.)

   Example: We will sample from the stream two times before and two times after the paddock is built and occupied. Each time we will collect samples from three upstream and three downstream locations.

9. What is your **control** (the untreated group that serves as a standard of comparison)?

   Example: Our control is the upstream sampling area.

10. What factors will you keep **constant** for all treatments? (The constants in an experiment are all the factors that do not change.)

    Example: Except for possible runoff from the horse paddock, all conditions will be the same for upstream and downstream sampling locations. As far as we know, there are no other proposed construction projects scheduled nearby.

INTERACTIVE RESEARCH PLANNING FORM 2 *(continued)*

11. What equipment and supplies will you need?

Example: We will need test kits necessary to measure nitrate, phosphate, turbidity, and dissolved oxygen, as well as equipment listed in Protocol 5.

12. What schedule will you follow?

Example: We will sample on four days—twice before the paddock construction begins, and twice after. We will need a double class period to sample, and another class period to analyze results.

13. What will you measure, and how will you display your data? Sketch an empty data table here, with the appropriate headings. (Think about what kind of table you will need to record the data from your experiment.)

On this graph, add labels for the x-axis and y-axis and sketch your expected results.

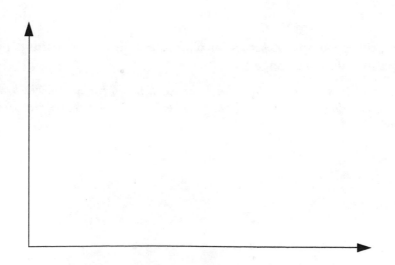

INTERACTIVE RESEARCH PLANNING FORM 2 *(continued)*

A Final Check: Evaluate Your Experimental Design

1. Does your planned experiment actually test your *hypothesis*?

2. Are you changing only one *variable* at a time? Which one?

3. Will your *control* be exposed to exactly the same conditions as your *treatments* (except for the *independent variable*)?

4. How many *replicates* will you have for each *treatment*?

5. Meet with another student or group to discuss these plans using the **Experimental Design Peer Review Form.** Then describe any changes you've decided to make based on this discussion.

PRESENTING RESEARCH RESULTS

RESEARCH REPORT FORM

Name _____ Date _____

1. What is the title of your research project?

2. What is your research question? Why is this question important, or how is it relevant to environmental issues?

3. Have other people investigated this question, or a similar one? Summarize what you have learned about this question from other students' reports, or from library or Internet research.

4. Summarize your procedures here.

RESEARCH REPORT FORM *(continued)*

5. Make a table here to summarize your data. Include calculations such as the averages of all replicates for each treatment.

6. Graph your data. (Remember: The independent variable goes on the x-axis and the dependent variable on the y-axis.)

7. What conclusions can you reach? (What did you learn from your experiment? Can you think of any other possible explanations for your results?)

8. If you looked into the research by other people on this subject, how do your results agree or disagree with what they found, and why do you think this may be the case?

RESEARCH REPORT FORM *(continued)*

9. What might you change to improve your experimental design?

10. If you had a chance to do another experiment, what would you change in order to learn more about the topic you studied? (Did you come up with questions you can't answer using your data? If so, that's a good starting point for planning future research. What new experiments might help to answer your new questions?)

POSTER GUIDELINES

Posters are one way in which scientists present their research results. When posters are displayed at conferences, researchers have the opportunity to discuss their findings and ideas with fellow scientists.

At a poster session, people tend to spend the most time looking at posters that are attractive, well organized, and easy to read. It's best to keep the text short and to illustrate your points with graphs, photos, and diagrams.

To make your poster effective, make sure that it is:

Readable—Can your text be read from 2 meters away? (20 points is a good font size)

Understandable—Do your ideas fit together and make sense?

Organized—Is your work summarized clearly and concisely, using the headings listed in the example below?

Attractive—Will your poster make viewers want to take the time to read it? Have you used illustrations and color to enhance your display, without making the text hard to read?

Here is an example poster layout:

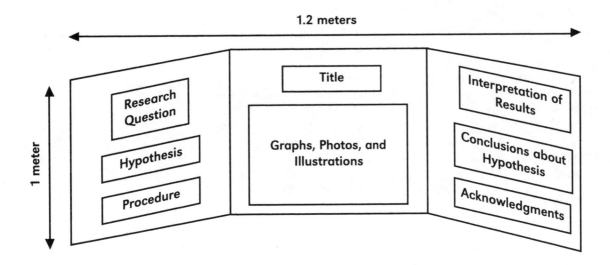

PEER REVIEW FORMS

EXPERIMENTAL DESIGN PEER REVIEW FORM

Name of Reviewer _____ Date _____

Project Reviewed _____

Is the research question clearly defined?

Very clear	❑	Comments about what was done well:
Mostly clear	❑	
Somewhat clear	❑	Suggestions for improvement:
Largely unclear	❑	

Are the procedures clearly described?

Very clear	❑	Comments about what was done well:
Mostly clear	❑	
Somewhat clear	❑	Suggestions for improvement:
Largely unclear	❑	

How well do the procedures address the research question?

Very well	❑	Comments about what was done well:
OK	❑	
Minor problems	❑	Suggestions for improvement:
Needs work	❑	

RESEARCH REPORT PEER REVIEW FORM

Name of Reviewer _____ Date _____

Project Reviewed _____

After reading a research report written by other students, answer the following questions. Remember to keep your answers friendly and constructive.

1. What was a particular strength in this experimental design?

2. Do you agree with the conclusions? Do they appear to be supported by the results of the experiment?

3. What suggestions can you make for improving this experiment or report?

POSTER PEER REVIEW FORM

Name of Reviewer _____   Date _____

Project Reviewed _____

KEY
1—Largely unclear
2—Somewhat clear
3—Mostly clear
4—Very clear

	(−) (+)
Does the poster include: Title, Research Question, Hypothesis, Procedure, Results, Conclusions, and Acknowledgments?	1 2 3 4
Is there a clear statement of the research question and hypothesis?	1 2 3 4
Does the experiment appear to be designed appropriately to address the research question?	1 2 3 4
Are the procedures described in enough detail for the experiment to be copied by someone else?	1 2 3 4
Are the data presented clearly?	1 2 3 4
Is there a clear explanation of the results?	1 2 3 4
Do the conclusions seem well supported by the data?	1 2 3 4
Were the presenters able to answer questions clearly?	1 2 3 4
Is the poster attractive and easy to read and understand?	1 2 3 4

TOTAL SCORE _____

Comments:
What was a particular strength of this experimental design?

What suggestions do you have for improving either this experiment or the poster presentation?

INTERACTIVE RESEARCH:
STORMWATER TREATMENT DESIGN CHALLENGE

STORMWATER TREATMENT DESIGN CHALLENGE

Consider the process cities must go through as they develop systems for collecting and draining runoff from storms. In designing these systems, scientists, engineers, and watershed managers must meet the specific needs and requirements of city residents and officials. Balancing these needs with available resources requires the use of mathematical analysis, scientific inquiry, and technological design as well as skills and knowledge related to cost, risk, trade-offs, and other aspects of critical thinking and creativity. In the scenario described below, you will need to use your knowledge of and skills related to watershed dynamics to solve a stormwater retention design challenge.

Materials

- Construction materials (see **Parts List and Cost Analysis Worksheet,** p. 170)

- 1.3 m x 1.3 m piece of Styrofoam, plywood, or other durable material

- AV equipment and other presentation tools

- Laboratory notebook

- **Parts List and Cost Analysis Worksheet** (p. 170)

- **Design Selection Matrix** (p. 171)

- **Design Proposal Form** (p. 172)

- **Team Questions** (p. 173)

- **Presentation Assessment Form** (p. 174) or alternative

Topic: water treatment
Go to: *www.sciLINKS.org*
Code: WD19

Setting the Scene

Over the last 10 years the city of Averyville has experienced rapid population growth, commercial development, and the construction of many new homes. A rigorous developmental plan has attracted high tech electronic companies to move into the city. This rapid commercial and private development has overburdened the city's antiquated drainage system, causing localized flooding from rainstorms and winter snowmelts. In addition, the present system for carrying stormwater is unable to filter the runoff with its increased sediment load. The residents of the small city fear that this could have a damaging effect on scenic Hahn Creek, which flows through the center of the city.

You are part of a student research team that has been asked by the city planning board to perform a preliminary investigation of the problem. Your team has decided to research stormwater retention and treatment, and to construct and test a scale model of a segment of the system that would provide solutions to current problems.

Background

During a rainstorm, water falls to the ground where it may mix with harmful contaminants such as sewage from leaky septic systems or oil from cars. The water and everything in it is known as **stormwater runoff**. Some of the water percolates or sinks into the earth and infiltrates into the groundwater. The rest of the runoff flows directly into streams, rivers, lakes, and other bodies of water or stormwater management units. These units are devices such as stormwater basins (sewers) and retention ponds. Retention ponds are human-made ponds used to collect runoff. Wet ponds (with or without filters) are natural ponds that are also used to collect runoff. Ponds are used partly because they enable some forms of bacteria to break down organic pollutants. This benefits the decomposition process.

In addition to sewage and oil, stormwater runoff may also contain fertilizer, antifreeze, gasoline, chemical wastes, household cleaners, herbicides, pesticides, and road sediments. Stormwater runoff comes into contact with these compounds as it travels over lawns, roadways, or agricultural fields. As you may know, these compounds are known as "non-point source" pollution because they come from many diffuse sources across wide areas. In contrast, point source pollution comes from a single source such as a wastewater treatment plant.

The Challenge

Build and test a model of a segment of a stormwater treatment system that adequately transports water and removes unwanted sediments and contaminants.

Design Criteria and Constraints

Treatment

▶ 85% of sediment added must be filtered after 2 storm events.

▶ 75% of storm volume must be drained after 2 storm events.

▶ Each storm event must be drained in 10 minutes or less.

▶ Treatment must not add new contaminants to the water.

Storm Volume and Rate

▶ Storm volume will be 1,500 mL of water containing known concentrations of sediments and contaminants for each storm event.

▶ Storm rate will be between 0.1 L/min and 1.0 L/min.

Cost

▶ Your system design must cost $10.00 or less.

▶ Use listed prices for items included in the **Parts List and Cost Analysis Worksheet** (p. 170).

▶ Use current catalogs to obtain prices for items that are not included on the parts list.

▶ For used items, assess cost as half the price of the replacement cost.

▶ Include maintenance costs and labor charges when system is used.

▶ The only items that can be added to the design with no cost are ones that are not human-made and are accessible to everyone.

Safety

▶ System components must pose no hazards to users or observers.

▶ Testing a storm event with the system must not pose any danger to the user.

Maintenance

▶ Your team must demonstrate routine removal of storm sediments and filter replacements.

▶ Your team must perform routine maintenance procedures between storm trials within 5 minutes.

Durability

▶ The system must be easy to transport without major repairs.

▶ The system must be capable of performing several tests without repair.

Restrictions

▶ Your system is limited to a maximum of 12 filtration and/or storage chambers.

▶ Your system must fit on a piece of Styrofoam or plywood with a slope of 10–15 degrees and no more than 1.3 m x 1.3 m in size.

▶ Excessive labor costs for operating the system during trials will be assessed at $1.00/minute. Your team may perform up to 5 minutes of routine maintenance between storm trials without accruing labor costs. However, if you need an operator to make adjustments or repairs during the trials, or if you need more than 5 minutes for adjustment and repairs between trials, labor costs will be assessed and added to the cost of your device.

The Design Process

Step 1. Define the Problem

1. Along with the members of your class team, read **Setting the Scene, Background,** and **Challenge.** This will give you an overview of the problem that your team is going to solve.

2. You also may want to consult with your teacher on doing further background research on this topic using Internet resources. Record all appropriate information in your lab notebook.

3. In your lab notebook, write a statement of the problem that you will be attempting to solve. Then make a list of the specific sediments and contaminants that may be in the stormwater in the city of Averyville (you may need to consult with your teacher). Your final problem statement should include the general specifications of the materials that must be treated by your system.

4. Read the **Design Criteria and Constraints.** Discuss with your teacher and members of your class team which parameters you will measure at the end of the design challenge to assess how well your system worked. Your final problem statement should be the problem that your design project is solving, so make adjustments if necessary.

Step 2. Identify Design Solutions and Select the Best Alternative

1. Examine the parts listed in the **Parts List and Cost Analysis Worksheet.** Brainstorm possible ways of using the materials to construct a treatment system that meets your specific problem. Make a list in your lab notebook of all possibilities developed by members of your team. Include a sketch for each alternative developed.

2. Using the same worksheet, calculate the cost of each of your alternative designs. Obtain costs for additional materials from your teacher. Record costs for each design in your lab notebook.

3. If necessary, brainstorm ideas for reducing costs of one or more alternatives. Refigure costs and record all changes in your lab notebook.

4. In order to select your best alternative, your team must determine the advantages and disadvantages of each alternative device. To do this, create a design matrix similar to the example below. List the specifications that you want to use to judge your alternatives and establish a scale to quantify each criterion. For example, you could use a scale of 1 to 3: (1 = poor, 2 = acceptable, 3 = good). The best alternative is selected based on the results of this analysis. Use the blank **Design Selection Matrix** or an alternative.

5. Your team may want to make modifications in one or more of the alternatives. For each modification, repeat the assessment process by completing the **Design Selection Matrix.**

Example Use of a Design Selection Matrix

Design Alternative	Expected Treatment Effectiveness	Cost	Safety	Expected Maintenance Cost	Expected Durability	Total
Idea 1	2	2	3	2	2	11
Idea 2	1	2	3	2	2	10
Idea 3	3	1	3	2	3	12*
Idea 4	2	1	3	1	2	9

*In this example, Idea 3 appears to be the best because it scored the highest for this combination of specifications.

Step 3. Build, Test, and Use the Best Design

1. Construct your stormwater treatment system using the materials from the **Parts List and Cost Analysis Worksheet** and any other acceptable materials that you have included in your design. As you construct your device, you may need to refine, eliminate, or add parts and/or specifications. Record all modifications in your lab notebook.

2. Test your device by using stormwater prepared by your instructor. You may need to test individual components in your system before you test the entire system.

3. Based on the results of your testing, you may need to make modifications in your design. If necessary, make a list of alternatives and repeat Step 2 to determine the best alternative.

4. Repeat the testing and modification process until the system is complete. Record all the steps of the process in your lab notebook.

Step 4. Evaluate the Constructed System

1. Use the **Presentation Assessment Form** to perform a self-assessment of your system.

2. Record the results of your assessment in your lab notebook.

Step 5. Plan Your Presentation

1. With your class team, plan a classroom presentation to illustrate how your system meets the specifications outlined in your redefined problem. You will need a presentation assessment tool to guide your plan. Use the **Presentation Assessment Form** or an alternative provided by your teacher. Begin preparing for your presentation by jotting down specific ideas about the advantages of your device. The whole class is trying to minimize costs and meet time and treatment specifications, so rather than claim that you have minimized costs, report precisely how much you have spent. Feel free to point out features that you think are good, especially those that are made of replacements for predetermined parts. Include a demonstration of the operation of your sampler.

2. Once your group is clear about the important details to be conveyed, determine what presentation aids you will use. You may want to prepare a handout for the class or create transparencies to show on an overhead projector. If time permits, you might include the use of a computer presentation.

3. Before your presentation, decide who in your group will cover each topic. Your presentation time will be limited and your group will need to state its case quickly and clearly.

Step 6. Present Your Work

1. Give your classroom presentation.

2. When finished, ask your audience for questions and feedback on what they considered the strong and weak points of your presentation.

3. Complete the **Team Questions** (p. 173).

4. Pass out the **Presentation Assessment Form** (p. 174) to get written feedback from your classmates.

FORMS FOR STORMWATER TREATMENT DESIGN CHALLENGE

STORMWATER TREATMENT DESIGN CHALLENGE
Parts List and Cost Analysis Worksheet

Item	Cost per Item ($)	Quantity Needed	Cost Subtotal
Plastic soda bottle (any size)	0.05		
Plastic tubing ($1/4''$ diameter)	0.50/ft		
Plastic tubing ($1/2''$ diameter)	0.80/ft		
Plastic tubing connector straight ($1/4''$ diameter)	1.80		
Plastic tubing connector straight ($1/2''$ diameter)	1.80		
Plastic tubing connector —T ($1/4''$ diameter)	1.00		
Plastic tubing connector —Y ($1/4''$ diameter)			
Duct tape	1.00		
Sand	Free		
Stopper	0.15		
Absorbent materials	See Instructor		
Other:*			
TOTAL COST			$

*Students may use materials other than those listed above. New materials must be assessed at full replacement cost. Used materials must be assessed at half the replacement cost. Students are responsible for documenting replacement cost.

STORMWATER TREATMENT DESIGN CHALLENGE
Design Selection Matrix

Use this form to help in selecting your best design idea. If you decide to carry out extensive revisions after pilot testing your design, you might want to fill out this form again to select the best modification of your original design.

Design Alternative	Expected Treatment Effectiveness	Cost	Safety	Expected Maintenance Cost	Expected Durability	Other Factors	TOTAL
Idea 1							
Idea 2							
Idea 3							
Idea 4							

SCALE
1 = poor
2 = acceptable
3 = good

STORMWATER TREATMENT DESIGN CHALLENGE
Design Proposal Form

Name _____ Date _____

Attach a sketch of your proposed design for a stormwater treatment system that meets the specified criteria and constraints.

Provide a brief written description of your sketch. Be sure to describe all parts of your proposed design.

Will you need any supplies that are not listed on the approved list? If so, what will you need, and how do you plan to get it?

What will your system cost? (Use the **Parts List and Cost Analysis Worksheet.**)

Team Questions

Name _____ **Date** _____

1. Compare the problem statement contained in the original Challenge to the problem statement you developed in Step 1. Are there differences between the two statements?

2. In later steps, did you need to rewrite the problem statement your team developed in Step 1? Did obtaining more background information help? Explain.

3. What were some of the tradeoffs that were made to select the best alternative design?

4. Describe the modifications, if any, that were made in your design as you built and tested your water sampler device.

5. What additional information about your design did you obtain from the actual testing of the device? Did you make any modifications after testing? Explain.

6. Are some areas of the assessment more difficult to complete than others? Why?

7. How does your assessment compare to those of other members of your team?

8. What parts of your presentation did you feel were very strong?

9. Describe any changes you would make in your presentation if you were to do it again.

PRESENTATION ASSESSMENT FORM

Presenters:_____

Assessed by: _____

Date:_____

EVALUATION SCALE

1—Inadequate in meeting requirements of the task

2—Minimal in meeting requirements of the task

3—Adequate in meeting requirements of the task

4—Superior in meeting requirement

Criteria	Evaluation (-) (+)	Weight	Points
The cost of system, including repair and maintenance, is less than $10.00	1 2 3 4	5	
Completed model fits on a 4' x 4' base	1 2 3 4	1	
85% of each sediment added must be filtered after 2 storm events	1 2 3 4	3	
75% of storm volume must be drained after 2 storm events	1 2 3 4	3	
Each storm event must be drained in 10 minutes or less	1 2 3 4	3	
New contaminants are not added to the water	1 2 3 4	1	
Demonstrate routine removal of storm sediments and filter replacements	1 2 3 4	5	
Perform routine maintenance procedures between storm trials within 5 minutes	1 2 3 4	1	
System is capable of performing several tests without repair	1 2 3 4	3	
System is safe to handle and operate	1 2 3 4	5	
Overall quality of presentation	1 2 3 4	4	
		Total Points:	

To determine the total presentation score, multiply the **Evaluation** by the **Weight** to get the **Point** score for each criterion. Then add the numbers in the **Point** column to get the **Total Points.**

Comments:

What was a particular strength of this stormwater treatment design?

What suggestions do you have for improving this design or the way in which it was presented?